# DEAR COMRADES

## HOOVER ARCHIVAL DOCUMENTARIES
General editors: Milorad M. Drachkovitch (1976–83)
Robert Hessen (1983–    )

The documents reproduced in this series (unless otherwise indicated) are deposited in the archives of the Hoover Institution on War, Revolution and Peace at Stanford University. The purpose of their publication is to shed new light on some important events concerning the United States or the general history of the twentieth century.

HERBERT HOOVER AND POLAND: A DOCUMENTARY HISTORY OF A FRIENDSHIP,
  Foreword by Sen. Mark O. Hatfield
*George J. Lerski, compiler*

NEGOTIATING WHILE FIGHTING: THE DIARY OF ADMIRAL C. TURNER JOY AT THE KOREAN
  ARMISTICE CONFERENCE, Foreword by Gen. Matthew B. Ridgway
*Allan E. Goodman, editor*

PATRIOT OR TRAITOR: THE CASE OF GENERAL MIHAILOVICH,
  Foreword by Hon. Frank J. Lausche
*David Martin, compiler*

BEHIND CLOSED DOORS: SECRET PAPERS ON THE FAILURE OF
  ROMANIAN-SOVIET NEGOTIATIONS, 1931–1932
*Walter M. Bacon, Jr., translator and compiler*

THE DIPLOMACY OF FRUSTRATION: THE MANCHURIAN CRISIS OF 1931–1933
  AS REVEALED IN THE PAPERS OF STANLEY K. HORNBECK
*Justus D. Doenecke, compiler*

WAR THROUGH CHILDREN'S EYES: THE SOVIET OCCUPATION OF POLAND AND THE
  DEPORTATIONS, 1939–1941, Foreword by Bruno Bettelheim
*Irena Grudzinska-Gross and Jan Tomasz Gross, editors and compilers*

BERLIN ALERT: THE MEMOIRS AND REPORTS OF TRUMAN SMITH,
  Foreword by Gen. A. C. Wedemeyer
*Robert Hessen, editor*

LENIN AND THE TWENTIETH CENTURY: A BERTRAM D. WOLFE RETROSPECTIVE,
  Foreword by Alain Besançon
*Lennard Gerson, compiler*

A QUESTION OF TRUST: THE ORIGINS OF U.S.-SOVIET DIPLOMATIC RELATIONS:
  THE MEMOIRS OF LOY W. HENDERSON
*George W. Baer, editor*

WEDEMEYER ON WAR AND PEACE, Foreword by John Keegan
*Keith E. Eiler, editor*

LAST CHANCE IN MANCHURIA: THE DIARY OF CHANG KIA-NGAU
*Donald G. Gillin and Ramon H. Myers, editors; Dolores Zen, translator*

IN DANGER UNDAUNTED: THE ANTI-INTERVENTIONIST MOVEMENT OF 1940–1941
  AS REVEALED IN THE PAPERS OF THE AMERICA FIRST COMMITTEE
*Justus D. Doenecke, editor*

BREAKING WITH COMMUNISM: THE INTELLECTUAL ODYSSEY OF BERTRAM D. WOLFE
*Robert Hessen, editor*

DEAR COMRADES: MENSHEVIK REPORTS ON THE BOLSHEVIK REVOLUTION AND THE CIVIL WAR
*Vladimir N. Brovkin, editor and translator*

# DEAR COMRADES

*Menshevik Reports on the Bolshevik Revolution and the Civil War*

*Edited and Translated by*

VLADIMIR N. BROVKIN

HOOVER INSTITUTION PRESS

Stanford University   Stanford, California

The Hoover Institution on War, Revolution and Peace, founded at
Stanford University in 1919 by Herbert Hoover, who went on to become
the thirty-first president of the United States, is an interdisciplinary
research center for advanced study on domestic and international
affairs. The views expressed in its publications are entirely those
of the authors and do not necessarily reflect the views of the staff,
officers, or Board of Overseers of the Hoover Institution.

www.hoover.org

Hoover Press Publication 398
Copyright © 1991 by the Board of Trustees of the
     Leland Stanford Junior University

First printing 1991
97  96  95  94  93  92  91      9  8  7  6  5  4  3  2  1
Simultaneous first paperback printing, 1991
26  25  24  23  21  20  19      9  8  7  6  5  4  3

Manufactured in the United States of America

Library of Congress Cataloging in Publication Data
Dear comrades: Menshevik reports on the Bolshevik revolution and
     the civil war / edited and translated by Vladimir N. Brovkin
               p. cm. — (Hoover archival documentaries)
(Hoover Press publication ; 398)
     Bibliography: p.
     Includes index
     1. Soviet Union—History—Revolution,1917–1291—Sources.
2. Mensheviks—History—Sources.   I. Brovkin, Vladimir N.
II. Series.
DK265.D34   1991      947.084'1—dc20      90-44818
ISBN: 978-0-8179-8981-1 (cloth)
ISBN: 978-0-8179-8982-8 (pbk.)
ISBN: 978-0-8179-8983-5 (ePub)
ISBN: 978-0-8179-8987-3 (mobi)
ISBN: 978-0-8179-8788-0 (PDF)

# Contents

# List of Documents

## NEW COURSE AND NEW REPRESSIONS
### (DECEMBER 1918–SEPTEMBER 1919)

### THE WHITE THREAT (1919)

### WAR COMMUNISM AND POPULAR RESISTANCE (1920)

### THE UNFORESEEN DICTATORSHIP (1920–1925)

# Acknowledgments

Many institutions and individuals have helped me prepare this collection for publication. I extend sincere thanks to the staff of the archives of the Hoover Institution on War, Revolution and Peace; Elena Danielson, the late Anna Bourgina, and many others were always ready to guide me through the numerous collections and materials deposited there and made my research at the archives a truly productive and enriching experience. I am also indebted to Mikhail Bernstam, senior research fellow at the Hoover Institution, for his published collections of documents on the Civil War in Russia, his vast knowledge of popular movements in Bolshevik Russia, and his observations during our several discussions. I would also like to express my gratitude to Boris Sapir of the Institute for Social History in Amsterdam; as a member of the Menshevik party and a scholar, he knew many leading Mensheviks personally. His observations and insights are uniquely valuable. My thanks go also to Marc Jansen of the Institute for Social History who, as an expert on the party of Socialist Revolutionaries, was most forthcoming and encouraging during my stay in Amsterdam.

This project was made possible by a Mellon Fellowship at the Center for Soviet and East European Studies at the University of California at Berkeley, with particular thanks to Gail Lapidus and Reginald Zelnik. A generous grant from the Social Science Research Council enabled me to conduct research at the Institute for Social History in Amsterdam and at the Russian Research Center at Harvard University. A fellowship from the Kennan Institute for Advanced Russian Studies made it possible for me to do research at the National Archives in Washington.

Finally, I am deeply grateful to Robert Hessen, the general editor of the Hoover Archival Documentaries, for his attentive scrutiny of the manuscript, many insightful comments and suggestions, and criticism and encouragement. Above all I am grateful to my wife, Karen, whose help was greater than I can describe.

# Abbreviations and Political Vocabulary

**CC**—Central Committee. A supreme body of party leadership.

**CEC**—Central Executive Committee of Soviets. Supreme legislative institution when the Congress of Soviets of Russia is not in session.

**Cheka**—Extraordinary Commission. Lenin's political police accountable to the Communist party leadership rather than to state institutions. A political terror police under Lenin's control.

**CPC**—Council of People's Commissars. The government, in theory accountable to the CEC: in practice ruling by decree.

**EC**—Executive Committee. A Soviet executive branch of a city government nominally responsible to an elected assembly (the soviet).

**GPU**—State Political Directorate. A successor to the Cheka after 1921.

**Kadet**—Russian KD or Constitutional Democrats. A party of Russian liberals outlawed by the Bolsheviks in December 1917.

**PLSR**—Party of Left Socialist Revolutionaries that split from the party of Socialist Revolutionaries in November 1917 and joined the Bolsheviks in a coalition government.

**PS**—People's Socialists. A party of moderate Socialists and liberals.

**PSR**—Party of Socialist Revolutionaries. A party of agrarian socialism that after October 1917 opposed the Bolshevik rule.

**Rev. Coms.**—Revolutionary Committees. Ad hoc bodies created by the Bolsheviks to seize power in various cities.

**Revolutionary Democracy**—A term used to describe Socialist parties that favored the February revolution and parliamentary democracy (hence Democracy), that is, the Mensheviks, the Socialist Revolutionaries, and the People's Socialists.

**RSDWP** (b)—Russian Social Democratic Workers' party (Bolshevik). The Mensheviks and the Bolsheviks, the two wings of Russian Social Democracy, were united in one political party until 1912. In March 1918 the Bolsheviks changed their name to RKP(b)—Russian Communist party (Bolshevik). The Mensheviks retained their original name; hence Menshevik and Social Democrat are interchangeable.

**RSDWP** (m)—Russian Social Democratic Workers' party (Menshevik).

**Socialists**—The use of this term changed over time in Russia. Generally, all non-Bolshevik left-wing parties were referred to as Socialist parties.

*SV*—*Sotsialisticheskii Vestnik* [Socialist Courier]. A Menshevik journal that began publishing in 1921 in Berlin.

**Trudoviki**—Literally a labor group, this name identified a group of Socialist Revolutionaries in the Fourth Duma and in 1917 in the preparliament. Alexander Kerensky belonged to this group.

# Note on Translation, Transliteration, and Dates

I have translated the documents in this collection into English from Russian, German, and French. Unless indicated, the original is in Russian. I have used the Library of Congress system of transliteration, except for names that are spelled differently by the authors themselves, for example, Gurewitsch, not Gurevich.

Documents of 1917 and early 1918 (through March) are dated according to the Julian calendar, which was used in Russia at the time. Dates after March 1918 are based on our present-day Gregorian calendar, which was adopted at that time. The Julian calendar is thirteen days behind the Gregorian one.

# Foreword

These documents are intended to broaden the existing data base on the social and political processes during the Russian Civil War, for the Communist system, the party, and the ideology as they emerged in 1921 were the products of that Civil War.[1] Bringing together testimony of participants and observers in political events from Petrograd and Moscow as well as from the cities and towns of European Russia, this collection does not attempt to document party history or record the major policy decisions of the Mensheviks, but to focus on the political reality they witnessed and described.

Because it would have been impossible to include reports covering all or even the most important topics pertaining to the social and political situation, the range of topics was limited to those the Mensheviks knew: conditions in urban industrial centers. Thus such important aspects of Russia's social and political history as peasant movements and military aspects of the Civil War are dealt with only marginally here. The documents focus on workers material conditions, aspirations, and political views and their involvement in politics, elections, strikes, and protest actions. Because workers were at the center of political life in Russia, these reports also cover the nature of local politics, conditions in the factories, and relations with and membership in political parties.

All documents here are drawn from the Boris I. Nicolaevsky collection at the Hoover Institution Archives. In selecting from the more than eight hundred boxes in the collection, I applied the following criteria: the documents had to contain little-known or unknown information on social and political conditions in Russia in 1917–1921. They had to deal with issues of then current politics. Preference was given to documents describing concrete events, rather than theories. Specific situations, colorful portraits, and attention to detail were important requirements. These documents include official statements and private letters of both unknown workers and experienced Menshevik journalists, of local party organizations and the Central Committee, and of right- and left-wing Mensheviks from various parts of the country.

As observers and especially as participants, the Mensheviks were not impartial to the events described. They held strong political views and were adherents of Marxism, which surely colored their perceptions of reality. Political views, as such, however, are not an obstacle to accurate reporting. That the Bolsheviks were Marxists does not disqualify *Pravda* from being used as a primary source.

As to the accuracy of the Menshevik press, one can argue that it was much more reliable than that of the Bolshevik press. The press of the Mensheviks and the Socialist Revolutionaries still operated on the old principles of journalism that were cast aside as "bourgeois" by the Bolsheviks—that is, the press must provide information to the public that is accurate and verified, even if damaging to those in power. For example, *Novaia Zhizn'* (New Life), an independent Social Democratic daily newspaper edited by Maxim Gorky, was a trustworthy source that published many sensational news items in 1917 and 1918. The Bolshevik approach, in contrast, was to see the press as one instrument of propaganda among others at the party's disposal. Factual accuracy was far less important than the political significance of the event in question or its propagandistic effect.

One could argue that the Mensheviks—a party opposing Bolshevik rule—would portray reality in its darkest colors. This may be true, just as the Bolsheviks, by the same logic, had a stake in presenting a rosy picture. Historians must ascertain the true situation. To do that, however, you need more than one source. As long as a multiparty, independent press existed in Russia (until July 1918), there was much information from diverse sources. Yet with the suppression of the independent press by the Bolsheviks in 1918, these sources ran dry. The Communists controlled what could and could not be published, and what was published had to correspond to the party line, which meant that many important events were simply not reported at all. The farther away from Moscow the event, the less information was available. Thus little is known to this day about workers' strikes, peasant uprisings, Red Army mutinies, and other expressions of discontent in Lenin's Russia.

On those rare occasions when disturbances were reported in the Bolshevik press, they were described in a coded language that labeled social and political phenomena in accordance with Marxist-Leninist notions of class struggle. The term *kulak*, for example, as Peter Scheibert points out, was not a social category, but a label to depict an enemy.[2] Likewise the label *bourgeoisie* was applied rather loosely to intelligentsia, white-collar workers, and even Socialists. When such labels could not be clearly pinned on, as in the case of some workers, for example, then the workers in question were said to be under the influence of bourgeois ideology or not sufficiently class conscious. Peasant rebellions were labeled kulak conspiracies, Red Army soldiers' mutinies were tagged as monarchist reactionary plots, and workers' strikes were called Menshevik and Social Revolutionaries' provocations and sabotage. By definition, there could not be a workers' political protest in a proletarian state, lest doubts be raised that it was a proletarian state.

The local Bolshevik authorities reported disorders as monarchist conspiracies because then they could act "decisively," as they put it, whereas if they reported that a strike had broken out, the Moscow Bolsheviks might be inclined to accuse them of a lack of vigilance on the ideological front. The Communists became so accustomed to reporting popular unrest in a coded language that without non-Communist sources it is difficult to determine whether the event in question was a monarchist conspiracy or a workers' strike. Bolshevik reports, however, have been taken at face value in Western historiography because there are often no other reports available. Thus although the official Communist version of events has been expressed in an ever-increasing number of books, the voice of the critics or witnesses has not been heard. The reports in this collection, therefore, provide an independent account on a number of crucial events in Lenin's Russia.

There are three types of documents in this volume:

1. Reports of local Social Democratic (Menshevik) organizations and individuals on specific events in a particular area
2. Reports of the Menshevik party leadership—the Central Committee—primarily to the leaders of the West European Socialist and Social Democratic parties
3. Personal letters of leading Social Democrats (Mensheviks) mostly to Pavel Axelrod—one of the founders of the party and at that time the official spokesman of the party in Europe

Each category has its advantages and limitations and at the same time complements the others.

The limitations of local reports are that they do not indicate whether and to what extent the events described were typical or exceptional. This could be remedied by compiling a great many reports from various sources, making it easier to identify major trends. The advantages of local reports are that they describe specific situations in detail, providing a close-up picture of provincial politics lacking in other, more general sources. In these reports local organizations, Menshevik journalists, and individual witnesses informed the Central Committee and the public about events the government-controlled press tried to conceal. The newspapers that published information critical of the Bolshevik government were almost always closed, at first for a limited time and in July 1918, forever. More than three hundred periodicals were shut down by the Bolshevik authorities from

October 1917 to July 1918, an event unmatched by any other government.[3] After July 1918 only two or three nonpolitical, non-Bolshevik newspapers remained in the entire territory of Russia, which is also why we know what was going on in the provinces in 1918 much better than we do in 1919 and 1920.

The limitation of the second category of documents as sources is that in writing to foreign Socialists, the Menshevik Central Committee (CC) described the situation as it saw it, making the analytic component stronger here than in reports on local events. The advantage is that the CC was much better informed on the overall situation than were local leaders or individual journalists. The CC was in a position to draw on a large store of evidence and include those episodes and facts it considered to be representative. Only verified and accurate information was included in these reports because the CC's credibility and reputation in the West were at stake.

The limitation of the third category of documents—personal letters— is that they are subjective by their very nature. An individual writing a personal letter not intended for publication does not have to be absolutely accurate. He or she may err, may not know something, or may be misinformed. Furthermore, personal letters may color or distort events, but they also convey intimate details. When Menshevik party leaders Iulii Martov or Fedor Dan wrote to Axelrod to bring him up to date on what was happening in Russia, they often revealed details that they would never have included in official pronouncements, bringing an added dimension to the overall picture. Only personal letters contain otherwise unrecorded conversations of key politicians and discussions of measures contemplated but never implemented.

Thus each type of document highlights political phenomena in a different way and from a different perspective. Because these reports were written by different people in different places at different times, they cannot possibly cover all the social, political, intellectual, and economic processes in a complex society at war. Nevertheless, these reports, covering local politics, elections, strikes, uprisings, and Bolshevik measures in response to popular unrest, give us a picture of daily life in Russian cities and popular attitudes toward war, peace, government policy, and opposition's criticism. Seen close up, conditions in a factory or in a small provincial town under the dictatorship of the proletariat can help one follow the zigzags of Bolshevik policy and factional infighting against the background of gradual suppression of all opposition parties and all opposition opinion in Soviet Russia.

It is astonishing that, despite Bolshevik repression, censorship, and disruption of transport and communications, these reports found their way West. Insofar as one can generalize, which is difficult because each document is unique, there were four ways for that to happen. The first, and simplest, was to publish a report in the Social Democrat press; however, that was only possible until July 1918 and then again during January and February 1919.

Even during those periods, however, not all reports could be published because of disrupted communications and Bolshevik censorship. Most reports were brought to Moscow by local Mensheviks; once in Moscow, the Central Committee took advantage of rare opportunities to send out reports or letters, above all to Pavel Axelrod, the party's official spokesman abroad, as well as to Central Committees of other Social Democratic parties in Europe. Materials could not be sent out of the country by mail because the Communist government censored Menshevik correspondence and on occasion seized materials in the mail. Thus in 1918 and 1919 the second way to get materials out was through individuals traveling abroad, usually Social Democrats, Socialist Revolutionaries, or Liberals who were going abroad for what they believed would be a short stay but turned out for most of them to be permanent exile.

The third way to send materials abroad was through visiting foreigners. To do this on a regular basis however, was possible only during 1920, when the British labor delegation, the Italian labor delegation, and the German Independent Social Democrats' delegation carried out large numbers of letters, reports, and official statements prepared by the Menshevik Central Committee. In fact, all the documents in this collection on 1920 arrived in the West in this fashion.

And finally, the fourth way to send materials abroad was through the diplomatic service. When Lenin's government recognized the independence of Georgia, Latvia, Lithuania, and Estonia in the summer of 1920 and the embassies of these countries opened in Moscow, the Social Democrats and Socialist Revolutionaries asked for and were officially granted the right to send mail through diplomatic channels.[4] Once a Menshevik or Socialist Revolutionary report had arrived in Moscow, it had a good chance of reaching the West.

Most astonishing, though, are the ways in which letters from Mensheviks in prisons and camps reached the Central Committee in Moscow. In some cases, those released from prison took letters—written with microscopic characters on a tiny sheet of paper on both sides—with them. One letter in the Nicolaevsky Collection was thrown out the window of a train en route to Siberia; someone found it along the railway tracks and sent it to the address indicated, adding a note: "We are indignant and we sympathize."[5]

By 1921 a more or less regular system of communication had been established between the Social Democrats in Moscow and in Berlin. *Sotsialisticheskii Vesnik* (Socialist Courier) was published in Berlin, and some fifty to two hundred copies of each issue were smuggled into Russia. In the other direction, Menshevik reports and letters flowed out of Russia by the methods described above. Especially important for the Nicolaevsky Collection were the Latvian Social Democrats and the Latvian embassy in Moscow. Hundreds of letters from Bolshevik camps are preserved in the Nicolaevsky Collection—an untapped source on early Soviet camp history. An example of one of them is included in this volume.

The Menshevik documents were only relatively safe in Berlin, for with the Nazis' coming to power in Germany, the Social Democrats, German and Russian, had to flee or be arrested. More than anyone, Boris Nicolaevsky, by then a member of the Menshevik Delegation Abroad (official party representatives), deserves credit for preserving the valuable documents in this volume and many others. The Nicolaevsky Collection is certainly one of the most important on twentieth-century Russian history.

Other important collections of documents on the Bolshevik Revolution and the Civil War have been published in the West, some by participants and observers. Nikolai Sukhanov's *Zapiski o Revoliutsii*[6] (Notes on Revolution) is perhaps the most well-known example. His portraits of political leaders and his vivid scenes of Petrograd in 1917 reflect a closeness to the situation sometimes missing in official proceedings or collections of resolutions and decrees. Of a similar nature is *Les Bocheviks par eux meme* by Boris Sokolov. Several other interesting collections of reports by participants were published in the West in the 1920s including *Les Bolcheviks a l'oeuvre* (The Bolsheviks at Work) by a Rostov-na-Donu Menshevik, Lockerman, as well as the Menshevik report to the British labor delegation, which visited Soviet Russia in 1920. Important collections of documents published by the opposition parties were the Socialist Revolutionary book *The Cheka* and the Left Socialist Revolutionry's *Kreml' za reshetkoi* [Kremlin behind bars], as well as materials of the Commission of Inquiry into the Atrocities of the Bolsheviks, which was created under General Denikin after the retreat of the Bolsheviks from the Ukraine in 1919.

In recent years Western scholars have published a number of important collections of documents on various aspects of the Bolshevik Revolution.[7] Some of these are reprints of Russian-language rare documents;[8] others concentrate on translating voluminous information into Western languages.[9] Two collections deal with the Menshevik party policy, and a new volume highlights the Socialist Revolutionary policy during the Civil War;[10] Mikhail Bernstam has published two collections of documents in Russian on social and political conditions during the Civil War.[11]

This collection is the first English-language publication of these documents. Some of these reports were published in local Menshevik newspapers and disappeared in the chaotic conditions of the Civil War; some reports could not be published in Russia because of Communist censorship, and others have never been published in Russia or in the West. Even those reports that reached Europe did not have much political effect in the West, first because Western Europe was too preoccupied with World War I in 1918 and with chaos in Germany and Central Europe in 1919 and 1920. Against such a background, news of strikes by Russian workers did not arouse much curiosity. Second, the Bolsheviks, who managed to present themselves as a workers' party, still enjoyed considerable popularity in leftist circles in Europe. Even in the worst days of Stalin's atrocities, the Western public was largely ignorant of the terror and famine in 1933[12] and the mass executions of the late 1930s. Although Stalin's crimes are now widely known and new revelations about them are being published in the Soviet Union, Lenin's period remains a taboo. The Soviet and Western publics are still largely ignorant about conditions of workers and peasants in Lenin's Russia. The Communist regime wants to maintain the illusion that things went wrong *after* Lenin. The Nicolaevsky documents, however, testify to the contrary: the Stalinist regime of lawlessness and arbitrary dictatorship was established under Lenin.

Because the reports in this collection are in chronological order, there is a certain overlap to some events and lack of coverage on others. Thus the following introduction briefly outlines Russia's internal conditions during the main stages of the Civil War.

## NOTES

1. This proposition is widely accepted in scholarly literature. See, for example, Sheila Fitspatrick, "Civil War as a Formative Experience," in Abbott Gleason, Peter Kenez, and Richard Stites, eds., *Bolshevik Culture* (Bloomington: Indiana University Press, 1985), pp. 57–76. Also Moshe Lewin, *Lenin's Last Struggle* (New York: Monthly Review Press), p. 12; and S. Cohen, "Bolshevism and Stalinism," in Robert Tucker, ed., *Stalinism* (New York: W. W. Norton, 1977), pp. 15–16.

2. Peter Scheibert, *Lenin an der Macht: Das Russiche Volk in der Revolution, 1918–1922* [Lenin in Power: The Russian People in the Revolution, 1918–1922] (Weinheim, West Germany: acta humaniora, 1984), p. 132.

3. Menshevik source, document 15; Soviet source, A. A. Goncharov, "Bor'ba Sovetskoi vlasti s kontrrevoliutsionnoi burzhuaznoi pechat'iu," *Vestnik MGU, seriia zhurnalistiki* 11, no.4:13–23.

4. This is clear from Martov's correspondence with other party leaders, as well as from other documents. For example, in a letter to Shchupak, dated December 12, 1921, Martov wrote that news came to Moscow "through Estonians" that only five copies of *Sotsialisticheskii Vestnik* had arrived. He also mentioned that Bruno Kalnin, a leader of the Latvian Social Democrats, was in Berlin and that

he, Martov, talked to him about "further functioning of that route." Nic-
olaevsky Collection (hereafter, Nic. Col.) series 21, box 60, folder 1. Bruno
Kalnin was much more explicit in his interview: "We, for example, sent to the
USSR Menshevik *Sotsialisticheskii Vestnik* through Latvian diplomatic mail."
Boris Vail, "Intev'iu s Bruno Kalnishem," *Forum* 4 (1983):72.

5. This handwritten letter is identified in the archive as "Pis'mo iz tiur'my" Nic.
Col., no.6, box 6, folder 4. The letter describes Bolshevik treatment of Socialists in the Butyrki jail in 1921.

6. For complete bibliographic information on books, see bibliography.

7. See, for example, Robert V. Daniels, *A Documentary History of Communism*,
vol. 1 (Hanover, N.H.: Published for the University of Vermont by University
Press of New England, 1984); Richard Lorenz, ed., *Die Russische Revolution
1917. Der Aufstand der Arbeiter, Bauern und Soldaten, eine Dokumentation*
[The Russian Revolution of 1917. The Uprising of Workers, Peasants, and
Soldiers, A Documentation] (Munich: Nymphenburger, 1981); John Keep, ed.,
*The Debate on Soviet Power: Minutes of the All-Russian Central Executive
Committee of Soviets, Second Convocation, October 1917–January 1918* (Ox-
ford, Eng.: Clarendon Press, 1979); Dimitri Von Mohrenschildt, ed., *The Rus-
sian Revolution of 1917: Contemporary Accounts* (New York: Oxford Univer-
sity Press, 1971); Robert C. Tucker, ed., *The Lenin Anthology* (New York: W.
W. Norton, 1975); and many others.

8. For documents published by the Mensheviks, see Petr Garvi, *Zapiski Sotsial
Demokrata (1906–1921)* [Notes of a Social Democrat (1906–1921)] (Newtonville, Mass.: Oriental Research Partners, 1982), and Boris Sapir, ed., *Theodore Dan. Letters, 1899–1946* (Amsterdam: International Institute for Social
History, 1985).

9. Wolfgang Eichwede, ed., *Sozial und Wirtschaftsgeschichte der UdSSR von 1917
bis 1941 in Quellen und Documenten* [Social and Economic History of the
USSR from 1917 to 1941 in Sources and Documents] (Bremen: forthcoming);
Abraham Ascher, ed., *The Mensheviks in the Russian Revolution* (Ithaca, N.Y.:
Cornell University Press, 1976); and *Texte der Menschewiki zur Russischen
Revolution und zum Sowjetstaat aus den Jahren 1903–1937* [The Texts of the
Mensheviks on the Russian Revolution and the Soviet State from the Years
1903–1937] (Hamburg: Junius, 1981).

10. Marc Jansen's volume of the PSR documents from the archives of the PSR will
be published by the Institute for Social History in Amsterdam.

11. Mikhail Bernstam, *Nezavisimoe rabochee dvizhenie v 1918 godu Dokumenty i
materialy* [Independent Workers' Movement in 1918, Documents and Materi-
als] (Paris: YMCA, 1982), and *Ural i prikam'e, noiabr' 1917–ianvar' 1919:
Dokumenty i materialy* [The Urals and the Kama Region, November 1917–
January 1919: Documents and Materials] (Paris: YMCA, 1982).

12. Robert Conquest, *The Harvest of Sorrow: Soviet Collectivization and the Terror
Famine* (New York: Oxford University Press, 1986), a detailed treatment of the
terror famine in 1932–1933.

# DEAR COMRADES

# Introduction

The Civil War in Russia (1917–1921) was a time of tremendous popular upheaval and the consolidation of Bolshevik rule. These two processes cannot be treated in isolation, for each was the extension of the other. Bolshevik rule was shaped in the Civil War, but the Civil War was the product of Bolshevik rule. There is no one date that marks the beginning of the Civil War because there were several civil wars going on at the same time. During 1917–1921 when fighting on one front quieted down, it intensified on another one with another enemy. In the early days of November 1917, when the Bolsheviks were fighting to gain control of Moscow, the Russian press referred to this as the Civil War. Several times during 1917–1921, the Civil War was declared over and yet continued year after year. Recent studies show that when the Civil War was officially declared over at the end of 1920 with the defeat of the White Armies, the war of the Bolsheviks with the peasant insurgents in central Russia was just entering one of its bloodiest stages.[1]

Just to list who was fighting whom during this period is a major undertaking. It was not simply the Whites fighting the Reds or, as the official Soviet historiography puts it, a civil war between the liberated proletariat and the overthrown propertied classes.[2] In the actual situation a variety of social and political forces fought each other or refused to fight for complicated reasons. Class divisions were accompanied by regional, national, economic, religious, and ideological cleavages. One can distinguish a civil war between organized armies operating from a certain territorial base marked by a front line, a civil war within one province or several provinces, a civil war fought by a central or regional government against a population under its nominal control, and a civil war by insurgent formations against their government.

The social and economic conditions in the huge country varied widely. Some parts of the country (the central industrial region and Petrograd) remained under continuous Bolshevik control, while others (the Urals and the Ukraine) changed hands several times. Still others had no indigenous Bolsheviks at all and were dragged into the empire by military conquest years after Red October. Yet though the mixture of political, military, and social forces changed considerably over time and from area to area, the following key combatants surfaced almost everywhere:

*The Bolsheviks'* goal was to destroy capitalism and bourgeois parliamentary order and establish a dictatorship of the proletariat (in practice a dictatorship of the Bolshevik party).

*The Mensheviks and the Socialist Revolutionaries'* (the Socialist opposition) goal was to defend parliamentary institutions and oppose Bolshevik dictatorship because they believed that progress toward the distant goal of socialism could only take place in a democracy.

*The Whites'* (organized into armies or itinerant, independent detachments) goal was first and foremost to overthrow the Bolsheviks and to restore what they believed to be law and order. Some Whites favored restoring the monarchy; others wanted to create a parliamentary republic.

*The Greens* (independent peasant formations of deserters from the Red or White armies) for the most part did not have a clearly defined positive program, but fought against Bolshevik intruders who were trying to conscript them and requisition their grain.

*The cossacks* (both as an independent force and as allies of the Whites) were concerned primarily with defending their traditional way of life, their communal institutions, and their land against the Bolshevik takeover.

*The Ukrainian national forces'* (government troops of independent Ukraine and volunteer formations) goal was an independent Ukraine.

*National minorities detachments* in various parts of the country, as well as the so-called Internationalists and the World War I prisoners of war—Germans, Austrians, Hungarians, and Czechs—also took sides in the Russian Civil War.

The diversity of the rival groups in the Russian Civil War led one historian to say that it was a war of all against all.[3] A closer examination, however, makes it apparent that each of the participants entered the Civil War against specific opponents and out of very concrete reasons. To untangle this chaotic record, we must follow the social and political processes that developed after October 1917 and that gave the initial impetus to the outbreak of the Civil War. Arising in reaction to the Bolshevik transformation of Russian society, few of the above-mentioned forces existed in October 1917. The officers and the cossacks, which already existed, were the first to offer armed resistance to the Bolsheviks. Defeated in January–February 1918, the Whites retreated to southern Russia into the steppes of Kuban and northern Caucasia.[4] Not until more than a year later, in the spring of 1919, did the Whites in the South become a factor in national politics and a major force in the frontline Civil War. In the East—the Urals and Siberia—the Whites came to power in November 1918.[5] In the Ukraine, the Bolsheviks defeated the Ukrainian government of Liberals and Socialists in January 1918[6]—the first salvo in a protracted struggle between the Moscow Bolsheviks and the Ukrainians. Most important, the peasant insurgents, later called the Greens, also did not exist in 1917, but took up arms against the Bolsheviks in response to Bolshevik policies in 1918.

## THE BOLSHEVIKS SEIZE POWER (OCTOBER 1917–JANUARY 1918)

The period from October 1917 to January 1918, however, was a happy one for the Bolsheviks. Intoxicated with victory, they enjoyed genuine support from workers and especially from soldiers.[7] Against all odds, they had won a big gamble and were now in power. Despite dire predictions that they would fall within a couple of weeks, they did not, and their position, although by no means secure, was not desperate either. Immediately embarking on a policy of radical economic reform, the Bolsheviks were in a great hurry to implement their Socialist reconstruction of industry as a historical showcase before they were ousted.

Documents 1 through 3—the previously unpublished letters of Menshevik party leaders Iulii Martov and Fedor Dan—are devoted to this period, which was so exhilarating for the Bolsheviks and so gloomy for the Mensheviks, who had suffered a defeat at the hands of their Marxist rivals in the Russian workers' movement. The letters, rife with interparty politics and the moves and countermoves of the key political figures in the first weeks after the Bolsheviks seized power, capture the spirit of the times: the workers' euphoria over the proletarian revolution, the Mensheviks' misgivings and hesitations, and the Bolsheviks' clever scheming and plotting to make sure that the coming Constituent Assembly would not reverse what had been fought so dearly for in October.

Iulii Martov's letters to Pavel Axelrod—his old friend, colleague, teacher, and cofounder of the Menshevik party—are perhaps Martov's fullest account of the events immediately following the October seizure of power. The letters not only narrate the course of events, but relate how Martov felt about being a key participant in the post-October political struggle. That the *Bolshevik* Revolution posed an insoluble dilemma for Martov and the Mensheviks comes forth clearly: on the one hand, he was disgusted with the Bolsheviks' dictatorial methods—violence, persecution of the press, arrests, and readiness to shoot their opponents from the very first days onward. On the other hand, as a Socialist, he felt embarrassed that the masses were supporting the Bolsheviks, something he could not bring himself to do. Martov's strategies in the post-October period were to side with the workers even though they were mistaken and thus win them over to the side of the Social Democrats and to oppose Bolshevik policies from within the soviets.

When the Bolsheviks defeated the cossacks and the Ukrainians in January 1918, they declared that the Civil War was over, and in the spring of that year, Lenin talked about a breathing spell and peaceful construction, having just concluded a peace treaty with Germany. The dissolution of the Constituent Assembly in January 1918 by the Bolsheviks, however, precipitated a confrontation with the Mensheviks and the Socialist Revolutionaries, who held the single largest number of seats in the assembly, far outnumbering the Bolsheviks. A letter from Fedor Dan—the coleader with Martov of the Menshevik party—to Pavel Axelrod (document 3) describes the charged atmosphere in Petrograd during the disbanding of the Constituent Assembly.[8] In expressing his anger and frustration at the Bolsheviks' action, Dan speaks for a whole generation of Russian intelligentsia to whom the convocation of the Constituent Assembly had been a dream for several decades. Now the dream was shattered. Particularly painful for Dan was that not just the Bolshevik leaders stood behind this action (Dan knew what to expect from them), but that the crowds of drunken sailors and soldiers (the embodiment of the *narod,* the revolutionary masses) were disbanding the Constituent Assembly on Bolshevik instructions. The goal of several decades seemed destroyed, as the mobs rejected the values of the Socialist intelligentsia. Dan's pessimism is somewhat offset by his report that the workers in Petrograd were indignant over the Bolsheviks' actions, giving him some hope that not everything was lost.

## SOVIET POWER WITHOUT THE SOVIETS (JANUARY–JUNE 1918)

The Mensheviks and the Socialist Revolutionaries did not recognize the Bolshevik dissolution of the Constituent Assembly, yet they were not willing at this stage to transform political conflict into a military confrontation. Adhering instead to a policy of peaceful competition with the Bolsheviks within the framework of the soviets,[9] their openly stated goal was to force the Bolshevik government to resign and to reconvene the Constituent Assembly. They believed this could be accomplished if and when the Socialist parties won majorities in the elections to the provincial soviets, which in turn would determine the majority at the subsequent Congress of Soviets, the supreme legislative body.

This policy was identical to the one the Bolsheviks pursued in the fall of 1917 under the provisional government when they criticized every step of the Mensheviks and the Socialist Revolutionaries and called for a different constitutional structure of political authority. In the spring of 1918, however, Menshevik and Socialist Revolutionary party leaders were optimistic about the success of their endeavor because they were convinced that the Bolshevik economic policies—nationalization of industry and banks—were bound to lead to an economic disaster and as a result antagonize a considerable part of the worker and peasant constituency.

Documents 4 through 13 cover the spring of 1918, a year starting with relative peace that turned out to be a prologue to the Civil War. These documents report on events in several provincial cities. Each incident taken alone may be dismissed as inconsequential, but taken together they add up to a picture of social and political upheaval. Explaining why workers' discontent grew into protest, these reports show how protests erupted into strikes and uprisings. When we are told that the arbitrariness of local Communists was the cause of the workers' discontent, it may not be convincing, but these reports describe exactly what such arbitrariness meant for the workers in Yaroslavl (a large industrial city in the central industrial region east of Moscow), Roslavl (a small industrial town in Smolensk province west of Moscow), or at the plant in Berezovskii (a small industrial town in the Urals); (see documents 8, 11, and 12). In the workers' own words, these documents disclose what workers read, what they liked in the theater, what their opinions were on local affairs, and what their daily concerns were at the factory. As Menshevik reporters describe the workers' thoughts about working conditions after the victory of the proletarian revolution, we also learn of their attitudes toward sex and family, as well as details of their attitudes toward political authority and political parties (document 5). Particularly striking is the degree to which the workers were interested and involved in politics. They came to rallies and meetings, followed closely the proposals of the various political parties, and voted for their representatives to the soviet.

Another thing we learn about is the growing resentment between the rank and file and their new Bolshevik bosses, who only months earlier had been ordinary workers on the factory floor. In theory, after the victory of the proletarian revolution in Russia, power was to belong to soviets elected by eligible voters—workers, soldiers, and peasants, the toiling masses—excluding merchants and businessmen, the bourgeoisie. In practice, however, local authority in the spring of 1918 was in the hands of self-appointed local Bolshevik leaders, commanders, and committees. The new bosses, yesterday's activists, did not want to reduce their newly acquired power and thus refused to hold elections. If they were compelled to conduct elections, they resorted to pressure and intimidation, falsified election returns, and, when there was no other option, disbanded the newly elected soviets. The peak of Bolshevik popularity was past. Bolshevik solutions were no longer attractive, and the electorate in the soviets was increasingly interested in the proposals of the opposition parties. Political struggles in provincial cities always ended with the Mensheviks and Socialist Revolutionaries' winning elections and the newly elected soviets' being systematically disbanded by the Bolsheviks.

A remarkable portrait gallery of these local Bolsheviks is presented in these Menshevik reports. Some, like those in Yaroslavl, held on tenaciously to the facade of democracy; after disbanding the soviet they called for new elections, but disbanded the new soviet when they lost for the second time. In Rostov-na-Donu, the cossack area, the Bolsheviks used outright threats; in Tambov, the black-earth region south of Moscow, they disbanded the soviet by armed force. Even more repugnant tactics were used in Roslavl, Smolensk province, where workers' representatives were seized and executed after it had been agreed that they were to negotiate on the workers' behalf (documents 8, 9, and 11).

The people who seized power after October in the provinces established their own dictatorships,[10] leaving the Bolsheviks in Moscow with only those local dictators to rely on. Those administering the "dictatorship of the proletariat" on behalf of Moscow in provincial towns requisitioned the best houses under the guise of strangling the bourgeoisie, created special food rations for themselves, and, most important, mistreated the workers more than their capitalist bosses ever had. Drunk with their newly acquired power, they were ruthless and ready to shoot, even at the workers, as they did in Kovrov and at the Berezovskii plant (documents 10 and 12).

## FROM REPRESSION TO CIVIL WAR (JUNE–OCTOBER 1918)

To save Soviet power, the Bolsheviks had to disband the soviets—the essence of the political transformation—by July 1918.[11] The workers responded with protest rallies, demonstrations, local strikes, and general strikes; in some cities they openly rebelled against the Bolsheviks. By July 1918 the confrontation between local Bolsheviks and workers had reached the stage of a civil war. Document 15 contains the most detailed and complete account of the Bolshevik repressions against the Socialists and the press from October 1917 to July 1918.

Iulii Martov's letter, dated June 16 (document 14), describes the escalation of Bolshevik repression in the spring of 1918. Listing cities where newly elected soviets were disbanded and where strikes and general strikes broke out in response, he recounts the dramatic expulsion of the Mensheviks and the Socialist Revolutionaries from the Central Executive Committee of Soviets—supposedly the legislative institution, a soviet parliament—on June 14 and expresses his fear that terror was going to intensify.

Undoubtedly, the Bolsheviks needed and wanted a civil war at this date,[12] for it is much easier to justify the use of armed force to crush an open rebellion than a general strike. Civil war allowed recourse to drastic measures, which, in the summer of 1918, were necessary if the Bolsheviks were to remain in power. Moreover, a civil war was good for party unity: only during a civil war could one demand unquestioning subordination of all factions to the party line or expel entire political parties in violation of the Bolsheviks' own laws, as was done with the Mensheviks and the Socialist Revolutionaries on June 14, 1918. Only under such conditions could the Bolsheviks arrest hundreds of duly elected deputies to the supreme legislative institution—the Congress of Soviets—as was done with the Left Socialist Revolutionary deputies on July 6, 1918. Civil war gave the Bolsheviks a chance to win back militarily what they were losing in the ballot box.

The workers, who lost their civil war against the Bolsheviks before it even started, never had a chance except where other forces opposed to the Bolsheviks joined them, as was the case with the Izhevsk workers in the Urals. Powerless vis-à-vis state power, the workers had no organizations of their own, independent of state authority, and were herded in big factories that could easily be occupied by the Cheka. Some factories simply shut down and fired all the workers, as was done in June 1918 with the Obukhov plant factory in Petrograd.[13]

The proletarian state could not tolerate workers' strikes, so yesterday's striker was tomorrow's unemployed. Having to find another job, which was almost impossible in the summer of 1918, or leave the city, workers made a large-scale exodus from the big cities.[14] In the summer of 1918, tens of thousands of workers fled to the countryside in search of food. In the long run the collapse of industrial production would have devastating consequences for the Russian cities, but in the short run it worked to the Bolsheviks' advantage because workers dispersed in villages looking for food were certainly less troublesome than in factories demanding their rights.

Some workers were drafted into the Red Army, where they had to obey orders and fight for Soviet power. Because the strikes were now officially labeled anti-Soviet conspiracies of enemies, those who took up arms, as did the Yaroslavl, Izhevsk, and Votkinsk workers, had to face an army of conscripted workers and peasants.

The Bolshevik Civil War in the cities against rebellious workers, Mensheviks, Socialist Revolutionaries, merchants, groups of intelligentsia, and other "enemies of Soviet power" ran parallel to another civil war raging in the countryside. As in the city war, there was no front line; the war was fought in every province and in every village. Whether a peasant war against Bolshevik requisition detachments or, from the other side, a Bolshevik war against kulaks (peasants) who refused to deliver grain to the authorities at fixed prices, the peasants were a much more formidable opponent than their urban counterparts. Thus it took the Bolsheviks several years to vanquish a majority population dispersed over an enormous territory, and at certain points they were close to losing. The Bolsheviks' problem in the countryside was that they had none of their own people there. For a few months, they relied on the Left Socialist Revolutionary influence, but by the summer of 1918, this was no longer possible. The Left Socialist Revolutionaries, like the Socialist Revolutionaries, defended the peasants' economic interests against the state.

In the case of peasants who were unwilling to deliver grain at low, state-controlled prices, Lenin decided to seize their grain. The Bolsheviks, however, did not have the manpower for such a grandiose undertaking. Their solution—to divide and conquer—meant that the hungry workers in the cities, many of whom had voted against the Bolsheviks, were now told to impose a proletarian dictatorship over the peasantry, now called petite bourgeoisie. Workers' detachments were mobilized and sent to the countryside to fight the peasants and confiscate their crops under that same divide and rule principle. The civil war between the countryside and the Bolsheviks now extended into a civil war between the peasants themselves. With peasants fighting peasants and workers fighting peasants, the Bolsheviks in big cities neutralized a large segment of their opponents.

In place of the soviets, which were discarded as counterrevolutionary and petit bourgeois, the Bolsheviks created the so-called committees of the poor to denounce those who had "surplus" grain. These committees then received a share of requisitioned booty as a reward. In addition to the "surplus" grain, the requisition detachments took any other food they could find. The hungry and irate peasants fought back and killed many Bolshevik officials and conscripted workers. In retribution, the Bolsheviks shelled or burned entire villages—now referred to as nests of counterrevolutionaries—took hostages from the recalcitrant peasants, and conducted mass executions. Thus any government official appearing in the villages was suspect, for whether it be a Bolshevik, a Menshevik, or a White officer, he wanted grain, horses, and recruits. The peasants now determined to defend their villages from *any* urban intruders, which meant that the countryside was neutralized as a potential reserve for an organized, urban-led, anti-Bolshevik movement. The peasants withdrew from national politics and from the national market, which in the long run would have catastrophic consequences. In the short run, however, the Communists were able to pump grain from the countryside to the cities for the coming winter.[15]

The summer of 1918 was a time of uprisings that flared up spontaneously, without much coordination. In some cases—Izhevsk, Votkinsk, and other industrial towns in the Urals—the workers were fighting on their own.[16] In other cases, Red Army soldiers rebelled against Soviet power, as they did in Saratov (the Volga basin) in May.[17] In still other cases, especially small towns in central Russia, peasants from the surrounding countryside attacked local Bolsheviks. In areas and towns in southern Russia, in the Ukraine, and in Siberia, detachments of White officers seized power. Most often, however, a combination of forces was at work. In Yaroslavl in July 1918, for example, a workers' detachment fought with White officers against the Bolsheviks during the famous uprising there.[18]

The Socialist Revolutionaries were particularly active in the Volga basin area, their traditional stronghold, and found an unexpected ally in the Czech legion. These Czech troops, nominally under the French high command, were on their way to Vladivostok for France, where they were to be deployed on the western front against Germany. The Bolsheviks, in an effort to recruit "Internationalists" among the Czech troops and use them for the cause of world proletarian revolution,[19] made obstacles to the Czechs' advance and tried to confiscate their weapons. The ensuing hostilities finally led to the Czechs' deciding to fight their way out of Russia. Here Trotsky made what many consider to be one of his greatest blunders: he issued an order to disarm the Czechs without adequate manpower. Instead, the Czechs began to disarm the Bolsheviks all along the trans-Siberian railway.

Having quickly come to an understanding with the Czechs, who needed an ally in Russia, on June 8, the Socialist Revolutionaries seized power in Samara on the Volga and formed the Committee of the Constituent Assembly from those members of the Constituent Assembly who happened to be present. This incident, which marked the beginning of one of the main stages in the frontline Civil War, could never have occurred had not the Socialist Revolutionaries been supported by thousands of rebellious workers and peasants in the Volga basin area. The Committee of the Constituent Assembly (Komuch) immediately created a people's army from the rebels. Within several weeks the rebels, aided by the Czechs, overthrew the Bolsheviks throughout the Volga basin north of Samara and in the Urals. On August 8 they captured Kazan and looked toward extending their offensive to Nizhnii Novgorod and to Moscow.

Thus by the end of the summer the Bolsheviks had been overthrown all along the trans-Siberian railway. In addition to Komuch claiming to govern the huge territory from the Volga to the Pacific, the Siberian duma and a number of independent White officers' military formations emerged as centers of authority. In the South, the poorly armed and badly understaffed

White Army continued to fight on in Caucasia. Although in most regiments officers served as privates, they fought well and their fortunes were beginning to turn.

By the late summer of 1918, the Bolsheviks' territory had shrunk to a dozen odd provinces around Moscow and the steppes of the lower Volga. Their control in the rural areas was nominal; basically, they controlled the cities and the railroads. That the Civil War could have ended with the Bolsheviks' defeat is shown by top-ranking Bolshevik officials' preparing foreign passports for themselves.[20]

Documents 14, 15, and 17 describe important details of these events, including the factional struggle in the Menshevik party over the policy toward the Komuch government. The documents convey the uncertain spirit of the time, as dramatic events unfolded that no one anticipated. Political leaders had daily to adjust and improvise to meet the unpredictable challenges of the situation.

How did the Bolshevik government manage to survive amid workers' general strikes, peasant rebellions, and the Czech–Socialist Revolutionary offensive? There is no simple answer, and a thorough discussion would take us too far from the material in the Menshevik reports. Nevertheless, there are some obvious reasons: Local uprisings and peasant rebellions toppled Bolshevik power only when aided by well-organized armies; otherwise, the Bolshevik forces could suppress local uprisings.

The Socialist Revolutionaries had a chance of winning in the summer of 1918, but were too dependent on Czech support. The Czechs were not committed to taking Moscow, even though they had decided to stay in Russia, at least for the time being, and support the Socialist Revolutionaries. The Socialist Revolutionaries on the Volga had neither the support of the Siberian government nor that of the White officers, who recognized the Constituent Assembly in words, but in fact were waiting for an opportune moment to get rid of the Socialist Revolutionaries and conduct armed struggle against the Bolsheviks on their own. Admiral A. V. Kolchak accomplished that when he overthrew the Komuch government in November 1918.

The Komuch government could unconditionally count on only the Izhevsk workers and peasant rebels, an improvised army of some thirty thousand. Because Komuch was fighting the Bolsheviks from the very first day, there was little time to organize a functioning administration and no unity in strategic matters among the Komuch leaders. They did not know whether to proceed with the offensive after the capture of Kazan or whether to assume a defensive position. The Mensheviks provided only half-hearted support. Local Menshevik organizations backed the Socialist Revolutionaries, but the Moscow Mensheviks pronounced themselves neutral. These divisions among bolshevism's opponents made it possible for the Bolsheviks in Moscow to defeat their enemies one at a time.

Perhaps the most important factor in the Bolsheviks' victory was their ability to mobilize a small but effective Red Army using the so-called Internationalists—that is, revolutionary elements from several nationalities, the Latvians, Hungarians, Jews, Poles, Chinese, and Russians—who would gain if the Bolsheviks stayed in power.[21]

Crushing the workers' resistance, the Bolsheviks arrested some, drafted others into the Red Army, and provided the possibility of upward mobility to still others. They neutralized the peasantry as a united anti-Bolshevik force by exploiting the antagonism between the well-off and the poorer peasants, successfully applying the divide-and-rule policy to defeat their numerous, heterogeneous opponents. Resorting to systematic, mass terror against entire political parties and several social groups as a matter of officially sanctioned state policy, the Bolshevik authorities, on the instruction of Moscow, took hostages from the civilian population, executed thousands of suspected oppositionists, shelled rebellious villages with artillery, and instituted the rule of Red Terror. Documents 16 and 17 describe these developments throughout the summer and fall of 1918. The Communists withstood the 1918 upheavals, but at great cost, for they had to abandon the idea that they could rule Russia by popular consensus. Their dictatorship, if it were to survive, would have to be fought for in a protracted, cruel, and bloody civil war.

## NEW COURSE AND NEW REPRESSIONS
### (DECEMBER 1918–SEPTEMBER 1919)

The year 1919 saw the most important battles in the frontline Civil War, although, as in 1918, at certain moments the Bolsheviks reckoned with the possibility of defeat. This time, however, their key opponents were not the Socialists (Mensheviks and Socialist Revolutionaries) but the Whites—well-organized volunteer armies led by former officers of the Russian Imperial Army—backed by the Allies: France, Britain, and the United States. In the beginning of the year, however, this course of events was not anticipated. The Bolsheviks scored major victories against the Socialist Revolutionary Komuch government on the Volga in the eastern front in the fall of 1918, having already recaptured Samara, the capital of the liberated area; the entire Volga basin; and the Urals. That the Komuch government was overthrown in November 1918 and that an undisguised military dictatorship was established by Admiral Kolchak enabled the Bolsheviks to portray themselves as the only heirs of the Russian Revolution.

There was no longer an alternative government between the Reds and the Whites.

The defeat of Germany in World War I in November 1918 meant the withdrawal of German troops from the Ukraine, opening up new possibilities for the Moscow Bolsheviks. The beginning of the revolutionary upheaval in Germany and in Central Europe likewise opened new avenues for action in the international arena, particularly in regard to the Socialist movement, all of which made the Bolsheviks more secure. Thus they tried to improve their image in the eyes of the European Socialists.

In document 18, Martov discusses and analyzes the changes in the Communists' internal policies in early 1919. He points out that the Cheka, which Lenin created in December 1917 as a kind of political police, had gone out of control by the end of 1918. Lenin meant it to be a merciless and effective strike force against all Bolshevik opponents; yet during the reign of unrestrained Red Terror in the fall of 1918, the Cheka usurped all power in many towns and villages. As Martov points out, local Chekas executed whomever they pleased, including some dissident Communists. These atrocities and arbitrary shootings provoked what Martov refers to as an "unheard of phenomenon," a "liberal" current in Bolshevism, on the part of some Bolsheviks in Moscow. Some Bolsheviks even went so far as to demand a total abolition of the Cheka and a restoration of the courts.[22] Some, like N. Osinsky (the pen name of Valerian Obolensky), publicly demanded full freedom of political activity for the opposition parties (the Mensheviks, the Socialist Revolutionaries, and the Left Socialist Revolutionaries).[23] Although some attempts were made to restore electoral procedures in the soviets, the reformers were particularly strong in the Moscow party organization. From Martov's account, we learn of the moderation in Bolshevik policies in Moscow; for a short time, from January to March 1919, a Menshevik newspaper, *Vsegda Vpered* (Always Forward), and the Socialist Revolutionary paper *Delo Naroda* (The Cause of the People) were allowed to publish. The contract for paper supplies for these newspapers was signed for seven months, making it look as though a limited amount of opposition would be tolerated at least that long.[24] As it turned out, *Vsegda Vpered* was closed after fifteen issues and *Delo Naroda* after ten—the last opposition party newspapers to be published in Moscow. The Cheka was not abolished, and local cliques continued to rule without elections.

Martov perceptively outlines some reasons for the limits to the Bolshevik reforms by showing that there is no contradiction between the concept of dictatorship and the lack of central controls over local Communist officials. The Communist dictatorship was no weaker when the Moscow Communists did not fully control the provinces. In fact the Communist party dictatorship was more secure when the local autocrats enjoyed greater autonomy and tightly controlled their provinces to further their own interests.

Martov's analysis of Bolshevik economic policies suggests that it is mistaken to regard Lenin's economic policy as a continuous whole. Rather, it should be seen as cyclical, with dynamics and zigzags. In the spring of 1918, Lenin was talking about a "new course," which was taken to mean a policy of moderation in contrast to the seizures of property after October. In June 1918, however, this moderation was abandoned in favor of the nationalization of industry and grain requisitioning, a policy later labeled *war communism*. In the spring of 1919, Lenin again spoke of a new course that would allow some degree of private trade. Again, after a short period, this moderation was abandoned until rebellions by peasants and sailors in the spring of 1921 forced the Bolsheviks to adopt the New Economic Policy (NEP). (There was very little new in it; it had been tried twice earlier, and each time the Communist zealots scored victories in the intraparty infighting and pushed the Communist party to a head-on attack on private enterprise.) Martov's analysis puts the chronology of the Bolshevik economic policy in a new perspective.

One of the most important questions is why did the Bolsheviks abandon moderation in the spring of 1919? The return to hard-line policies of war communism—grain requisitioning, Red Terror, and arbitrary executions by the Cheka—renewed the anti-Bolshevik uprisings and swelled the ranks of volunteers to the White Armies, bringing them about two hundred miles away from Moscow by October 1919. These Bolshevik policies prolonged and intensified the Civil War and turned the Bolshevik party even more into a military organization at war with its own population.

It is possible that the decisions affecting Bolshevik party policies were shaped more in the provinces than in the capital and that the Moscow Bolsheviks had to sanction the arbitrary dictatorship of the local cliques because they had nobody else to rely on in the provinces, least of all the hostile and often insurgent local population. In many cases the choice was between a dictatorship of hard-line Communist cliques or losing the province to the insurgents or the Whites. The accounts of provincial politics in the Menshevik reports suggest that the local autocrats lacked control not only by the electorate but also by their Moscow superiors. The farther a provincial town was from Moscow, the more the local dictators could get away with. For instance, some dictators arrested Socialists for subscribing to a Menshevik paper legally published in Moscow, whereas others refused to legalize the opposition party despite the supposedly binding law of the CEC (document 20) and continued with requisitions and executions (document 28). In many localities, the *uezd* (district-level) Chekas continued to operate as masters in their provinces even though a ruling had been made that they were to be phased out.

The Menshevik reports on conditions in the provinces are not dissimilar from the reports in *Pravda*. At that time, *Pravda* reflected the views of moderate Bolsheviks who wanted to curb the powers of the Cheka and restore at least some measure of accountability to the local administration. In one report, for example, *Pravda* described an incident in Nizhnii Novgorod province where, under the guise of requisitioning, local authorities took away peasants' personal belongings, clothing, samovars, and so forth. When the peasants resisted, an armed detachment was called in to suppress what was described as a kulak uprising. *Pravda* commented that "the detachment arrived and executed those who were pointed out by the local party organization. The detachment left, but everything remained as earlier. . . . In one village fifty people were executed in this fashion."[25] Many similar accounts were published in *Pravda,* echoing the more explicit reports of the Mensheviks and the Socialist Revolutionaries. Drunkenness, corruption, unlawful requisitions, and settling personal feuds under the guise of class struggle were the salient characteristics of provincial Communist administrations.

One document describes the situation of a Communist commander of a punitive detachment in Smolensk province in the summer of 1919 who reports that the local authorities requisitioned even peasants' personal belongings for their own use and that the peasants hated the commune. He frankly describes his pacification measures: ambushes in "bandits" homes, taking hostages, and arrests.[26]

These problems with local administrations were discussed at the Eighth Party Congress in March 1919, during which numerous speakers admitted that the situation was appalling. As Viktor Nogin of the Moscow party organization put it: "In that commission [of the Central Committee on party development] we have received such an endless number of horrifying facts on drunkenness, debauchery, bribery, robbery and reckless actions on the part of many officials, that it is simply hair-raising."[27]

Grigorii Zinoviev, the Petrograd party boss, said that in some localities, "the word commissar has become a swear word, a hated word. A man in a leather jacket, as they say in Perm, has become hateful for the people."[28] Said another speaker, "We see that somehow the soviets are beginning to slowly die out, that in the end a process is going on as a result of which only the Executive Committees remain. And the soviets are liquidated, although this is against the Constitution."[29] In other areas Communists were surrounded by an "intense hatred."[30] Yet despite these frank admissions, the Communist congress could not find any solution other than a purge of the party. There was no more talk of restoring free elections to the soviets, for this was considered too risky in view of the Menshevik popularity among the workers and Socialist Revolutionary and kulak influence in the countryside.

The revival of Menshevik popularity in the spring of 1919, just as in the spring of 1918, can be seen by the Menshevik paper *Vsegda Vpered* reaching the circulation of one hundred thousand a week after it resumed publication. But as the demand rose, the Communists (as mentioned earlier), to limit circulation, imposed restrictions on the amount of paper the Mensheviks could obtain. The Communists' toleration of an opposition paper lasted only two months, revealing the degree of their insecurity over the Mensheviks' political influence. Document 25 describes the manifestations of what must have been serious infighting among the Bolsheviks over the fate of the opposition press. The paper was closed, and then a promise was made that the permit for publication would be granted; then the permit was withdrawn, and finally the Cheka arrested the entire Menshevik Central Committee, including Martov. A statement signed by Felix Dzerzhinskii, the head of the Cheka, explained that "the arrested Left Socialist Revolutionaries and the Mensheviks will be held as hostages and their fate will depend on the behavior of both parties."[31]

Strengthening the hand of the hard-liners was the intensification of the workers', peasants', and soldiers' protests while under the conditions of the new course in the spring of 1919. In February and March, serious strikes broke out in Petrograd, Tula, Bryansk, Tver, and many other cities.[32] George Leggett depicts the dénouement of the Putilov plant workers' strike in Petrograd as follows:

> Describing these events, *Izvestiia* reported that fighting broke out between striking workers and Red Army soldiers and in the shooting a number of people had been wounded. The strike was suppressed and the Cheka went to work, holding summary trials. Many executions followed, taking place in a remote locality called Irinovka, near the fortress of Schlusselburg. The procedure was to line up the victims against the wall, blindfolded, and to shoot them down sometimes in batches by machine-gun fire.[33]

*Delo Naroda,* in one of its last issues, attempted to publish an account of the strike in Tula, but the censors banned it; the paper came out with blank columns under the title EVENTS IN TULA. Fortunately, a Tula worker who was a participant in and witness to these events some months later published his account of the events in Tula (see document 24). Although less is known about the disturbances in Bryansk,[34] the Red Army soldiers there did join the strikers, and the ensuing liquidation of "disorders" was cruel and bloody. Dozens of workers were arrested and jailed, and local Menshevik and Socialist Revolutionary leaders were taken hostage by the Communist authorities.[35]

Workers' demands in the spring of 1919 were strikingly similar to their demands in 1918. Protesting against the unfair distribution of food, privileges for the Communists, destruction of independent unions, and high-handed, arbitrary rule by local Communists, they also demanded free elections to the soviets, release of all political prisoners, and freedom for political activity for the Mensheviks and the Socialist Revolutionaries. Document 23, a resolution of workers at the Motovilikha metal industry plant in the Urals, is representative of these demands. (Perhaps unique to that resolution is a demand that the leather jackets of the Cheka agents be donated to manufacture shoes for children.)

Because of tight Communist control over the press and the flow of information, little is known about the workers' political attitudes during the Russian Civil War, except from Soviet official sources. In many books these resolutions are treated as though they authentically reflect popular attitudes on the basis of having been adopted by a unanimous vote. Yet to accept them as such is to misunderstand the nature of the Bolshevik dictatorship. Compulsion, intimidation, coercion, and arrests were applied systematically and consistently throughout the Civil War years in every strike or protest for which records are available. Moreover, the Bolshevik measures against the strikers in the spring of 1919 were harsher than in 1918, when frightened Bolshevik authorities often made concessions to or concluded agreements with the strikers, only to violate them later (document 11). In 1919, however, the local Chekas were more firmly entrenched than in 1918. After a period of Moscow-sponsored lawlessness and arbitrary murders during the Red Terror in the fall of 1918, local Communists felt much more confident. Thus the strikes in Tula, Bryansk, and Motovilikha ended badly for the workers: in almost every case, plants were shut down, mass arrests conducted, and hostages taken.

In late December 1918 and early January 1919, a relatively small force of the Siberian White Army, led by General Anatolii Pepeliaev, overran Perm province (in the Urals) and the Reds hastily withdrew, marking the beginning of the White offensive on the eastern front. Although figures on Bolshevik terror reported by the Bolsheviks' political opponents are usually distrusted, in this case, immediately after the White Army drove the Reds from the city of Perm, an American Red Cross official visited the area and filed this report: "Perm front: Have seen this district, extensive proof savage cruelty, Bolsheviki occupation, over 2000 civilians, men, women, murdered locally in cold blood without warning or trial, many peasants and small shop keepers. Some bodies show fearful mutilation before death."[36] According to a British parliamentary report, one hundred strikers in the Motovilikha plant in the Perm province were executed by the Bolsheviks in December 1918,[37] which was not many compared with the bloodbath in neighboring Izhevsk and Votkinsk. When these towns were retaken by the White Army in March 1919 and the victims of Red Terror counted, the total, from November 1918 to March 1919, exceeded seven thousand.[38]

The Whites' success could only be explained by worker and peasant insurgents striking the Communist forces from the rear; the best fighting units in the Siberian White Army were detachments of Izhevsk and Votkinsk workers. Throughout the spring of 1919, the White Army in the Urals continued its offensive, pushing slowly toward the Volga River. Focusing on the frontline shifts in the Civil War often obscures that it was the insurgent movements, not the armies, that were the decisive factor in the frontline Civil War. It is estimated that more than 100,000 insurgents operated against the Bolsheviks in the Urals area alone in the spring of 1919,[39] which means that the Civil War was not a civil war between organized armies, but rather that the Whites and later the Reds simply poured into an area that was already in rebellion against an existing authority. The insurgent movements, however, were only successful if later backed by an advancing army; both the Reds and the Whites were almost always able to suppress local insurgencies by bringing in a superior force to the affected area.

The Whites' successful offensive in the East made the Bolsheviks draft more peasants into the Red Army. According to Western intelligence, in September 1919 there were 120,000 Red Army soldiers on the eastern front (the Urals), 180,000 on the southern front (black-earth area south of Moscow), 35,000 soldiers on the northern front (Pskov province area in the approaches to Petrograd), and 130,000 on the western front (Belorussia)—a total of 465,000 troops.[40] This expansion of the standing armies brought about mass desertions; according to the documents in the Smolensk archives, mass desertion reached catastrophic proportions. Lobanov, a Communist speaker at a regional party conference, said that the problem started at the beginning of March 1919; by June, in Bel'sk *uezd* alone, twenty-six hundred deserters were apprehended. To put an end to the problem of desertion, Lobanov recommended (1) confiscating cattle, (2) executing the most active deserters, and (3) sending punitive detachments into the districts.[41]

In Ryazan province near Moscow, 54,697 deserters were apprehended in the forests.[42] From White sources we learn that the deserters from the Reds made up the majority of the fighting force of the northern White Army, which grew from twenty-five hundred to thirty thousand in the

Pskov area.[43] Moreover, these deserters hated the Bolsheviks; so if Petrograd were to be taken, fears were that a Communist bloodbath could not be avoided. Similarly, in South Russia the volunteer White Army of General Anton Denikin took in so many deserters from the Reds that by July 1919 their number exceeded the strength of the original White Army force.[44] A Western authority estimated that the total number of deserters in 1919 exceeded one million.[45]

As we have seen, in the areas adjacent to the front lines, deserters from the Reds often joined the Whites, but in central Russia most deserters formed their own detachments, known as the Greens. The political outlook of the Greens varied a great deal from area to area. In the Urals the peasants joined the Whites in the spring of 1919. Shortly thereafter desertion from the White Army gained momentum, and the Greens behind the White lines began to cripple the Whites' war effort.[46] In the Ukraine independent peasant detachments, which were often anti-Semitic, fought against the Reds and the Whites and also engaged in pogroms against the Jews.[47] For the most part the Greens defended their local areas from any outside intruders, Red or White.

A survey of the Communist press for the summer of 1919 makes it clear that desertion from the Red Army and the rise of the Green movement were major problems for the Bolshevik authorities. Special days were announced whereby deserters could return without punishment. In almost every city a commission for the struggle with desertion was set up. The Petrograd Bolsheviks decided to resolve the problem of desertion in June 1919 by announcing that deserters who return voluntarily would be pardoned. It was said that many returned and that

> in those cases when the parents and the brothers of these deserters had been taken as hostages, these latter were set free; . . . those who in the course of specified dates, that is up to 20 July, came back voluntarily, would be enlisted in the ranks of the Red Army, in case they were fit, without any punishment; and those whose relatives were taken as hostages by that time would be released and the confiscated property would be returned. All those persons older than twelve years of age found in the forests during the search after the date indicated in point one, and those who will not have a permission, will be shot on the spot.[48]

The Bolshevik war against deserters—the Greens, or "bandits," as they were referred to in official media—affected every province and every district in the supposedly Bolshevik-controlled territory. In its magnitude, this war far eclipsed the frontline Civil War with the Whites. As Robert Conquest puts it,

Yet in general the Civil War was a contest between two well armed but unpopular minorities. And if in considering the period from 1918, we are habituated to turn our main attention to it, it is for inadequate reasons: it was a regular war, of organized armies, rival governments, high commands, conducted for the capture of key points, of central cities. Its campaigns and battles are clear on the ground; its prominence in the eyes of the world plain and dramatic. Yet in its scope, and even more in its casualties and its effect on the country, it may be reasonably held as less pervasive and less massive than the Peasant War of 1918–22 which overlapped it and outlasted it.[49]

This aspect of the Civil War has not received adequate attention.[50]

By the summer of 1919, the White offensive in the East had run out of steam. Once their area had been liberated from the Bolsheviks, the Izhevsk and Votkinsk workers were demobilized. The enthusiastic reception of the White forces by the local population gave way to disillusionment and hostility. As a U.S. dispatch to the State Department pointed out,

> Reliable reports indicate that the Kolchak units, freed from all restraint, are looting the districts through which they are retreating. . . . All reports indicate that the Siberian army is completely disorganized, demoralized, and in panic. There is jealousy and intrigue among commanding officers. I am reliably informed that a large number of line officers are abandoning their units and fleeing to the rear, that a great many have been shot.[51]

Soldiers began to desert the White Army. Two Ukrainian regiments crossed over to the Reds; peasant uprisings broke out in the rear. The Kolchak regime began to slowly collapse, slowly because Siberian distances provided some room for maneuver. Thus in June 1919, the Bolsheviks were beginning to roll Kolchak's forces back, but then they had to face a new peril—General Anton Denikin.

## THE WHITE THREAT (1919)

Denikin's extraordinarily successful offensive in summer 1919 from the foothills of Caucasia to the threshold of Moscow was largely made possible by peasant insurgencies behind the Red lines. In April 1919 alone, there were ninety-three separate armed uprisings against the Bolsheviks in the Ukraine.[52] Two of the most serious were the rebellions of Nikolai Hryhoriiv and Nestor Makhno, a popular peasant leader. To fight Hryhoriiv and Makhno, the Bolsheviks withdrew most of their reserves from the Denikin front, which made it easier for the volunteer army to break up the Red defense lines.[53] (Several months of Bolshevik rule in the subjugated Ukraine had given rise to widespread resistance.[54])

Perhaps the most notorious operation undertaken by the Bolsheviks in the spring of 1919 was the "de-cossackization" of the cossack areas. This policy, which had a decisive impact on the course of the Civil War, was adopted at the initiative of the Communist Donburo. The Communist Central Committee directive of January 1919 stated: "Taking into account the experience of the Civil War against the cossacks, it is necessary to recognize the unique correctness of the most pitiless struggle against all upper strata of cossackry, by means of their extermination to a man." The policy specified "*large-scale terrorism*" [emphasis in original] against the wealthy cossacks, including exterminating them, confiscating their grain, completely disarming the population, and arming reliable elements.[55] The Donburo immediately set out to implement this directive and to issue its own even more bloodthirsty edicts, ordering large-scale arrests, the taking of hostages, and the setting up of tribunals. According to an eyewitness,

> Most of the time the tribunals dealt with cases on the basis of lists. Sometimes it took only a few minutes to consider a case. And the sentence was almost always the same: shooting. . . . Old cossacks from various families were shot, officers who had voluntarily laid down their arms were shot. Even cossack women were shot.[56]

These brutal methods were applied indiscriminately not only against a social class, but against entire populations. Mass executions in some villages were discovered through mass graves.[57] Bordering on genocide, this bloody episode resulted in the Don and the Kuban cossacks' rising en masse against the Communists and breaking the Bolshevik hold on the Don, the Kuban, and the Ukraine.[58] Thus the less secure the Communists were in their capacity to hold power, the more readily they resorted to violence and executions.[59] (General Denikin, on the entry of the White troops,[60] formed a Special Commission to Investigate Bolshevik Atrocities. Documentary evidence collected by this commission in the presence of the Allied representative widely publicized the atrocities of the Kharkov and Kiev Cheka.)

General Denikin's astonishingly successful offensive in summer 1919 and equally astonishing rout in the winter of 1919–1920 cannot be properly understood without examining the dynamics of popular movements. In this regard the Menshevik reports are of particular interest. Documents 29 and 30 describe internal conditions on the territory controlled by the Whites; documents 32, 33, and 34 deal with popular attitudes in the territory controlled by the Reds. The authors of these reports did not know about their colleagues' observations on the other side of the front line, which makes all the more striking the similarity of their accounts. Documents 32 and 33 are Menshevik delegation reports on the area immediately adjacent to the front line—Tula and Bryansk in October 1919—at the most critical stage of the frontline Civil War for the Bolsheviks, who after the fall of Orel were making plans for the evacuation of Moscow. In case Denikin's offensive was not stopped, the schedule for departure was worked out and lists were made of those to be evacuated to the East.[61] It was widely believed that Tula might be the next city to fall to the Whites, which would have been catastrophic for the Bolsheviks not only because of Tula's strategic position (the last major city before Moscow), but also because of the two armaments plants there that produced rifles and bullets. The Bolsheviks were well aware of workers' political attitudes in Tula and neighboring Bryansk because it was in those cities that strikes and disturbances had broken out earlier in the year (document 24), and thus the memories of arrests and hostage taking were still painful and fresh.

When Orel fell and the Bolsheviks received news of how enthusiastically the population welcomed the Whites, they had to somehow lessen popular antagonism to Communist rule;[62] intensified propaganda was the Bolshevik answer. Finally, in desperation, they allowed the Mensheviks to campaign for Soviet power in the frontline area. Even in this situation, however, local authorities were reluctant to allow the opposition party representatives to speak, agreeing only under pressure from Moscow. The Menshevik compaigners state in their report to their Central Committee that their mission could not be called successful: hostility to the Communists was widespread, and the possibility of Denikin's arrival did not cause the workers to man the barricades. Even the Mensheviks—who had always had tremendous influence in Tula, winning all local elections in 1917 and in 1918 until they were expelled—failed to convince the Tula and Bryansk workers to support Soviet power.

The letter of the Kiev Mensheviks to the European Socialists (document 29) is explicit on workers' attitudes in the Ukraine and speaks of workers' hatred of the Bolshevik regime. One might be tempted to dismiss these Menshevik allegations on the grounds that the Social Democrats, an opposition party, were likely to emphasize workers' negative attitudes to the Bolsheviks: by the same logic, however, the Social Democrats should also have emphasized workers' negative attitudes to the Whites (between the two evils, the Whites and the Reds, the Mensheviks considered the Reds the lesser evil). Yet the letter of the Kiev Mensheviks states that the overwhelming majority of workers supported an extreme right wing, and the Mensheviks reporting from Bryansk, in Soviet territory, wrote of an atmosphere of sympathy toward Denikin. Attitudes are difficult to measure, especially in the conditions of dictatorship without free elections; thus Menshevik reports on workers' attitudes should be treated with caution. They do, however, seem to undermine the claim that Russian workers' choosing between the Whites and the Reds chose the Reds.[63] The true picture is much more complex and diverse, for worker apathy, withdrawal from politics, sympathy to the Whites, and anti-Semitic feelings were as much of the spectrum as was a preference for Soviet power.[64]

In the summer of 1919, Denikin's armies benefited from the peasants' and cossacks' anti-Bolshevik insurgencies and the workers' benevolent neutrality.[65] The propertied classes and the church, of course, greeted the volunteer army as a savior and a liberator (*spasiteli i izbaviteli*). The question is, why did the volunteer army fail to translate these favorable sociopolitical conditions into a lasting victory? The answers, however, go far beyond the scope of this introduction, and many await further research. Thus we will give only a brief outline here.

Documents 29, 30, and 31 deal with the conditions in the White-held territory. In general, these reports confirm the conclusions of some Western historians, notably Peter Kenez,[66] that the leaders of the White movement alienated the very social groups—Russian workers and peasants, Socialist intelligentsia, Ukrainian intelligentsia, Ukrainian peasants, Jews, and even cossacks—that were sympathetic or neutral to them. As Kenez points out, the Whites wrote off the workers as a hostile class,[67] which, according to Menshevik reports, meant arrests, curbs on unions, and arbitrary rule. Far more significant, however, was the entrepreneurs' attempt to re-establish control over factory floors. The time of the workers' committees was over; there would be no dictatorship of the proletariat. This forthright reimposition of authority made it obvious to the workers who the bosses would be in the new conditions. Resentment began to accumulate.

That the White Army antagonized the peasants is clear from the admission of General Petr Wrangel in a letter to General Denikin:

> At the very time when the Volunteer armies were victoriously advancing on Moscow, and your ears were listening to the sound of the bells of Moscow, in the hearts of many of your subordinate commanders alarm crept in. The armies—without training and subsisted by robbery, afflicted with drunkenness, in which its chiefs led, and disorganized by their example—were not the armies to save Russia. Without an organized rear, without one prepared position or chain of communications, retreating through places where the population had learnt to hate it, the Volunteer army, once the retreat began, was forced to move precipitantly.[68]

In many instances the officers punished peasants who had seized property under the Bolsheviks, and the sentiment soon emerged that the Whites were no better than the Bolsheviks. Among the many independent observers who came to this conclusion was Admiral N. A. McCully. His report to the State Department included the following:

> During Denikin's advance in August and September 1919, the service of supply was neglected and became so inefficient, that the troops had no other resort except to live off the country. Official permission to do this quickly degenerated into license and the troops were responsible for all kinds of excesses. Localities that welcomed them as Deliverers within a month came to detest them.[69]

The White Army's slogan was Russia, United and Indivisible! which implied restoring the empire and in practical terms meant no tolerance for the national aspirations of cossacks, Ukrainians, Jews, and others. General Denikin, however, never committed himself by restoring the monarchy and was reputed to have preferred a parliamentary order. Although the policy of no compromise on the national question led to a virtual war with the Ukrainian government, the officers were more cautious with the Don and the Kuban cossacks' autonomous aspirations because the White Army depended on the cossacks' military strength. The Don and Kuban cossacks shared with the volunteer army a hostility to bolshevism that was the core of their alliance. They had, however, profoundly different goals that increasingly diverged; in the end the crisis of the cossack-White officers' partnership contributed more than anything else to the catastrophic collapse of the front in November 1919.

The cossacks' main goal was to drive the Bolsheviks out of their territory, not out of Moscow. The farther the front was from the cossacks' homeland, the less vigor they demonstrated on the battlefield. As discipline deteriorated, requisitions increased, as did violence against the civilian population, especially the Jews. Successes at the front actually weakened the volunteer army's alliance with the cossacks; the farther North the front, the less they needed each other. In addition, Nestor Makhno's detachments of peasants struck the White forces in the interior of the held territory. Without the active support of the peasants or the cities, the White front collapsed and with it the Whites' rule.

No documents can adequately describe the tragedies suffered by the Russians, Ukrainians, Jews and others during the Civil War or the defenselessness of the local population vis-à-vis armed bands, armies, and administrations. In some areas people traveling to a neighboring town would ask, "What kind of authority do you have in town? (*kakaia vlast' u vas tam?*) Ukrainian, Red, White, Green, anarchist, or some other?" The collapse of Denikin's regime, which exposed millions of local residents to a new Bolshevik conquest, caused panic to break out. Railway stations were packed by thousands of desperate people trying to get a ticket, but a ticket to where? Odessa? Novorossiisk? Those who could not obtain a ticket went on foot. From the air a British pilot observed refugees fleeing from Kuban.

> As to the sentiment generally of the Cossacks with regard to the Soviets, about 100,000 of them fled from their homes when Red forces occupied the territory eastward of the Sea of Azov. This number is quite well verified not only by the reconnaissance of aviators who reported a stream of refugees sixty miles in length—women, children, cattle, pigs and whatever could be taken along—fleeing southward in middle March 1920. From other sources, the fact undoubtedly existed. It is the only definite ·fact bearing on the attitude of the populations toward the Reds, and whether they were justified or not in doing so, nevertheless this number of peasant population of the Cossack territories believed themselves in such danger from the Reds that they abandoned everything they could not carry along and fled from their homes.[70]

Many of them would die of starvation and disease on the road, many would be captured by the advancing Reds, and many would be executed as White sympathizers or as enemies of Soviet power. Even some of those who made it to the ports only delayed the final denouement. When the fall of Odessa approached, thousands tried to obtain a seat on a ship to safety, but Allied and Russian ships could only take a limited number. Desperate crowds formed on the pier as shouting, crying, panic-stricken people tried to make their way to the ships. An American officer, reporting on how difficult it was to preserve order and carry on with the evacuation when the cutoff number was reached, described an unforgettable scene: When no one else could be taken on board, an old, white-haired Russian officer and four women were next in line. No exceptions could be made, for there were thousands still on the pier. The old man went on his knees, crying, and pleaded with the officer to take him and his family along. He had to be refused, even though it meant death for him when the Bolsheviks arrived. The officer's report continued: "It is estimated that not less than twelve thousand women and children and six thousand men, women and children of the literary, scientific and professional classes who should have been evacuated, were left behind."[71]

## WAR COMMUNISM AND POPULAR RESISTANCE (1920)

By the end of 1919 and the beginning of 1920, the White Armies had suffered irreversible defeats. After a hectic retreat to the Black Sea, they evacuated whatever forces remained to the Crimean peninsula under General Wrangel. Although they may have cherished hopes of launching new offensives against the Reds, by this time their forces were no match for the Red Army. In early 1920, for the first time since October 1917, it appeared that no internal enemies of Soviet power were strong enough to threaten the Bolshevik regime. Just as in early 1919, this newly acquired sense of security was expected to lead to a new moderation in domestic policy, for there was now no serious justification for temporary and extraordinary measures. Indeed the death penalty was abolished, except in the frontline areas; some soviet assemblies were revived; and elections were being held, including some where opposition parties could take part. The similarities with the atmosphere of early 1919 were striking.

Alas, the policy of moderation gave way to renewed repression. The year 1920 was one of brewing discontent over the policies of war communism—centralization, militarization, and continued grain requisitioning—strikes, and an ever-broadening wave of peasant rebellions and merciless Bolshevik repressions. Thus 1920 saw a new cycle of confrontation between the Bolshevik authorities and the peasants and workers that led the Bolsheviks to the brink of disaster in March 1921.

Of greatest concern to the Mensheviks was the militarization of labor (militarizing the industrial relations at a factory) using a new system of command and subordination. Bolshevik editorials demanded that the differences between workers and soldiers be erased. Some workers were drafted into the Red Army and then worked at their factories as soldiers; some military formations not needed for frontline duty were deployed on the labor front, thus implementing Leon Trotsky's utopia of labor armies.

The new virtues in the proletarian state were unquestioning obedience and subordination. Such notions as an eight-hour day, independent unions, and workers' control, which brought so much popularity to the Bolsheviks in 1917, were forgotten. New attitudes were on the rise in the Bolshevik party, along with new ethics and new ethos. The Bolsheviks now saw social and political problems in terms of war categories: implementing a policy was now an offensive on the industrial front, the food supply front, the transport front, or the ideological front; a revision of policy or a failure was now a retreat; policies were implemented by commanders ruthless in their pursuit of deserters and traitors. These and many other war concepts were to be firmly entrenched for decades to come.

A strike was now perceived as an act of sabotage, labor desertion, or treason, and the reaction to strikes was dismissal, exile, or imprisonment. Lack of space makes it impossible to include the numerous Menshevik reports on the strike movement in Soviet Russia; however, almost all strikes developed according to an identical scenario with minor variations. Labor protests usually began over economic issues and new measures introduced with the militarization of labor, such as fines, reduction of bread rations, and short-term imprisonment. Almost always no concessions to strikers were made, and the reported number of instigators (*zachinshchiki*) arrested and deported or imprisoned in the camps varies from several dozen to several hundred. The Mensheviks did not even know their names; they disappeared to an unknown fate.

A strike in a large industrial city (Tula, May–June 1920) is reported in document 36, which describes the workers' grievances, causes for the strike, Bolshevik measures against the strike, workers' responses, and the Social Democrats' role. In what was becoming a widely practiced tactic, the Tula Bolsheviks denounced the strikers as Polish (because Soviet Russia was at war with Poland, this accusation amounted to a charge of high treason) agents and Black Hundreds a (right-wing anti-Semitic organization in imperial Russia, thus an extreme reactionary). Projecting the unity of the proletarian vanguard with the masses meant that protest could only originate with counterrevolutionaries, White Guardists, agents of foreign capital, hidden Mensheviks, kulaks, or enemies of the people. Those Communists who convinced themselves of this projected their frustration and hatred on these handy scapegoats. How many of the Tula Bolsheviks truly believed that thousands of the striking workers, were Polish agents is unknown. It was, however, convenient to label a strike a White Guardist conspiracy, for it made it possible to absolve oneself from the responsibility of failure and at the same time to implement "merciless measures against counterrevolution." The workers' role in the proletarian state was redefined to be an obedient follower of the proletarian vanguard. As a Tula Communist said in connection with the strike, "It is necessary to put an end to it once and for all. It is necessary to make the workers obey blindly and obediently all demands of Soviet power." Mass arrests, deportations, and exiles of strikers in Tula were not uncommon.

Now more than ever the Social Democrats considered it their duty to inform Westerners of the workers' situation in the proletarian state. In fact, after the latest expulsion from the soviets (document 39) and after the only remaining independent union in Soviet Russia—the Printers' Union led by the Social Democrats—was destroyed, informing the West became an important means of political struggle for the Social Democrats in Russia. Without press of their own inside the country, they tried to bring pressure on the Communists by publicizing what the Communists wanted to conceal.

In a letter to Pavel Axelrod (document 35), Raphail Abramovich, a member of the Menshevik Central Committee, described the cycle of Menshevik confrontations with the Bolsheviks in 1920. Menshevik successes in local elections, combined with workers' strikes and the Mensheviks' report to the British delegation on conditions in Soviet Russia, brought the Bolsheviks' patience to an end. The Mensheviks knew too much and, what was worse, said too much. From the Communists' point of view, reporting to the West on executions of rebellious peasants (document 38), on arrests of labor leaders (document 39), on the imprisonment of strikers (document 36), and on the luxurious lifestyles of prominent Bolshevik leaders (document 37) amounted to high treason and must be dealt with accordingly.

Document 39 describes in detail the concerted attacks on Menshevik local organizations during 1920. This document was not written for communication abroad, but to inform local organizations of what was happening in other areas of the country. Although a variety of circumstances led to the wholesale arrests of the Menshevik leaders throughout the country, several were typical: success in elections, workers' unrest or strikes, and gathering information on the misdeeds of local officials.

These Menshevik revelations were particularly damaging in the summer of 1920, when the Communists convened the Second Congress of the Communist International. A big propaganda show—orchestras playing, choruses singing the "Internationale," lavish receptions, and Potemkin villages of happy laborers in a Socialist motherland—was under way to convince foreign visitors that they were in the country of the victorious proletariat. The Communists were determined to win the battle on this front. Cheka agents kept an eye on the foreign delegates and strictly controlled access to them; workers' collectives were carefully selected to demonstrate the iron unity of the party and the working class.

Martov and his Social Democrats, however, met with the British delegation and furnished it with a voluminous report.[72] Martov also met with Wilhelm Crispien and Arthur Dittman of the Independent German Social Democratic party and with G. M. Seratti of the Italian Socialist party.[73] The information thus provided strengthened some Western Socialists' reservations about the first proletarian state and would play an important role in the coming struggle within Western Socialist parties between the left-wing admirers of Moscow, soon to become Communists, and the moderates, who would increasingly distance themselves from Moscow's "socialism."

## THE UNFORESEEN DICTATORSHIP
## (1920–1925)

In 1920 the Social Democrats' party leadership also tried to formulate a positive program, which culminated in the draft of a new party platform known as the April thesis. Its key message was that the Mensheviks accepted the reality of Soviet power in Russia and saw as their immediate task implementation of those democratic provisions of the Soviet constitution that only existed on paper, namely, power of the elected assemblies of workers and peasants—the soviets—not the Communist party committees. The Mensheviks also demanded guarantees for freedom of speech, assembly, press, and political activity.

This was a dangerous line to follow in Soviet Russia because it raised a problem that the Communists have had difficulty resolving: namely, how to reconcile the regime's claim that power belonged to workers and peasants' elected representatives in the soviets, when in reality that power belonged to the Communist party bureaucracy, which is not accountable to any elected body. All Communist factions felt that their monopoly on power had to be maintained, which meant that there was no place for an opposition party in Soviet Russia, no matter how loyal. The Constitution was a farce, a declaration of principles long since forgotten.

Certain propositions of Martov and the Central Committee were unacceptable to the Right Mensheviks. Document 40 presents their views on and analyses of the Soviet system. The Right Mensheviks regarded Martov's attempts at accommodation with the Communists as wishful thinking at best and as a capitulation to the Communists at worst. From the Right Menshevik's point of view, the problem with Martov's thesis was that he recognized the Communists as a workers' party and thus, for the sake of nonexistent Soviet democracy, abandoned the principle of parliamentary democracy and made the Communist dictatorship appear as a mere distortion of Soviet democracy.

In their perceptive analysis of the Soviet political system, the Right Mensheviks left no doubt that they considered Communist rule in Russia to be neither proletarian dictatorship nor proletarian democracy, but simply different from any existing models. Perhaps one of the most interesting and original ideas in document 40 is that the Soviet sociopolitical system was a formation unforeseen by Marxism. Relying on a Marxist methodology of social analysis, the authors conclude that Marxism did not include a system of the Soviet variety in a conceivable framework of sociopolitical formations.

Yet the authors of the document did not break with Marxism. Operating with such classic Marxist notions as commodity exchange, class struggle, market forces, means of productions, and so on, they applied Marxist class analysis methodology to analyze the "unclass" nature of the Communist regime. The classes did remain in Soviet Russia, not in relation to means of production, but in relation to an omnipotent state; not in relation to property, but in relation to access to privilege and control over means of production and other people. The authors referred to a rise of a new estate (*soslovie*)—the Communist party. Trying to interpret why the Bolshevik regime developed the way it did, they reiterated the classic Menshevik propositions: that Russia was not ready for socialism; that the level of development of its industry, culture, and political consciousness was too low; that it was impossible to skip stages of historical development; and that the Bolshevik experiment was doomed to failure.

To many, the Right Mensheviks' conclusions may seem to have been proven wrong. The Bolsheviks built what they called socialism and destroyed private enterprise (or so it seemed to them). From the Mensheviks' point of view, however, socialism was much more than merely building industry with convict labor, and a developed industrial infrastructure was only one of many prerequisites for embarking on a transition to socialism. Like many European Socialists of their time, the Mensheviks believed that socialism would liberate labor from poverty and exploitation. For them, socialism was inconceivable without parliamentary democracy because only in conditions of democracy could labor become free. In Soviet Russia, for the sake of building socialism, labor was deprived of even elementary freedoms.

In the historical perspective, Russia's backward, premodern society, which the Mensheviks considered unripe for socialism, was probably indeed at a stage when advanced Western ideas on socialism could only be understood in the narrow sense of fighting on the industrial front. Culture and democratic consciousness cannot be created overnight. In that sense the Menshevik proposition was correct, although inadequate; remaining Marxists, they put too much emphasis on the objective forces of history and not enough emphasis on the subjective will of Lenin and his party to subordinate society. Like so many others in their age, the Right Mensheviks believed that it would be impossible in the long run for a minority party to coerce the workers into submission and that it would be impossible to coerce millions of peasants to abandon market relations. The Bolshevik regime had to either collapse or adjust to the laws of history. It is possible that here too the Mensheviks will be proven right. Private enterprise and capitalist market relations may be restored because a centralized command economy does not perform well in comparison with private enterprise. Some measure of the rule of law and the accountability of officials may have to be introduced to restrain pervasive corruption and privilege (which in itself would be an acknowledgment that Bolshevik socialism had run into a dead end). In the short-term historical perspective, however, the impossible was made possible. It was not the masses, the classes, or the popular movements that determined Russia's future, but the state in the hands of a new ruling class. The Bolsheviks proved that Marx was wrong; the Mensheviks were the first to witness and report it.

They paid dearly for their revelations and their criticism. As Lenin was embarking on his great retreat—the New Economic Policy—political repression intensified. Document 42 describes the plight of thousands of Russian Socialists in Soviet prison camps who were seized in the streets and in their homes in 1922–1923 for their political views. The Communists did not forgive those who dared to think and write as free men and women. For decades to come, under all Soviet leaders, those who did found themselves in the camps, which makes all the more important the testimony of the first generation of Soviet critics—the Mensheviks.

*NOTES*

1. This has been pointed out in several recent studies. See, for example, Oliver H. Radkey, *The Unknown Civil War in Soviet Russia: A Study of the Green Movement in the Tambov Region, 1920–1921* (Stanford: Hoover Institution Press, 1976), p. 32; Robert Conquest, *The Harvest of Sorrow: Soviet Collectivization and the Terror Famine* (New York: Oxford University Press, 1982), p. 50; Peter Scheibert, *Lenin an der Macht: Das Russische Volk in der Revolution, 1918–1922* [Lenin in Power: The Russian People in the Revolution, 1918–1922] (Weinheim, West Germany: acta humaniora, 1984), p. 156; and Mikhail Heller and Aleksander Nekrich, *Utopia in Power: The History of the Soviet Union from 1917 to the Present* (New York: Summit Books, 1986), p. 100.
2. *Kratkaia istoriia SSSR* [Short History of the USSR], 2 vols., (Moscow: Nauka, 1983) 2:118–22.
3. Theodore H. von Laue, "Stalin in Focus," *Slavic Review* 42, no. 3 (1983):387.
4. Peter Kenez, *Civil War in South Russia, 1919–1920* (Berkeley: University of California Press, 1977), pp. 94–95.
5. For a vivid description of the political atmosphere in Omsk and the circumstances of Kolchak's coup d'état, see "Kak eto bylo," *Byloe* 21 (1923):245–50.
6. For a discussion of this subject, see Yaroslav Bilinsky, "The Communist Takeover of the Ukraine," in Taras Hunczak, ed., *The Ukraine, 1917–1921, A Study in Revolution* (Cambridge, Mass.: Harvard University Press, 1977), pp. 104–28.

7. William Rosenberg, "Russian Labor and Bolshevik Power after October," *Slavic Review* 44, no. 2 (1985):219; Diane Koenker, *Moscow Workers and the 1917 Revolution* (Princeton, N.J.: Princeton University Press, 1981), pp. 212, 342; S.A. Smith, *Red Petrograd: Revolution in the Factories*, 1917–1918 (Cambridge, Eng.: Cambridge University Press, 1983); and David Mandel, *The Petrograd Workers and the Soviet Seizure of Power* (New York: St. Martin's Press, 1983), pp. 324–27.

8. This letter was not included in the recently published collection of Dan's letters by Boris Sapir, who was unaware of its existence. Boris Sapir, ed., *From the Archives of L. O. Dan* (Amsterdam: Stichting International Insituut voor Sociale Geschiedenis, 1987), p. XIII.

9. I discuss the competition in the soviets in greater detail in *The Mensheviks after October: Socialist Opposition and the Rise of the Bolshevik Dictatorship* (Ithaca, N.Y.: Cornell University Press, 1987), ch. 5.

10. Scheibert, *Lenin an der Macht,* pp. 34, 41, 45.

11. I deal more extensively with the crisis in the summer of 1918 in "The Mensheviks under Attack: The Transformation of Soviet Politics, June–September 1918," *Jahrbuecher fuer Geschichte Osteuropas* 32, no. 3 (1984):378–91.

12. Sheila Fitspatrick, "Civil War as a Formative Experience," in Abbott Gleason, Peter Kenez, and Richard Stites, eds., *Bolshevik Culture* (Bloomington: Indiana University Press), p. 74.

13. "Zakrytie Obukhovskogo zavoda," *Novaia Zhizn'* no. 122 (June 26, 1918); Grigorii Aronson, *Rossiia v epokhu revoliutsii* (New York: Walden, 1966), p. 192; Serge de Chessin, *L'Apocalypse russe: La Revolution bolchevique 1918–1921* [The Russian Apocalypse: The Bolshevik Revolution, 1918–1921] (Paris: Plon-Nouritt, 1921), p. 78 and Mandel, *Petrograd Workers,* p. 410.

14. V. Z. Drobizhev, ed., *Rabochii klass Sovetskoi Rossii v pervyi god proletarskoi diktatury* [The Working Class of Soviet Russia During the First Year of the Proletarian Dictatorship] (Moscow: Moskovskii Gosudarst vennyi Universitet, 1975), pp. 83–103.

15. A great many documents on peasant uprisings are in the PSR archive. Part of the PSR archive is in series no. 7 of the Nicolaevsky Collection (hereafter, Nic. Col.), but the main body of the archive is in the Institute for Social History in Amsterdam.

16. Stephen Berk, "The Class Tragedy of Izhevsk: Working Class Opposition to Bolshevism in 1918," *Russian History,* no. 2 (1975):176–90. The fullest collection of Soviet sources on the Izhevsk uprising is in Mikhail Bernstam, ed., *Ural i prikam'e noiabr' 1917–ianvar' 1919: Dokumenty i materialy* [The Urals and the Kama Region, November 1917–January 1919. Documents and Materials] (Paris: YMCA, 1982).

17. The most detailed information on the uprising in Saratov is in the *Izvestiia Saratovskogo Soveta* at the Hoover Institution Library, particularly the following articles: "Sobytiia 18 maia," *Izvestiia,* no. 95 (May 20, 1918):2; "Listovka krasnoarmeitsev i frontovikov," ibid.; and "Zasedanie Soveta," *Izvestiia Saratovskogo Soveta,* no. 100 (May 26, 1918):1.

18. The leaders of workers' detachments were Abramov and Savinov. For taking part in the uprising, they were expelled from the Menshevik party. "Rezoliutsiia TsKa," Nic. Col., no. 6, box 5, file 2.

19. There is a large body of literature on the subject. See, for example, Victor M. Fic, *The Bolsheviks and the Czechoslovak Legion* (New Delhi: Abhinav Publications, 1978), pp. 13–14; L. I. Iakovlev, *Internatsional'naia solidarnost trudiashchikhsia Zarubezhnykh stran s' narodami Sovetskoi Rossi, 1917–1922* [International Solidarity of the Toilers in Foreign Countries with the Peoples of Soviet Russia, 1917–1922] (Moscow: Nauka, 1964); and A. Kh. Klevanskii, *Chekhoslovatskie internatsionalisty i prodannyi korpus* [Czechoslovak Internationalists and a Betrayed Legion] (Moscow: Nauka, 1965).

20. Karl Helfferich, "Moia Moskovskaia missiia," a handwritten manuscript in Russian. Nic. Col., series no. 128, box 198, file 19. Helfferich was the German ambassador in Soviet Russia in August 1918.

21. According to official Soviet data, ten thousand "foreign internationalists were fighting for Soviet power" in 1919 in the Ukraine alone. V. I. Miller, "Velikii Oktiabr' i proletarskii internatsionalizm," *Voprosy istorii KPSS*, no. 10 (October 1985):145; see also Marc Jansen, "International Class Solidarity or Foreign Intervention," *International Review of Social History* 31, part 1 (1986):68–79.

22. According to Leggett, Kamenev's recommendation to abolish the Cheka was made on January 8, 1919, and the Bolshevik Central Committee rejected it on February 3, 1919. George Leggett, *The Cheka: Lenin's Political Police* (New York: Oxford University Press, 1981), p. 396. Without identifying the names, Boris Nicolaevsky suggested that "an influential group inside the CPC insisted upon the liquidation of the VeCheKa and on the transfer of its functions to the reorganized People's Commissariat of Justice," B. Nicolaevsky, "Pervaia popytka istorii mashiny Sovetskogo terrora," *Sotsialisticheskii Vestnik*, no. 1 (January 1958):55.

23. N. Osinskii, "Novye zadachi stroitel'stva Sovetskoi respubliki," *Vlast' Sovetov*, no.2 (February 1919):7–17.

24. "Voix de Russie. Petrograd 19 fevrier 1919," *La Republique Russe*, no.9 (May 15, 1920):2.

25. "Po Rossii. Nizhegorodskaia guberniia," *Pravda*, no. 73 (April 4, 1919):4.

26. The original document is entitled "Donesenie Roslavl'skomu uezdvoenkomu," WKP 119, the Smolensk archive, Harvard University.

27. *Vos'moi s'ezd RKP(b). Protokoly*, p. 169.

28. Ibid., p. 220.

29. Ibid., p. 200.

30. Ibid., p. 204.

31. S. P. Melgunov, *Krasnyi terror v Rossii* [Red Terror in Russia] (New York: Brandy, 1979), p. 27.

32. Strikes in Tula and at the Putilov plant in Petrograd are briefly mentioned by Thomas Remington, *Building Socialism in Bolshevik Russia: Ideology and Industrial Organization (1917–1921)*, Series in Russian and East European Studies, no. 6 (Pittsburgh, Pa.: University of Pittsburgh Press, 1984), pp. 109–10. A list of Putilov workers demands is in K. Iakovleva, "Zabastovki za pervuiu chetvert' 1919 goda," *Matelialy po statistike truda vypusk*, no.5 (1919) and in Leggett, *The Cheka*, p. 313. As far as the number of workers involved in strikes is concerned, the British parliamentary report stated that "Further confirmation of the reported opposition of a section of the working population to Bolshe-

vik rule is found in a recent Bolshevik wireless message, which states that sixty thousand workmen are on strike in Petrograd, demanding an end to fratricidal war and the institution of free trade." Document 54, "Summary of a Report on the Internal Conditions in Russia," in *A Collection of Reports on Bolshevism in Russia: Abridged Edition of Parliamentary Paper, Russia No. 1* (London: His Majesty's Stationery Office, 1919), p. 60.

33. Leggett, *The Cheka*, p. 313. I cannot resist citing an example of Soviet falsification of history: Gogolevskii wrote about the Putilov workers' strike in March 1919, saying that the workers "gave a firm and decisive rebuff to the underground petty bourgeois group." A.V. Gogolevskii, *Petrogradskii Sovet v gody grazhdanskoi voiny* [Petrograd Soviet in the Years of the Civil War] (Leningrad: Nauka, 198), p. 44.

34. Local Bolsheviks reported to Moscow that rebellions in March and April embraced "almost all uezds in Orel province." Orel, Bryansk, and Gomel were singled out as cities where Red Army soldiers' rebellions took place. As usual, uprisings in the countryside were referred to as "kulak rebellions." It was stated that almost everywhere deserters were the leaders. *Perepiska sekretariata*, vol. 7, p. 416.

35. Eyewitness account of Ia. Matokhin, "K sobytiiam v Bryanske," *Delo Naroda*, March 29, 1919.

36. W.H. Anderson to Department of State, April 5, 1919, file number 861.00 4204, *Records of the Department of State*.

37. Sir C. Eliot to Earl Curson from consul in Ekaterinburg, March 3 (1919), "Labourers opposing Bolsheviks were treated in the same manner as peasants. One hundred labourers were shot at Motovilyky [Motovilikha] near Perm." Document 49, *A Collection of Reports*, p. 54. The same figure is cited in V. Miakotin, "Zhutkaia kniga" *Na Chuzhoi storone*, no. 7 (1924):267.

38. Bernstam, *Ural i prikam'e*, p. 471.

39. According to a Socialist Revolutionary who was in the area at the time, there were 150,000 peasant rebels in the area; see V. Bobrov, "Po Sibiri i Uralu," *Narod*, no. 1 (August 17, 1919):2.

40. British Military Mission at Reval, "Strength of the Red Army. Report on Bolshevism, Appendix X." This report was sent to the Department of State. A note attached to the cover letter said, "Information has been received from Berlin that this report was written by Lieutenant Colonel Wilson, British Military Observer at Reval," file no. 861.00 7847, *Political Affairs, Records of the Department of State*.

41. "Piataia Bel'skaia partiinaia konferentsiia RKP(b)," WKP 254, the Smolensk archive.

42. *Report (Political and Economic) Russia No. 1,* Document 162, p. 46.

43. American legation in Copenhagen July 15, 1919, to Department of State. The military attaché noted that "the statements made here can be taken as based upon actual facts," file no. 861.00 5051, *Political Affairs, Records of the Department of State*.

44. These data are in the article "Prizyv Generala Vrangelia," *Narodnaia Gazeta*, no. 110 (August 16, 1919).

45. As John Erickson wrote (*The Soviet High Command, 1918–1941: A Military*

*Political History* [Boulder, Colo.: Westview Press, 1984]), p. 685, "According to the Red Army archives quoted here, in 1919 one million deserters were recaptured or voluntarily returned to their units."

46. On the situation on the Kolchak-held territory, see the testimony of a Socialist Revolutionary: V. Bobrov, "Po Sibiri i Uralu," *Narod*, no. 1 (August 17, 1919):2.

47. I. Derevenskii, "Bandity," *Byloe*, no. 24 (1924):252–74.

48. "Ot chrezvychainogo Komiteta Revoliutsionnoi Okhrany Karel'skogo uchastka," *Izvestiia Petrogradskogo Soveta*, no. 155 (July 12, 1919):1.

49. Conquest, *Harvest of Sorrow*, p. 50.

50. In the above-cited diplomatic dispatch to Lord Curson, the British consul in Ekaterinburg reported that "Russian authorities have just commenced investigation of Bolshevik crimes and therefore it is difficult to obtain precise data as to the number of persons killed, although, as far as we can judge, it runs into several thousand in Perm' Government." *A Collection of Reports*, p. 54.

51. From General Gray to the secretary of state, August 6, 1919, file 861.00 5009, *Political Affairs, Records of the Department of State*.

52. Even Soviet historians did not dispute this. See *Istoriia Grazhdanskoi Voiny v SSSR*, vol. 4 (1959), p. 71; see also Arthur E. Adams, "The Great Ukrainian Jacquerie," in Hunczak, ed., *The Ukraine, 1917–1921*, p. 266.

53. Michael Malet, *Nestor Makhno in the Russian Civil War* (London: Macmillan, 1982), p. 36.

54. In a letter to Petrovskii, a commissar of internal affairs of the Ukraine, a local Communist, Fedorchuk, complained that slogans of Hryhoriiv (Grigor'ev) such as "instead of land they gave us chrezvychaikas and instead of freedom, commissars from among those who had crucified Christ" were popular among the peasants. The text of the entire letter is in "Krasnyi terror," *Na Chuzhoi Storone*, no. 4 (1924):214–15.

55. Sergei Starikov and Roy Medvedev, *Philip Mironov and the Russian Civil War* (New York: Alfred A. Knopf, 1978), pp. 110–11.

56. Ibid., p. 115.

57. Ibid., p. 118.

58. For a demographic analysis of cossack losses during the civil war, see Mikhail Bernstam, "Storony v Grazhdanskoi Voine," *Vestnik Russkogo Khristianskogo Dvizheniia*, no. 128 (1979):300.

59. According to Kenez, "The Bolsheviks had carried out more than a thousand bloody murders during the last days of their rule [in Kharkov]," *Civil War in South Russia*, vol. 2, p. 157.

60. Several published reports of the Commission to Investigate Bolshevik Atrocities are in the Nicolaevsky Collection. Findings of this commission were also published in the following articles: "V tsarstve zla i smerti," vol. 5; "Eshche o Kievskoi Cheka v 1919 godu," vol. 10, 1925; and a letter of Martyn Latsis (deputy head of the Cheka) to local Chekas: "Vsem Chrezvychainym Kommissiiam," vol. 5, 1924, *Na Zhuzhoi Storone*, Berlin. See also *In the Shadow of Death (A Document): Statement of Red Cross Sisters on the Bolshevist Prisons in Kiev* (London: Russian Liberation Committee, 1920) on the Kharkov

Cheka, see K. Alinin, *Tche-ka: The Story of the Bolshevist Extraordinary Commission* (London: Russian Liberation Committee, 1920), pp. 61–64.

61. Simon Liberman, *Building Lenin's Russia* (Chicago: n.p. , 1945), p. 36.

62. Kenez has suggested that the fall of Orel created an atmosphere of crisis in Moscow "worse than anything the Reds had experienced since the spring of 1918." *Civil War in South Russia*, vol. 2, p. 214.

63. Remington, *Building Socialism in Bolshevik Russia*, p. 101; see also a Soviet source, *Ocherki istorii Kievskikh gorodskikh i oblastnykh partiinykh organizatsii*, p. 226, claiming that the workers' masses rose with enthusiasm against Denikin.

64. A British observer of events in South Russia wrote, "When the Bolshevists rule them they welcome the Volunteer army with enthusiasm. After a month or two of the Volunteers, they are ready to welcome the Bolshevists again, all the old scores being already forgotten. In another month, they wish the Volunteers had stayed." C. E. Bechhofer Roberts, *In Denikin's Russia and the Caucasus, 1919–1920* (London: W. Collins Sons, 1921), p. 77.

65. On peasants greeting volunteers as liberators, see Kenez, *Civil War in South Russia*, vol. 2, p. 156. For Bolshevik accounts of peasant detachments' attacking them in the rear at the time of Denikin's offensive, see I. Lantukh, "Iz istorii grazhdanskoi voiny na Ekaterinoslavshchine," *Letopis' Revoliutsii*, no. 2 (1926):51–55.

66. Kenez, *Civil War in South Russia*, pp. 158, 159, 197.

67. Ibid., pp. 102–3.

68. This letter was included in the dispatch of Rear Admiral N. A. McCully, U.S. Navy, to the secretary of state, February 18, 1920, file no. 861.00 7082, *Political Affairs, Records of the Department of State*.

69. Ibid. Dispatch dated May 19, 1920, file no. 861.00 7081, "Present Conditions in Don, Kuban' and Terek," *Political Affairs, Records of the Department of State*.

70. Ibid.

71. Rear Admiral N. A. McCully, U.S. Navy, to the secretary of state, subject: Odessa, fall of, made by Lieutenant Commander Hamilton Bryan: "Report on the Evacuation of Odessa (30 January–9 February 1920)," file no. 861.00 6649, *Political Affairs, Records of the Department of State*.

72. The full text of the Menshevik report to the British delegation is in Nic. Col., no. 6, box 5, file 37. Much of the Menshevik information is incorporated in *British Labour Delegation to Russia 1920. Report*.

73. V. Sukhomlin, in a letter to P. Axelrod dated August 29, 1920, named specific Western Socialists with whom Martov met in Moscow and to whom he had given "many documents and a manuscript." Nic. Col., no. 16 box 45, file 6.

# DOCUMENTS

# The Bolsheviks Seize Power
## *(October 1917–January 1918)*

# Iu. O. Martov to P. B. Axelrod

19 November 1917, Petersburg

Dear Pavel Borisovich!

At last it seems I have the opportunity to write you a letter and to send it; from the moment of Lenin's coup the border has been shut even more hermetically, and there is no possibility, it seems, of maintaining contact. More than ever before I feel your absence and the difficulty of maintaining contact with you at a time when both the revolution and our Social Democracy are going through the moment of their sharpest and most dangerous crisis. The worst one could have expected has happened—the seizure of power by Lenin and Trotsky at a time when even those who are less insane than they are could have made irretrievable mistakes on the assumption of power. But what is even more terrible is that the moment has arrived when conscience does not allow us Marxists to do what seems imperative: side with the proletariat even when it is mistaken. After painful vacillation and hesitation I decided that in this situation it is better to wash my hands of everything and step aside for awhile rather than to remain in the role of opposition in the camp where Lenin and Trotsky are determining the fate of the revolution.

The coup was predetermined, as is now clear, by the entire preceding development. In September, the Kornilov conspiracy [General L. G. Kornilov ordered the troops under his command to march on Petrograd in August 1917. As is generally acknowledged, this revolutionized the Petrograd garrison and workers and thus contributed to the Bolshevik cause. See J. D. White, "The Kornilov Affair: A Study in Counterrevolution," *Soviet Studies* 20 (1968).] revealed first the terrible resentment of the propertied world against the revolution; second, the internal decomposition of the coalition government, where Savinkovs [Boris Savinkov—before 1917, a terrorist and a member of PSR—in the summer of 1917, commissar of the provisional government; in September 1917, expelled from the Socialist Revolutionary party for his role in the Kornilov affair] were Kornilov's accomplices; and third, the still intense revolutionary enthusiasm of the workers and soldiers' masses and their readiness to rally again to the side of the soviets and their leaders when necessary to safeguard the revolution. At

Nicolaevsky Collection, series no. 17, papers of Iu.O. Martov, box 51, folders 1–2.

the same time, the Kornilov conspiracy, with all its far-reaching branches, as well as the soldiers' revolution at the front, which overthrew counterrevolutionary generals and officers, apparently disorganized the army so definitively that the task of concluding peace immediately, even without honor, was put point-blank to the Democratic Conference. [This conference took place in Petrograd from 27 September to 6 October 1917. Convened to resolve a government crisis, it consisted of representatives of various political parties and public organizations.] Both our and the SR [Socialist Revolutionary] Defensists seemed to be aware of this. The majority in the Menshevik faction turned out to be for rejecting the coalition [with the Kadets] and for creating a general democratic government. [Most likely Martov means a government of all Socialist political parties.] Bogdanov [B. O. Bogdanov, a Defensist Menshevik, during 1914–1917, was a worker representative in the labor group of the Central War Industries Committee. After the February Revolution of 1917, Bogdanov became one of Tsereteli's key associates and a prominent leader in the Petrograd soviet and the Central Executive Committee.], Isuv [I. A. Isuv, a leader of the Moscow Mensheviks and a member of the Moscow soviet; in 1917 he was a Revolutionary Defensist after the December 1917 Menshevik party congress supported Martov's policy; in 1918 he became a leader of the Menshevik opposition faction in the Moscow soviet.], Khinchuk [L. M. Khinchuk became, after the February Revolution, a key Menshevik leader in Moscow and was the chairman of the Moscow soviet until September 1917. He was also a member of the Menshevik Central Committee; politically, he was a Revolutionary Defensist. At the end of the civil war he defected to the Bolsheviks and died in Stalin's camps.], Cherevanin [N. Cherevanin (F. A. Lipkin) was a member of the Social Democrat's Central Committee and was known as an economic expert in the Menshevik party. In 1917, he served on the economic council of the Petrograd soviet. Although initially a Defensist, by the fall of 1917, Cherevanin was moving closer to Martov's political position.], and many other Defensists favored that course. Fedor Il'ich [Fedor Il'ich Dan (Gurvich), a key leader of the Menshevik party and, in 1917, chairman of the Central Executive Committee, was the leader of the party center that supported Tsereteli's policy on war and coalition with the Kadets until September 1917. In the political jargon of 1917, Dan's and Tsereteli's policy was called Revolutionary Defensism and their supporters, a majority in the Menshevik party— Revolutionary Defensists.] was also for it at first and only later, clearly yielding to the pressure of Tsereteli [I. G. Tsereteli—a member of the Central Executive Committee and a minister in Kerensky's government— played a much bigger role in 1917 than his official positions would suggest, shaping the outline of the provisional government's policy in addition to his leadership of the Central Executive Committee. A Revolutionary Defensist, Tsereteli supported the June offensive. He embodied the link between the soviets and the provisional government and defended to the end his firm belief that the Socialists had to rule in a coalition with the Liberals (Kadets) to prevent civil war. He was the architect of several governmental coalitions in 1917, including the last one in September, which Martov criticized in this letter. See W. H. Roobol, *Tsereteli, A Democrat in the Russian Revolution: A Political Biography* (The Hague: Nijhoff, 1976).], Liber [Mark Liber (M. I. Goldman)—a member of the Central Committee of both the Jewish Bund and the Mensheviks in 1917, a leader of the Central Executive Committee, a Revolutionary Defensist, and an outspoken supporter of Tsereteli's policy—remained throughout his life a staunch opponent of bolshevism and died in Stalin's prisons in the late 1930s], and Skobelev [ M. I. Skobelev was a member of the Central Executive Committee of the Soviets and minister of labor in the provisional government, May–September 1917.] was inclined to repeat the experiment of a coalition [with the Kadets] again. But what was most characteristic was that all the Caucasians who had arrived from the provinces, headed by Zhordaniia [Noi Zhordaniia—the leader of the Georgian Mensheviks and in 1917 a member of the Menshevik Central Committee—initially supported Tsereteli's policy. By the fall of 1917, as Martov relates, Zhordaniia became critical of the continued coalition with the Kadets. After the Bolsheviks seized power in Petrograd, Zhordaniia became the head of government of independent Georgia until 21 February 1921, when the Red Army invaded Georgia and occupied the country.] and Ramishvilli [I. I. Ramishvilli was a leader of the Georgian Mensheviks and in 1917 a member of the EC of the Petrograd soviet.], demanded that the coalition be broken. They sharply criticized Tsereteli's entire policy. The situation was such that I spoke at the [Democratic] Conference as the official spokesman for the delegation of the soviets and for the majority of the Menshevik faction. [Several factions in the Menshevik party usually presented their own diverse political views not only at party gatherings but also in multiparty assemblies, like the Democratic Conference.] A considerable minority in the SR party favored breaking the coalition as well. Nevertheless, the coalition was restored with the same Tereshchenko [M. I. Tereshchenko was minister of finance (March–May 1917) and minister of foreign affairs (May–October 1917) in the provisional government.] as the head. To compensate for this, [they created] the preparliament and gave it a consultative role. [Created at the Democratic Conference, the preparliament's name emphasized that it was a temporary legislative institution preceding the Constituent Assembly, which was to be elected just three weeks later.] It is my firm conviction that, had our influential leaders displayed at least some steadfastness, the Right SRs, the SRs, and even Kerensky himself would have agreed to try a purely democratic cabinet with a simple program: to start peace negotiations immediately, to convene the C[onstituent] A[ssembly] immediately, and to fulfill the promise to transfer [the authority over] land to the Land Committees. [The Land Committees were created by the provisional government on 21 April 1917 for "preparation of the agrarian reform." For a discussion of the structure and activity of Land Committees, see Marc Ferro, *The Russian Revolution of February 1917* (Englewood Cliffs, N.J.: Prentice Hall, 1972), pp. 282–86.] This became our program in the preparliament. Soon afterward some Defensists, including Fedor Il'ich [Dan], went along, more or less, with us. (Tsereteli and Chkheidze [N. S. Chkheidze—member of the Menshevik Central Committee; before 1917, the head of the SD fraction in the Fourth State Duma; after the February 1917 Revolution, the first chairman of the Petrograd soviet; a Revolutionary Defensist; and a supporter of Tsereteli—favored coalition with the Kadets and lost his chairmanship of the Petrograd soviet to the Bolsheviks in early September 1917.] left for Caucasia.) The breakdown of the army and imminent economic bankruptcy have finally begun to convince even the most stubborn ones.

In September the minister [of defense], Verkhovskii, declared in the Defense Commission that the situation was so bad that it was necessary to conclude peace immediately, even if it were a separate and shameful peace. The navy minister, Verderevskii, supported him. The economics ministers (Konovalov, Gvozdev, Prokopovich) [A. I. Konovalov: minister of trade and industry; K. A. Gvozdev: minister of labor; S. N. Prokopovich: minister of food supplies in the last cabinet of the provisional government] and the [minister of] transportation, Liverovskii, leaned toward the same. This time Tereshchenko managed to overthrow Verkhovskii thanks to a new fit of weakness on the part of Dan, Skobelev, Gots [A. R. Gots—a leader of the PSR, a member of the PSR Central Committee, and a member of the EC of the Petrograd soviet—favored continued coalition with the Kadets.], Avksent'ev [N. D. Avksent'ev, a political leader of the PSR right wing and a close associate of Alexander Kerensky, in October 1917 was the chairman of the preparliament.], and others, but the breach had already been made. Even Kuskova [E. D. Kuskova, an influential publicist and politician, was famous in Socialist circles for her brochure *Credo,* which was understood as the Russian version of Marxist revisionism.], some Trudoviki [*Trudoviki* before February 1917 was a faction closely associated with the PSR in the Fourth State Duma with Kerensky as their leader. After February 1917, *Trudoviki* merged with the PSR and became its most moderate wing.], and the Right SRs decided to take an energetic step. (To be sure, Potresov [A. N. Potresov—a founder of the RSDWP, a member of the Menshevik Central Committee, and, in 1917, an outspoken Defensist—supported the war policy of the provisional government.] and Ortodoks remained faithful to the program *jusqu' au bout* [to the end].)

On 24 October, a resolution was adopted in the preparliament by the entire left side (except Trudoviki and some Plekhanovites, with several Defensists abstaining), to begin negotiations on a general peace immediately. Doing this, they reckoned, would prevent a sharp conflict with the [Second] Congress of Soviets, which was to open on 25 October and discuss the question of transferring all power to the soviets. But it was too late. On the night of the twenty-fourth, Lenin's military revolutionary committee had a number of strategic positions occupied by its sailors and soldiers, and in the morning Petrograd learned of the accomplished seizure of power. The technical side of the undertaking was carried out masterfully, whereas the fighting ability of Kerensky's government turned out to be equal to zero, even though just a day earlier he had announced in the preparliament that "all measures had been taken," that "any attempt [at an uprising] would be crushed at once," and so on.

All this happened because, after the Democratic Conference, which had restored the coalition with its program of vague promises, a catastrophic flight of the masses to Lenin began. The soviets began to go over to the Bolsheviks one after another without any new elections: the middle-income peasants [*seredniak*, Because most soldiers were former peasants, Martov uses this term in regard to soldiers as well.] and workers were defecting to the Bolsheviks. All factions, except the Bolsheviks, became a pitiful minority in Piter [Russian for Peter, a widely used name for Saint Petersburg] soviet in the course of a few weeks. Chkheidze and the entire presidium of the soviet were overthrown. The same occurred in Moscow with Khinchuk and in almost all the big cities. [For a detailed discussion of the nature of the workers' vote in Moscow, see Diane Koenker, *Moscow Workers and the 1917 Revolution* (Princeton, N.J.: Princeton University Press, 1981), pp. 215–27.] Simultaneously, this epidemic seized the army. Not being able to overthrow existing army committees, which comprised almost the entire army intelligentsia and not yet daring to establish an undisguised autocracy of soldiers, the regiments, divisions, and army corps, bypassing the [army] committees, began to send delegations, evermore numerous and clamorous, to Peter[sburg] with the demand that peace be concluded immediately. More and more often this was followed by a demand to transfer power to the soviets.

Nevertheless, it probably would not have come to a straightforward insurrection because the urban masses were passive and did not go beyond passing resolutions. Apparently, the experience of 3–5 July had left its mark. [In history 3–5 July 1917 is known as the July days, when demonstrations against the provisional government were organized by the Bolsheviks and when the government suppressed what it believed was the Bolshevik attempt to seize power. For a detailed treatment of the July days, see Richard Pipes, *The Russian Revolution* (New York: Knopf, 1990), pp. 385–439.] The army continued to endure as long as there was food and as long as it was not cold. Had the Socialist majority proceeded at a quicker pace toward the formation of a "government of immediate peace" (which could only have been coalition-free), perhaps Lenin might have lost hope for a successful insurrection. Intense struggle against Lenin and Trotsky was going on within the Bolshevik ranks. Zinoviev, Kamenev, and Riazanov were trying to postpone the denouement. [In September and early October 1917, Lev Kamenev and Grigorii Zinoviev opposed the Bolshevik seizure of power and leaked to the press that the Bolsheviks were preparing an insurrection. In the 1920s, this was labeled the *October treason* and used against them.] Apparently Lenin understood the urgency and cut this knot with a sword.

The way the seizure [of power] was carried out and the very fact that it was done on the eve of the [Second] Congress [of Soviets], where the Bolsheviks had a slight majority, was so disgusting that one could not deplore our and SR Defensists' decision to walk out of the congress immediately and to abandon Smolny [a building in Petrograd where the Second Congress of Soviets took place, which until March 1918 was the seat of the Bolshevik–Left Socialist Revolutionary government; the name Smolny quickly became identified with the Bolsheviks, hence Bolshevik regime equals Smolny regime] forever. We [a faction of Menshevik Internationalists led by Martov] nevertheless contended with this mood and insisted that there should be no walkout without giving Lenin a fight. What we proposed was to present an ultimatum at the very beginning demanding cessation of hostilities (the siege of the Winter Palace where the ministers had barricaded themselves was going on at this time) and starting negotiations on a peaceful resolution of the crisis in order to create a democratic government with a program acceptable to all. Our admonitions did not work. Partly due to indignation, partly to an illusion that Lenin would not hold out for even three days in Peter[sburg], the Mensheviks, SRs, and People's Socialists [a left Liberal party, which, in the political context of 1917, can be placed between the Kadets and the Socialist Revolutionaries] decided to walk out [of the congress] at the very beginning. We [about 40 people] remained and presented our ultimatum. It was supported by the left SRs and by the *Novaia Zhizn'* group [so called after its newspaper, *Novaia Zhizn'*, edited by Maxim Gorky and N. N. Sukhanov; politically a Social Democratic organization close, if not identical, to Martov's Internationalists]. The congress disregarded it, and we walked out a couple of hours after the Defensists. The *Novaia Zhizn'* group remained for several days and then also walked out in protest against political terror.

The following days dissipated all illusions regarding the coup as being hopelessly weak. All the troops in Peter[sburg] and the surrounding area actively supported the Bolsheviks. As it turned out, there was no one behind Kerensky. Even the majority of cadets and all cossacks refused to fight. The garrisons in a number of cities immediately recognized the Soviet government and defended it with arms. There were vacillations at the front, but the leaders [of the army] immediately realized that the soldiers would not go against a government that would begin to carry out the peace program. As far as the workers are concerned, there is no doubt that they were passive at first and that their sympathy for the coup was definitely paralyzed by concern for the future, by fear of unemployment and violence, and by lack of trust in the strength of the Leninists. But when the news came that Kerensky was leading the cossacks on Peter[sburg], ardor seized the masses, and the Red Guards fought in Gatchina [a suburb of Petrograd] almost as valiantly as the Kronstadt sailors.

At first our Defensists built a convenient theory for themselves: that this purely pretorian coup did not rely on the proletariat and that it would burst like a bubble in a few days because it could not cope with the economic crisis or get hold of the state apparatus and would choke in the blood of anarchy [*pogrom* in original, which cannot be translated as pogrom here because what is meant is not an anti-Jewish pogrom but general, free-for-all violence] that it had unleashed. I warned them not to be too optimistic. The coalition [with the Kadets] had been so rotten internally and had alienated the masses from their former leaders to such an extent that even the most paradoxical government of adventurists and utopians could hold out on credit until the masses were convinced that it was unable to resolve the problems of foreign and domestic policy. That is why we stated from the very beginning that there were two courses of development possible: Either, after passing through all the logical stages of terror, incitement to violence, and extreme embitterment of the entire petit bourgeois democracy, Lenin's adventure would lead to the momentous June days [most likely Martov is referring to the June days in Paris during the 1848 revolution; the expression became synonymous with crushing workers' revolutions] for the Russian proletariat or to the Russian 9th of Thermidor [Because it was customary for Russian Socialists to use the terminology of the French Revolution, the 9th of Thermidor became synonymous with the establishment of a counterrevolutionary regime after a revolutionary upheaval.]; or the difficulties the usurpers face will make them understand that the proletariat plus the democratic petite bourgeoisie and the intelligentsia, not the proletariat plus the soldiery, will be able to cope somehow with the legacy of war and revolution. Then it will be possible to talk to them about surrendering the power they seized to the Socialist coalition, which they will also join, to carry out not a program of social anarchy but a program of starting peace negotiations and convening the Constituent Assembly immediately.

At first, the Defensists rose up in arms against the very idea of negotiations with the "usurpers" and, in the beginning, were ready to draw all the logical conclusions from this. They supported the civil servants' strike [The civil servants' strike started in various departments in the first days of November. It is noteworthy that the employees of the Ministry of Labor (a bastion of Defensist Mensheviks) were among the most resolute organizers of the strike, which lasted nearly two months with varying degrees of endurance in different departments. At the end of November, some "saboteurs" and "enemies of the people," as they were labeled by the Bolshevik press, were arrested. See John Keep, ed., *Debate on Soviet Power: Minutes of the All-Russian Central Executive Committee of Soviets, Second Convocation, October 1917–January 1918*. (Oxford, Eng.: Clarendon Press, 1979), p. 312.] in all departments against Soviet power. Alas! Dedicated Socialists, indignant over Bolshevik methods, united in this strike with hordes of old-time civil servants inherited from the old regime and untouched by the coalition [government] who were guided by their hatred not just of Leninists but of all democrats. They [Defensists] also supported adventuristic attempts to overthrow the Leninists by armed force [an uprising of cadets of military schools in Petrograd on 29 October 1917, see below], the same kind of *coup de force* the Leninist coup had been, and were ready to conduct the entire struggle under the banner of the "legitimate" provisional government, which had been odious to the working class and which not a single city or a single regiment at the front had risen to defend. In this vein they managed to do a lot of harm. Despite the admonitions of Fedor Il'ich [Dan], somebody gave permission to several officers in Peter[sburg] to raise the cadets for an attempt to take the Bolsheviks by surprise. The matter ended with the shooting of these unfortunate ones [cadets] and their mass lynching by the sailors and soldiers. As a result, the insurgent masses received their first "christening with blood," whereas the city duma and the Defensists, who headed the struggle against the new government, became contemptible to the masses as the first perpetrators of bloodshed. (During the seizure of the Winter Palace, casualties were very low.)

It was even worse in Moscow. The SRs (the military and the duma) [the Socialist Revolutionaries in the Moscow city duma] tried to prevent the [Bolshevik] seizure of power and caused [Martov's use of the word *caused* here suggests that he puts the responsibility for the street battles in Moscow at the door of the Moscow duma. From the point of view of Martov's political opponents—the duma members—the Bolsheviks caused bloodshed by trying to seize power.] a street battle that lasted six days with appalling results (at least two thousand [casualties]). The masses of soldiers won here as well. [It is significant that Martov does not mention workers among those fighting for the Bolsheviks. As Diane Koenker put it, they displayed "non-participatory support" for the Bolsheviks. See Koenker, *Moscow Workers,* pp. 342–44.] Voitinskii [V. S. Voitinskii—a center-right Menshevik and a commissar of the provisional government at the front in 1917] got involved in the adventure of Kerensky, who fancied marching on Petersburg with one thousand cossacks in order to win it back [30 October 1917]. All this only strengthened the Leninists.

The Defensists' more serious attempts to form a new government (without the Kadets and without the Bolsheviks), relying on the troops at the front, fortunately ended harmlessly [This was an attempt to form a new government in Mogilev in mid-November. Viktor Chernov—one of the key leaders of the PSR—tried to convince his party colleagues that it would be wise to give up the struggle for the capitals, now in Bolshevik hands, and instead to assemble the All-Russian Peasant Congress, still solidly Socialist Revolutionary, in a provincial city. Mogilev was chosen because it was the seat of the army headquarters. See V. Chernov, *Kommentarii k Protokolam TsKa PSR,* Nic. Col., series no.7, Records of the PSR, box 10, folder 3.] thanks to the wisdom of the army committees. They finally understood that even if they were not going to be betrayed by the soldier masses, it was pointless to knock out the soldiers piece by piece, that is, one soldier regime by another [Bolshevik regime, by a new government formed in Mogilev and relying on the army at the front] and that it meant embarking on the road of pretorian, or Mexican, revolutions. In the end, the less fanatical Defensists [less than irreversibly opposed to the Bolshevik regime] understood this well and, under pressure from Fedor Il'ich [Dan], abandoned attempts to form a new government and overthrow the Leninists by force. [Chernov, in his account of his efforts to form a new government in Mogilev, does not mention the role played by Martov and Dan. According to Chernov, his efforts were hampered by Gots and Avksent'ev, his colleagues in the PSR Central Committee, who wanted to create an anti-Bolshevik center in Kiev. See *Kommentarii k Protokolam TsKa PSR.*] This was made all the more easy because as soon as Trotsky declared peace, it became obvious that the soldiers, even those critical of the Bolsheviks, would not go *against* them.

In the meantime, the boycott against Lenin on the part of employees in all institutions, dumas, and so on acquired such broad proportions that it put the new government in a tragicomic situation. The government's decrees remain on paper in nine-tenths or even ninety-nine–one hundredths of Russia, and even in Peter[sburg] they have not succeeded in subordinating a single department to themselves. Terror was the first consequence of this boycott. All bourgeois newspapers and many Socialist ones as well were shut down. At the plants, the Mensheviks and SRs were beaten up and driven out. Some were arrested. *Pravda* and other Bolshevik papers, as well as ministers themselves, were inciting mob law and violence.

To strengthen themselves, the Leninists rushed posthaste toward the conclusion of peace so coarsely and clumsily that even their supporters began to understand that in such a way one can only come to a separate peace and even a despicable separate peace. However, they started out on a course of social demagoguery, decreeing "workers' control," which removed the entrepreneur entirely from the management of a plant, and, in order to please the Left SRs, declaring "equalized land use." They announced a moratorium on apartment rent and now promise "equalized apartment use." The officers' food rations were reduced to the soldiers' level, and they now promise immediate nationalization of the banks. They are doing all of this so incompetently, so irresponsibly, and so foolishly that even Luper and Drumont [Edouard Adolphe Drumont—French publicist and politician known for his book *La France juive* (1886) wherein he denounced Jewish influence in the Third Republic. Later his anti-Semitic ideas found expression on the pages of a newspaper he founded (1892), *La Libre Parole.*] could not have surpassed them. Among the masses of common people [*obyvatel'skie*], all of this, of course, only inflames hatred of any kind of socialism and of the workers.

We are trying to convince our Mensheviks [Defensist Mensheviks or, as they later came to be known, Right Mensheviks] that the first precept we must follow in such a situation is not to participate, under any circumstances, in the destruction of the proletariat [Martov means not to participate in attempts to overthrow the Bolsheviks by force because in his mind, such attempts, if successful, would lead to severe reprisals against the workers, Bolshevik or not. The expectation of a right-wing backlash was very much in the minds of Russian Socialists in 1917, partly as a legacy of the 1905 revolution.], even if it is going along the wrong path. It seems that in this regard we were successful. That is to say that the majority of Defensists, both ours [i.e., Menshevik] and the SRs, are now less belligerent. Even Tsereteli seems to have firmly taken this stand. He is less firm in acknowledging that the only way out of this situation lies in concluding an agreement with the Bolsheviks in order to create a general democratic government (from the SRs to the Bolsheviks). He has abandoned the idea of a coalition [with the Kadets], but, together with Skobelev, Liber, and others, he is still dreaming of creating a government consisting of the Mensheviks, the SRs, and the P[eople's] S[ocialists], even though the facts (the Constituent Assembly returns) indicate clearly that without the support of the Bolshevik masses, such a democratic government would be even more suspended in midair than the Leninist one is. Moreover, it is impossible to win these masses over from Lenin, as they [Defensists] dream, in two or three weeks. At any rate a majority was formed [at the Central Committee session on 31 October 1917] in our Central Committee to seek an agreement with the Bolsheviks to resolve the crisis. F[edor] Il'ich, Gorev, Cherevanin, and Erlikh [Henryk Erlikh—a Revolutionary Defensist in 1917, elected to the Central Committee in December 1917, and a leader of the Jewish Bund] are with us on this point. But eleven members of the Central Committee resigned (Gvozdev, Golikov, Zaretskaia, Skobelev, Liber, Baturskii, Roman, Iurii, and others). [The full list of those who resigned from the Menshevik Central Committee in protest against negotiations with the Bolsheviks is as follows: M. I. Liber, B. S. Baturskii, L. I. Goldman, F. A. Iudin, K. A. Gvozdev, A. N. Smirnov, P. A. Garvi, K. M. Ermolaev, S. M. Zaretskaia, P. Kolokol'nikov, B. N. Krokhmal', and Central Committee candidates M. I. Skobelev, B. O. Bogdanov, and Golikov.] A number of our prominent Defensists quit, but Tsereteli convinced them to return after the negotiations with the Bolsheviks fell through. *In terms of practical policy,* this problem has lost priority (at least for a while).

In the very first days negotiations began on the initiative of the Railroad and Post/ Telegraph Union, under pressure from the army committees with our participation as intermediaries [the Menshevik Internationalist faction], together with the Left SRs and the *Novaia Zhizn'* group. When the Bolsheviks realized how difficult it was to subordinate the state apparatus in the conditions of boycott on the part of Democracy [democratic parties and organizations], they began vacillating. The Left SRs, who had stayed in the CEC [Central Executive Committee], now also threatened to walk out. The workers and some soldiers began passing resolutions on the inadmissibility of civil war [In this context civil war means armed struggle between Kerensky's forces and the Bolsheviks.] and the desirability of an agreement. Lenin was forced to allow the CEC and the CC [Central Committee] of his own party to conduct negotiations. These began at the moment when the Right SRs, the Peasant Soviet, and the P[eople's] S[ocialists], still full of illusions that it would be easy to achieve victory over the Bolsheviks, had an implacable attitude. Only our CC, after initial false steps, stood firmly for an agreement, for during the preliminary talks we detected grounds for an agreement. The new government would be a "cabinet of experts" [In Russian, *delovoe ministerstvo* is a cabinet whose ministers are chosen for their business qualities regardless of political affiliation. In fact, however, party affiliation of ministers could not have been irrelevant. Martov wants to indicate here that the participants in the negotiations attempted to put an emphasis on joint work of qualified leaders, not on who represented which party in a new government.], which would include those Bolsheviks least offensive to the right wing of Democracy (Lunacharskii's, [A. V. Lunacharskii in 1917 was a member of a Trotsky-led interdistrict group of Social Democrats and worked on *Novaia Zhizn'*. By the fall of 1917, Lunacharskii joined the Bolsheviks and became commissar of enlightenment in the Bolshevik government.] Pokrqvskii's [M. N. Pokrovskii in the fall of 1917 was a Bolshevik leader of the Moscow soviet and as of November, its chairman; from May 1918 until his death he was the deputy commissar of enlightenment. In the 1920s he became one of the most distinguished Marxist historians of Russia.], and Aleksei Rykov's [A leading Bolshevik, during World War I he was exiled to Siberia, served on the presidium of the Moscow soviet in 1917, became people's commissar of internal affairs after October, and was executed in 1938.] names were mentioned.) From the Mensheviks and SRs, persons with expertise would be included, and the cabinet would be led by Chernov. Until the convocation of the Constituent Assembly, the government would be responsible not to the CEC, but to a new institution to be composed of both old and new CEC [The old CEC, led by the Mensheviks and Socialist Revolutionaries, was elected at the First Congress of Soviets in June 1917. The new CEC is the Bolshevik-led one elected at the Second Congress of Soviets on 26 October 1917 after the Mensheviks and the Socialist Revolutionaries walked out. The old CEC refused to recognize the new CEC because a great number of soviets were not represented in it. The proposed agreement would have been a compromise between the Bolsheviks, the Mensheviks, and the Socialist Revolutionaries.], the Peasant Soviet, Petrograd and Moscow dumas, trade unions, and so forth. The negotiations seemed to be going on quite amicably. But at this very moment, the Leninists, who at one point had been pressed by Kerensky's detachment, began to win. They demoralized the cossacks' ranks and strengthened Lenin's position. When we pointed out that, as a moral symbol of the negotiations' success, it was imperative to stop the reign of terror, to open the [Peter and Paul] fortress, and to establish a cease-fire on the internal front (to which Kerensky sent his agreement), the Bolsheviks responded at first with procrastination and then with refusal. The negotiations were wrecked, and all the intermediaries recognized that the blame for this fell on the Bolsheviks. This caused a split among the Bolsheviks, which, it seems, is the first good result of our policy. Zinoviev, Kamenev, Riazanov, Nogin, Rykov, Miliutin, Lozovskii, Larin (he is now a Bolshevik!), and some others, declaring that the Lenin-Trotsky policy was leading to the destruction of the proletariat, resigned their posts as ministers (four) and relinquished other duties. Although Zinoviev, Lunachar[skii], and Teodorovich soon returned in remorse, others remain in opposition.

After this a period of inactivity began. We could only campaign against

Bolshevik terror and for the necessity of an agreement. When the right elements of Democracy attempted to resurrect the old government or set up a new one at the front, we (here Tsereteli was with us) hindered them. However, it seems that soon everyone became convinced that it was impossible. The Bolsheviks, for their part, did not lose any time and bombarded Russia with demagogical decrees.

On 12 November elections to the C[onstituent] A[ssembly] began in Petrograd and a number of provinces (some had to be postponed). We expected widespread absenteeism on the part of the masses. The meetings were not attended, most papers did not come out, and there were many cases of violence inflicted on the campaigners of all parties except the Bol[sheviks]. But it turned out differently. In Peter[sburg] more than 80 percent of the electorate went to the polls; in workers' neighborhoods up to 90 percent. Almost all the soldiers and an overwhelming majority of the workers and the poor voted for the Bolsheviks (415,000 out of 900,000 votes), who won six seats out of twelve. Since the August elections to the duma, the number of their voters increased from 180,000 to 415,000. The Kadets have shown almost the same success: 250,000 votes (instead of 120,000) and four seats. All other parties have disappeared. We received only 10,000 (in August 25,000). The Potresovites [followers of A. N. Potresov, see above], who had come out with a separate election slate, received 16,000 votes, the P[eople's] S[ocialists], 18,000, and the Plekhanovites [supporters of Plekhanov, known as the father of Russian Marxism and one of the founders of the RSDWP. In 1917, however, Plekhanov found himself on the extreme right wing of the Social Democratic movement. See S. H. Baron, *Plekhanov, the Father of Russian Marxism* (Stanford: Stanford University Press, 1963).] less than 2,000 votes.

Although final returns are not available, the general picture in the provincial cities is the same, except for an even bigger success for the Kadets. They are often number one, or immediately follow the Bolsheviks. The SRs are in third place almost everywhere; we are in fourth place or even lower. Generally, we do not exist as a party of the masses anywhere (Caucasia excluded), regardless of whether we campaign amicably or (as in Peter[sburg] and Kharkov) come out with two factional election slates. [Disagreement among the Menshevik factions was so strong that Internationalists and Defensists drew separate election slates that competed against each other.] Everywhere in the cities we have 5–10 percent of the vote, consisting of the elite of the working class and part of intelligentsia. The masses follow the Bolsheviks, the Kadets, and the SRs. According to available data, the Constituent Assembly will have a strong wing of the Bolsheviks and Left SRs siding with it, a similar or even stronger wing of the Kadets, and a Socialist center headed by the SRs.

The majority would depend on its [the center's] vote. (Therefore, there has to be either a bloc with the Bolsheviks or with the Kadets and those to the right of them.) There will be a small number of our delegates. I think thirty people, but F. I. [Dan] thinks not more than twenty. So far, judging by the returns in the cities, I almost certainly will not make it to the CA. (Out of the four places where my candidacy was on the slate, it fell through in Peter[sburg], and data from Kharkov and Moscow are inauspicious. That leaves only one front where there is any chance, but elections are due there in a few days.) F. I. [Dan] has rather uncertain chances in one province. Abramovich [Rafail Abramovich—a member of the Menshevik CC and a center-left Menshevik closely associated with Martov; at the same time, one of the leaders of the Jewish Bund] seems to have failed. Martynov [A. S. Martynov, a leading Social Democrat, one of the founders of the party, a close associate of Martov's, and a member of the Menshevik CC] has some chances in two provinces where elections are due in the coming days. Ermanskii [O. A. Ermanskii—a Menshevik Internationalist, a member of the Menshevik Central Committee (May 1918), and a close associate of Martov's] is in the same situation. Only the Caucasians are going to get through; they did not nominate a single non-Caucasian there [Caucasia]. You [Axelrod] also have chances in Moscow city and in Kiev province. The [Menshevik] faction will consist of provincial delegates and some very right-wing Defensists (Dement'ev and others). [In fact, the Menshevik faction in the Constituent Assembly consisted of twenty Social Democrats. See Oliver H. Radkey, *The Election to the Constituent Assembly of 1917* (Cambridge, Mass.: Harvard University Press, 1950), p. 21.] (In some places in the provinces, the elections can be characterized as Istambul-like on the part of the Bolsheviks.)

The election returns have inspired the Bolsheviks and had an immediate effect on the behavior of the Left SRs and the Railroad Union. The Left SRs split from the Right SRs at the Conference of Peasant Soviets and declared their part [of the conference] to be an Extraordinary Peasant Congress. They entered into an agreement with Lenin's CEC, merged the two institutions, and added representatives from the Railroad and Post/Telegraph Union, other trade unions, and military organizations. According to the agreement the parties who walked out of the [Second] Congress of Soviets can enter this institution with a number of representatives proportionate to their strength at the Second Congress of Soviets. According to [our] calculation, if all representatives enter the Bolsheviks will have half the votes and all others the other half. Despite the demand on the part of our workers, we [the Menshevik CC] too have decided that to enter under the given political conditions would camouflage the [Bolshevik] masquerade. Even now the real power is not in the hands of the CEC, but in the hands of Lenin and Trotsky, who have reduced their own parliament to the role of the Bulygin duma [a limited franchise institution permitted in 1905 for the first time and designed to play a consultative role in legislation under the czar]. The latter can be explained by the fact that the CEC members have an extremely low cultural level, which will not rise with the admixture of Left SRs. Moreover, the presence of all political parties in the CEC now would have covered the dark scheming against the Constituent Assembly, which is clearly going on. The Leninists are almost openly preparing for the disbandment; it is becoming apparent that they will not have a majority and that the Kadets will be very strong. The disbandment of the Constituent Assembly will be a terrible blow to the revolution. If the Constituent Assembly has forces to resist, a civil war will start between the proletariat and the petit bourgeois Democracy. This civil war can only end in the destruction of the proletariat and the victory of the Kadets. If, however, the Constituent Assembly is powerless to resist the coup d'état, which is possible, the worst form of soldier dictatorship would reign, compromising the proletariat. That is why I thought it necessary to put the question point-blank. If the new parliament declares that from the moment of convoking the Constituent Assembly all power will be passed on to the Constituent Assembly, we will enter this parliament, but only in this case. It is preferable that the Bolsheviks not be able to say, in the event of a direct attack on the Constituent Assembly, that their "people's soviet" unites all Socialist currents. The Left SRs did a lot of harm by making an agreement [to enter the Bolshevik government. In fact, when Martov was writing this letter, the Bolshevik–Left Socialist Revolutionary agreement was far from final. The difficult negotiations were not completed until December 1917. See A. I. Razgon, *VTsIK Sovetov v pervye mesiatsy diktatury proletariata* [The CEC of Soviets in the First Months of the Dictatorship of the Proletariat] (Moscow: Navka, 1971), pp. 33–37.] without guarantees of recognition for the Constituent Assembly and without a repudiation of terror by the Bolsheviks. They [Left SRs] also carried the Railroad Union with them.

This is the situation. It is tragic. Try to understand that what we face, after all, is a victorious uprising of the proletariat, that is to say that almost the entire proletariat is behind Lenin and expects social liberation from this coup. It has challenged all antiproletarian forces. In such conditions not to be in the ranks of the proletariat, at least in the role of opposition, is almost unendurable. But the regime's demagogic forms and the pretorian background of Lenin's rule do not provide enough assurance for us to join them, especially in this period when the new government has not yet consolidated its authority and, struggling against the passive resistance of society, is resorting to violence of all kinds. Yesterday, for example, after the

Moscow duma, they [Bolsheviks] dissolved the Petrograd duma and fixed new elections for the day after tomorrow. Tailoring the electoral law, they introduced Bonapartist changes [All political parties protested against the dissolution of the Petrograd and Moscow dumas. The decree on the dissolution was issued on 16 November. By Bonapartist changes in electoral procedure, Martov means a number of unilateral, dictatorial, and, from the point of view of non-Bolshevik parties, illegal changes in the election procedure. According to John Keep, "The dissolution of the Duma clearly foreshadowed similar action against the Constituent Assembly." Keep, ed., *Debate on Soviet Power*, pp. 336–37.] and did all this simply by decrees, bypassing the new "people's soviet."

Furthermore, because they do not want an "agreement" with bourgeois Democracy and Socialist intelligentsia, the new rulers are compelled to surround themselves with careerists of the most disgusting type. (Many new functionaries have already been exposed as criminal elements and people of the old regime.) To make things worse, our boycott of Smolny [the Bolshevik government] not only made the Bolshevik masses hate us (particularly us), but also was extremely embarrassing for our own workers. Many workers are leaving the party. They say, "You used to sit with the Kadets in the preparliament, but you don't want to be in a Bolshevik workers' parliament." I am afraid that our "absenteeism" will not be understood in Europe either. But changing the situation will only be possible, I think, if our (and the SRs') right wing agrees to enter [The next word is missing. It is most likely an epithet.] Lenin's parliament in order to campaign there. Perhaps the Extraordinary Party Congress scheduled for the 27 [of November] will venture to do that. If not, we may find ourselves without any real means of bringing influence to bear on the working masses. (Very often they don't let our speakers speak at the factories.)

[First word is missing.] Therefore, I do not think that Lenin's dictatorship is doomed in the near future. The army at the front is going over to his side, apparently irrevocably. Germany and Austria have in fact recognized it [Lenin's government], and the Allies are likely to assume a wait-and-see posture. As long as the army is not disillusioned by Lenin's peace, there may not be any real force available for counterrevolution. Much more dangerous for him, of course, is the economic collapse.

As you may guess, our spirits are quite low. One is witnessing the destruction of the revolution and feels unable to do anything about it. Partly because of this, I advised the CC to respond to you with a recommendation not to go now. I mean that your presence in Stockholm may still be very much needed.

I would not want to deliberately villify the Bolshevik dictatorship in Europe's eyes because, objectively, this could help enemies of the revolution and of socialism. But I am saddened by the idea that our German, French, and Italian comrades will not understand our absenteeism from the "new revolution." That is why I would like to send a special declaration with an explanation for Europe from us, as a faction affiliated with Zimmerwald [an International Socialist Commission elected at the Conference of Socialist Parties opposed to war in September 1915 in Zimmerwald in Switzerland. The word *Zimmerwald* became synonymous in Socialist circles with the Left Social Democrats or Internationalists' repudiation of the war.]. I have not been able to do it in time to send it with this letter. I'll do it by the next time, but I ask you to familiarize Rakovskii [Kh. G. Rakovskii—a Social Democrat who before 1914 belonged to the Menshevik party and during World War I was an Internationalist and attended the Zimmerwald conference. Thus at the time of Martov's writing this letter, Rakovskii was a Social Democrat of a similar political outlook. In 1918, however, Rakovskii began to play a leading role in the Ukraine, as a Bolshevik. From 1918 to 1923 he was the chairman of the Ukrainian Council of People's Commissars; he died in Stalin's camp.] with my information. He probably feels that the manner in which the Bolsheviks have tackled the problem of peace is adventuristic. I would be very grateful if you could, with someone's help, compose a report, based on my information, on the position taken by the Menshevik Internationalists for *Leipz[iger] Volkszeitung*. It is important that the German left know that we found it impossible to support the Bolsheviks. Please tell Rakovskii that I received his letter about Dobrodzhan's [The name in the original is *Dobrozhan*. Most likely it is a Russian version of the name of a well-known Romanian Social Democrat and later a Communist—Aleksandru Dobrogeanu-gherea. During World War I, he belonged to the left wing of the Socialist party of Romania, and in 1921, he was one of the founders of the Romanian Communist party. He died in Stalin's camps in 1937.] son only now and that I do not see how one could help him at this time. Most likely Trotsky does not have diplomatic relations with Romania. I will try to raise the alarm in the press.

Greetings from all our [comrades]. How are you? You must have seen Goldenb [Io. P. Goldberg—a Russian Social Democrat who changed his affiliation from the Mensheviks to the Bolsheviks several times during his political career. In 1905–1910, he was a member in the Central Committee of the RSDWP; from 1914 to 1919, a Menshevik. After the October overturn, he remained abroad; in 1920, he switched sides again, this time to bolshevism.] and learned from him about what is going on here.

I shake your hand warmly.

Iu. Tsederbaum

## DOCUMENT TWO

## Iu. O. Martov to P. B. Axelrod

1 December 1917 [Petersburg]

Dear Pavel Borisovich!

Several days ago (about a week), I sent you an enormous letter about what's going on here. I hope you have received it. Now I have another chance to write you a letter about the following:

As far as I know, Haase [Hugo Haase, one of the founders and the first chairman of the Independent Social Democratic party of Germany (USPD), which split away from the Sozialdemokratische Partei Deutschlands (SPD) in 1917 over war and peace policy, demanding "Peace without winners or losers." Politically, the USPD was the closest party to Martov-led Mensheviks. At the end of 1919, Haase was assassinated in Berlin.] and Ledebour [Georg Ledebour, cofounder of the USPD and outspoken critic of the Sozialdemokratische Partei Deutschlands's support of the war effort. On some issues, he was to the left of Haase, especially early in 1919. For many years, he remained close to Martov and to his criticisms of bolshevism.] are in Stockholm now. We consider it very important that they be informed why we Internationalists have found it impossible to take any part in the realization of the so-called dictatorship of the proletariat. Unfortunately, we have not had time to draft a special declaration for the Europeans, and I am enclosing, just in case, a project of our resolution, which has been submitted to the Extraordinary Congress [a Menshevik party congress that took place from November 30 to December 9, 1917. Most likely, Martov enclosed the resolution he presented at the congress. The entire text is in "Iz materialov s'ezda. Proekty rezoliutsii po tekushchemu momentu," *Novyi Luch'*, no. 2 (3 December 1917, Petrograd):4.] of our party, now in session. During the last few days, the Leninist regime has enriched itself by another deed: it has declared the entire Constitutional Democratic party [Kadets] outlawed (without any external grounds) and staged the first undisguised assault on the Constituent Assembly. [On 27 November 1917, the Constituent Assembly was scheduled to open. On 28 November, the Bolsheviks outlawed the Kadet party and arrested some of its leaders. Martov doubt-

---

Nicolaevsky Collection, series no. 17, box 511, files 1–2.

lessly refers to these events.] Its members (the SRs) who gathered for private consultations (less than a hundred of them have arrived [in Petersburg] so far) were disbanded by armed force. They [the Bolsheviks] "decreed" that the Constituent Assembly will convene only when at least four hundred delegates have been elected and then made their way [to Petersburg]. But because all the Kadets will have been arrested and because about 150 elected Bolsheviks will most likely deliberately not show up, another month will go by before a necessary quorum can be assembled from all the distant localities. Such is Lenin's captious and vile plan. By that time, a part of the SR [delegation] will probably have been arrested as well and the dictatorship can last ad infinitum. It is essential that our German comrades understand that

1. Even though a mass of workers is behind Lenin, his regime is becoming more and more a regime based on terror, exercised not by the proletarians but by sansculottes—a mixed bag of armed soldiers, Red Guards, and sailors who are turning into state pensioners, just as happened with the French sansculottes

2. To attempt to govern (and even more so to conduct Communist experiments) against the will of the overwhelming majority of peasants (not fewer than twenty million voters at the elections chose the moderate SRs) and against the will of the entire urban Democracy (civil servants, social [organizations], private [sector] employees, technicians, free professions, teachers, and so on) cannot lead to anything but disaster

3. The regime of terror, the trampling of civil liberties, and the outrages against the Constituent Assembly in the name of class dictatorship are nipping in the bud the seeds of democratic education that the people had acquired during the eight months [of the revolution in 1917] and preparing fertile soil for any kind of Bonapartism

4. The civil war and the disintegration of the country (the Ukraine, the cossack territories, the Crimea, Siberia, and even "Bashkiria" have declared their total autonomy [from Lenin's government], and Caucasia in fact governs itself) make the Leninists absolutely helpless in negotiations with the German government; they are caught in a soldiers' tumult they themselves unbridled

5. Even though we do not want to play into the hands of the bourgeoisie, who will inherit the situation after the Bolsheviks' bankruptcy, and even though we categorically reject the idea of forming "a bloc of all honest people" against Lenin and Co. (as a matter of fact some right Socialists would like to do that), still we now have to concentrate all our efforts on denouncing and exposing Leninist policy in the hope that the best elements

among the workers following him [Lenin] will understand whence they have been led and will form a nucleus capable of directing the course of the dictatorship along a different path

Our stance is that the majority in the Constituent Assembly (Socialist) must unite and find an agreement between the Leninists and all others [Socialists] on the tasks of concluding peace, regulating industry, and carrying out agrarian reform. Terror and Soc[ialist] utopian experiments must be repudiated.

What we expect from the Germans [German Socialists, particularly the independent USPD] is that they, insofar as possible, will hinder their own imperialists' attempts to use the madness of Trotsky's foreign policy for the purpose of finally grasping Russia by the throat. An international peace conference is urgently needed.

If you have a chance, tell Rakovskii that his letter to Lenin's government has produced an unfavorable impression. *All* of us laugh when we read that he is urging the Leninists to make Romania convene the Constituent Assembly and [establish] a free press. How can one expect this from our sweet Trotsky, who is disbanding the Constituent Assembly here—*il est bien qualifié pour cela*—and who has shut down at least a *hundred* Socialist newspapers all across Russia.

The congress [the Menshevik party congress] is running smoothly so far (today is the first day), but it is hard to say if all will end well. Because of Lenin's war with Kaledin [General A. M. Kaledin's war with Bolshevik forces was the first incident of the frontline Civil War between the Whites and the Reds that would erupt in full strength in 1918 and especially in 1919. In October 1917, General Kaledin refused to recognize Lenin's government and assumed full powers in the Don area. After initial successes, his forces were defeated by the Bolsheviks by the end of February 1918.], forty Caucasians who were going to come, headed by Zhordaniia to help us out, could not come [because the war zone, the Don area, was on their route from Georgia to Petrograd]. With their help, our left wing could have formed, together with the center-left of F. I. [Dan], Cherevanin, and others, a solid majority in order to get on with a truly Social Democratic policy, the kind of policy that would not turn our unavoidable struggle with Leninism into part of a general campaign against the working class as now conducted by the entire bourgeoisie and petit bourgeoisie. (But Leninist terror is leading to this exact thing.) Without the Caucasians, such a majority may turn out to be small and unsteady. Then the decomposition of the party will continue, which is much more dangerous in the given conditions than only Potresov's wing [Some of Potresov's supporters did leave the

Menshevik party, but the majority remained to oppose Martov's policy from within.] splitting away, which would have been the case had the Caucasians come. (Most likely they will go to Plekhanov [that is, to Plekhanov's organization Edinstvo (Unity)] under the impact of Lenin's Bashi-Bukovstvo [From Bashi-Buzuk, a type of a Turkish soldier in the eighteenth and nineteenth centuries. The expression was used to denote a particularly rude, cruel, and unruly person; here implies Bolshevik cruelty and unruliness.] because they are inimically inclined toward the working class in its current appearance.)

I shake your hand warmly. Greetings from all our [comrades]. Please let the Germans understand that they should write in *Leipz[iger] Volkszeitung* without ardor about the Leninists and in no way allow an apologia. When the true picture of the "truly Russian" "dictatorship of the proletariat" after its collapse is clearly seen in Europe, the Scheidemans [Philipp Scheideman, the leader of the SPD. For the left-wing Social Democrats, his name became synonymous with supporting the war effort. Scheideman became minister president of the first republican government in February 1919.] of all countries will use it to discredit all that is left wing in socialism for centuries. Let them, therefore, disassociate themselves from everything specifically Leninist.

You know, Pavel Borisovich, only now can we clearly see the Jacobin nature of Leninism that you revealed in 1903 in your article in no. 65 of *Iskra*.

IU. TSEDERBAUM

## DOCUMENT THREE

## F. I. Dan to P. B. Axelrod

8 January 1918, Petrograd

Dear Pavel Borisovich:

You will learn about what's going on here from newspapers and from an oral report [Dan apparently sent this letter with a person traveling abroad and also asked him to deliver an oral message.], for I have no doubt that, as the Bolsheviks blatantly lie here, where the truth is in everyone's sight, they lie even more blatantly abroad, where they have a monopoly on information.

I will write a few lines in a hurry. Everything must be done in a hurry now because a whole lot of people, ours [the Mensheviks] and the SRs', including I[raklii] G[eorgievich] [Tsereteli], Skob[elev], me, and others, have to live in semilegal conditions or even go into hiding because of possible arrests but even more so because of the danger of lynching and mob violence on the part of the savage soldiery and the Red Guards.

The fact is that the city [Petrograd] and Soviet power itself are at the mercy not just of the Petrograd garrison, which has become unreliable [for the Bolshevik authorities] in its majority, although still passive, but at the mercy of the Kronstadt and Helsinfors sailors and the Red Guards who have turned into well-paid mobsters ready for anything.

It so happened that I was not present at the session of the Constituent Assembly, but according to the unanimous testimony of the participants, the newspapers do not convey even roughly the unbearably shameful and disgraceful position the assembly found itself in, thanks to Bolshevik bedlam and the rude interference of armed sailors who crammed the galleries and the hall itself. Swearing, shouting, and whistling filled the hall. It all reminded one more of a pub than of an assembly of even the most pitiful consultative institution, let alone of the supreme Assembly of People's Will. No doubt, the world has not seen anything like it. It took a combination of Bolshevik banditry, soldiers' debauchery, and specifically Russian crassness to create such a shameful scene. But even in this atmosphere, which would have overstrained a cart horse, Tsereteli, after endless interruptions and shouts of "blood sucker," "executioner," and the like, in a situation when rifles and pistols were aimed at him, managed to make them

Nicolaevsky Collection, series no. 16, box 45, file 9.

listen. His speech and declaration produced an enormous impression, and in a commonly shared view, it was the only dignified performance.

At the same time, the shooting of unarmed peaceful demonstrators was going on in the streets. In contrast to the demonstration of 28 November [The Constituent Assembly was scheduled to open on 27 November. The Bolshevik government postponed the opening. Dan refers here to the demonstration in protest of this action.], the great majority [of participants] were workers. About forty thousand of them came from the various districts [of Petrograd]. They were walking peacefully, of course, and all the Bolshevik stories about some shots on the part of the demonstrators are brazen fabrications. They were shot at without warning, primarily by sailors and Red Guards armed to the teeth with their hand grenades at the belt. The shooting produced an enormous impression. The entire Nevsky district is seething with indignation against the Bolsheviks. They are not given a chance to speak [at the rallies]. They are being recalled from the soviet and from the Red Guards. The same is happening in other districts, although not with such intensity. News is coming in from various places in the provinces about new elections to the soviets and the replacement of the Bolsheviks by the Mensheviks and SRs. The Bolshevik dictatorship is falling apart. The workers are pulling away from it, and it is degenerating into the most ferocious hegemony of the soldiery and the hired pretorian Red Guards.

Tomorrow, January 9 [This day is associated in Russian history with Bloody Sunday in 1905, the day when a peaceful demonstration was fired on by czarist troops. The parallels between the two shootings were obvious to contemporaries.], the burial of the victims of the shooting will take place. The funeral is likely to be impressive, but unfortunately, new shootings may occur because the Bashi-Bukovstvo [Bashi-Buzuk; see document 2] act not only like the sailors and the Red Guards do, but worse: they disband groups of people on the streets and threaten to shoot them as a matter of course. All newspapers are closed today; all printing shops have been occupied by a [special] detachment. In our printing shop, they tore to shreds all the manuscripts and scattered the type. Those two or three pitiful leaflets that managed to come out are being confiscated, torn to pieces, and burnt on the streets. The SRs' Central Committee premises have been occupied by the Red Guards. The editorial office of their paper has been occupied as well. I am not even talking about the Kadets. [Dan is implying that the Kadets were subjected to severe repression.] We [the Menshevik CC] are compelled to gather for work secretly because we are sure that if not today, then tomorrow, our Central Committee will be assaulted as well.

The licentious practices of sailors and Red Guards have reached unbelievable proportions. And because, as of tomorrow, the bread ration will be decreased to a quarter of a pound a day and in three or four days, unless a miracle happens, there won't be any bread at all, it is frightening to think of what must be going on in Petrograd. The abominable murder of Shingarev [A. I. Shingarev (1869–1918), a Kadet party leader and member of the Second, Third, and Fourth State Duma. From March to May 1917, minister of agriculture in the provisional government; from May to July, minister of finance, elected member of the Constituent Assembly. Arrested by the Bolsheviks on 28 November 1917 and murdered by the sailors in a hospital in January 1918.] and Kokoshkin [F. F. Kokoshkin (1871–1918), a Kadet party leader and member of the Kadet Central Committee. Arrested by the Bolsheviks on 28 November 1917 and murdered, along with Shingarev, by the sailors in a hospital in January 1918.] gives an idea about the kind of bloodthirsty bacchanalia the Bolsheviks have set loose, but no longer can control.

Definitely, confusion is in their minds. A third of their own faction in the Constituent Assembly protested against its disbandment. [This important piece of information is not mentioned in Soviet historiography.] In the CEC too, demoralization has begun. Riazanov [D. B. Riazanov (1870–1938), real name Goldendakh, belonged to a small group of "conciliators" within the Bolshevik leadership who favored "conciliation" with the Mensheviks and the Socialist Revolutionaries and protested Lenin's dictatorial methods on numerous occasions. In later years Riazanov helped imprisoned Socialists in many ways. In the 1920s, Riazanov was the director of K. Marx and F. Engels Institute in Moscow. Died in Stalin's purges.] made a speech against the Council of People's Commissars. This belated and cowardly opposition, however, is no longer capable of leading to anything. [ Dan is referring here to the opposition within the Bolshevik party, apparently, those who resigned from Lenin's government on 5 November 1917. They failed to prevent the disbanding of the Constituent Assembly.]

Because the cause of [concluding] peace is irrevocably ruined as well and because the Germans, who are tired of Trotsky's eloquence, presented the Bolsheviks with such conditions that they are afraid to say what they are to this very day, I think that this regime is living through its last days. But it will spend them in such filth and blood that I am afraid democracy will not be its heir. (This very minute I was informed by telephone that the Red Guards have come to the dormitory of the SR members of the Constituent Assembly and arrested twenty-six deputies.) Anarchy on the one hand and fierce hatred of the revolution, the proletariat, and democracy on the other, against the background of general apathy and disillusionment of workers' and soldiers' masses—all this is not fertile soil for strengthening democracy. And if we add to this that we are threatened again by German invasion then, alas, the most probable outcome is merciless reaction.

You truly cannot imagine the kind of wailing that is resounding all over Russia, where whole cities are being destroyed and streams of blood are being shed. In the guise of the "dictatorship of the proletariat" reigns the dictatorship of the lumpen in soldiers' uniforms whose "socialism," all of it, to the last drop, boils down to primary accumulation by the most barbaric, truly medieval methods: robbery, violence, and incredibly usurious trade. In this fashion, wealth is pumped into new pockets, and all of these "Socialists," with all those crooks, swindlers, and rogues clinging to them, are nothing but the petite bourgeoisie newly reborn in Russia. Today it plunders the property of others, and tomorrow, when these other people's goods become *its* goods, it will demand the most ferocious and merciless suppression of all those who deny the sanctity and inviolability of property. It will become the most reliable pillar of support for the most bloodthirsty order. It seems that all the conditions are ripe for the appearance of "the White general."

As you see, I am not very optimistically inclined. It seems to me that only an unusually fortunate combination of circumstances, both internal and international, could save us. Meanwhile we see an announcement that an "Internationalist" meeting (and this after the shooting of workers) has taken place; that Mister Hogland [(1884–1956), a Swedish Social Democrat, who, during World War I, belonged to the "internationalist" Zimmerwald group], Rakovskii [Rakovsky; see Document 1], and other representatives of the "International" spoke together with Zinoviev [Grigorii Zinoviev headed the Bolshevik organization in Petrograd and was a member of the Bolshevik Central Committee. In November 1917, he resigned from the CPC to protest the breaking off of multiparty negotiations to form a new government. When in March 1918 Lenin's government moved to Moscow, Zinoviev remained in Petrograd, as the leader of the Petrograd Commune.]; and that the Obukhov workers [The Obukhov state plant, which employed thousands of workers in early 1918, was one of the biggest plants in Petrograd. During the spring of 1918, the Obukhov workers were in the vanguard of the independent workers' council movement (*upolnomochennye*), which opposed the Bolshevik dictatorship. It was against the Obukhov workers that the Bolshevik authorities used a lockout. At the end of June 1918, the plant was closed and all workers were fired for an anti-Bolshevik strike. It is important that the evidence on Obukhov workers' opposition to the Bolsheviks dates to as early as January 1918.] (some of whom were among those shot at) greeted them with shouts of "Murderers!"

I am sure that if the International does not understand what the Prussian General Hoffman understood and that if the International does not repudiate in a timely manner even the slightest solidarity with those hangmen of freedom, those murderers of unarmed workers, those who strangled the Constituent Assembly, those who in Russia, which has just emerged from czarist slavery, speak from the podium of the Constituent Assembly about a "lousy democratic republic," as the Bolshevik speaker Bukharin has done, if the International does not repudiate all this, then, the banner of international socialism will be disgraced for decades in Russia, not only in democratic circles, but in the eyes of the workers as well.

It is imperative to do everything possible to inform the International about what the Bolsheviks are doing in Russia and to inform Russia about the opinion of the International. If they [the Bolsheviks] are not disgorged from the International Socialist milieu, it will mean that all kinds of renegades and hangmen can be tolerated in the International. It will mean that one can cover direct preparation for the most ferocious counterrevolution with the banner of the International.

Well, it is time to finish. As soon as there is another opportunity I will write again if—one has to be mindful of this every minute!—it is still possible for me to write. Meanwhile, I shake your hand warmly.

Yours,

F. DAN

# Soviet Power without the Soviets
## *(January–June 1918)*

DOCUMENT FOUR

## Regional Party Conference in Moscow

On January 13–15, the conference of our party organizations of the Central Industrial Region took place in Moscow. Because of the tremendous difficulties involved with traveling on the railroads now and because of a decline of activity in many of our organizations, the conference was much less well attended than might have been expected. The following organizations were represented at the conference: Yaroslavl—two delegates, Vladimir, Kovrov; Ivanovo Voznesensk (Vladimir province)—each city, one delegate; Kolomna and Spaso-Tushinskaia organizations—two from each; Orekhovo-Zueyvo and Podolsk—one delegate from each; Bogorodskaia organization (Nizhnii Novgorod province)—two; Tver—one; Rzhev (Tver province)—one; Kaluga—one; Orel, Bryansk, Bezhitsa (Orel province)— each city, one delegate; Tula—two; and Kineshma (Kostroma province)— one delegate. In addition, the regional party bureau, the representatives of the Moscow party committee, the Moscow province organization, the editorial board of *Vpered* [Forward], a representative of the Central Committee, and itinerant party propagandists were present. The agenda included reports from local organizations, the report of the regional party bureau, and a discussion of the current situation, the struggle with unemployment, and, finally, organizational and financial matters such as the creation of a regional periodical.

The first item on the agenda—reports from local organizations—which are usually dry and formal, this time was listened to by all the participants with unabating interest. For the first time since the Bolshevik coup, party members from various parts of the central industrial region (this Bolshevik kingdom) were exchanging observations, impressions, and characterizations of Bolshevik "power" in the provinces.

The picture of the Bolsheviks' playing the master and the gallery of types holding power made the reports vivid, colorful, and exceptionally interesting. The general impression produced by the delegates' reports is as follows: The party organizations have shrunk considerably in comparison with the "pre-Bolshevik" period, membership has decreased, and dues are coming in poorly. In most places, Bolshevik terror has prevented using the

This document first appeared in *Party News*, the journal of the Menshevik Central Committee: "Oblastnaia konferentsiia v Moskve," *Partiinye Izvestiia*, nos. 1–2 (January 1919, Petrograd):21–25. Nicolaevsky Collection, series 279, box 678, folders 15–16.

campaign of elections to the Constituent Assembly for propaganda and organizational work. In some organizations, workers—Mensheviks—are so terrorized by the soldiers and Red Guards that they regain strength and resume work with great difficulty. On the other hand, all delegates unanimously stated that *a sharp turnaround* has been noticeable in the mood of the working masses recently. Mass unemployment and famine cause disillusionment in Bolshevik socialism, and the latest events, such as the disbanding of the Constituent Assembly and the shootings at the demonstration in its defense, caused a number of mass protests and made many, even among those sympathetic to the Bolsheviks, have second thoughts. They are beginning to listen willingly to the speeches of the Mensheviks, who were not allowed to speak only a short time earlier. *Only the soldiers* are quite satisfied with the Bolshevik regime, although their numbers in the cities have diminished. (But this does not prevent them from playing the same role in the soviets.) Streaming into the villages, they disband local zemstvos and terrorize the peasant population, thus becoming a new base of Bolshevik power, this time in the villages.

The turnaround in the workers' attitudes opens new possibilities for our organizations. In the entire Bryansk region this can be seen in numerous new elections to the soviets. Almost everywhere the Bolsheviks have found themselves in the minority. This, however, does not prevent the local "commissars" from ignoring such soviets and in other places (like Tula) from ignoring the new election results. In such cases, however, the Bolshevik rule comes across to workers as a rule of naked force, and this in turn makes campaigning easier for our organizations. Recently, many local organizations have in fact begun campaigning both in the press and at workers' rallies. Almost everywhere they need fresh forces and visits of party campaigners and lecturers from the capital.

According to the report of the regional bureau, its work has slowed down due to a lack of funds and weak financial support from local organizations. Nevertheless, for the six months of its existence, the bureau has carried out large organizational and agitational work. It has organized seventy-two trips around the region to provincial conferences or to organize workers' rallies. It has registered one hundred cities or towns where there are our organizations, totaling seventeen thousand members. It has published eight leaflets of the CC and disseminated 300,000 copies. At the present time, the financial situation of the bureau is such that it can function no longer without decisive support from local organizations.

The conference unanimously agreed that the regional bureau should continue to function because it renders a lot of assistance to local organizations. Now, at a time of tremendous dislocation of railroads and post/telegraph communications, the bureau is the only connecting link between all organizations of the Moscow region and the Central Committee. That is why the conference decided that all organizations must make a special payment of 10 percent of their assets to the regional bureau. After that, they should continue with their regular payments both to the CC and to the regional bureau. The conference elected a new bureau consisting of nine members. The main task of four of them will be to travel throughout the region. The newspaper *Vpered* will become the official party paper for the region. The budget of the regional bureau has also been worked out. Comrade Kipen delivered two interesting reports, one on the current political situation and the other on unemployment. These reports were the subject of lively debates, which ended with the adoption of a resolution in line with the decisions of the latest party congress.

The conference results have been fruitful, and its participants have demonstrated their political consciousness, thoughtfulness, earnest attitudes to the questions considered, and a sense of great political responsibility. All this produced a good impression and made the participants hope that an increase in our activity in the Moscow region will be possible in the near future.

---

DOCUMENT FIVE

---

## Open Letter of the Don Committee of the RSDWP

March 1918, Rostov-na-Donu

The Don Committee brings to the attention of readers and the editorial boards of contemporary Russian press that it is deprived at the present time of the possibility of publishing any periodical to replace *Rabochee Slovo* [Workers' Word], shut down after thirteen issues, and *Rabochee Delo* [Workers' Cause], which was also strangled by the Bolshevik authorities. The circumstances surrounding the closings so vividly illustrate the actions of the institutions and agents of so-called Soviet power in the provinces that they deserve to become public knowledge.

---

A copy of this letter—a newspaper clipping from a Georgian newspaper *Bor'ba* [Struggle], no. 74 (23 May 1918, Tiflis):3—is in the Nicolaevsky Collection.

*Rabochee Slovo* was coming out when madness and horror seized our city during the entry of Soviet troops. [Soviet troops entered Rostov-na-Donu in February 1918 and remained until May. Before February, the city was in the hands of General Kaledin, and in May 1918, German troops entered the city after they had occupied the Ukraine. For a detailed account of the Bolshevik rule in Rostov-na-Donu in March and April 1918, see another report of a Menshevik from Rostov-na-Donu: A. Lockerman, *Les Bolcheviks a l'oeuvre* [The Bolsheviks at Work] (Paris: Riviere, 1920).] Our paper published a vivid and truthful account of executions, outrages, looting, crimes, and willfulness of the new masters of our city. In the course of several days, the paper acquired the sympathy of the entire local Democracy, of the working masses, and of the city population at large. The paper's circulation grew to forty thousand copies, which must have caused the fall of the inept *Izvestiia* and of the Left SRs' petty daily. The local rulers could not forgive this. On 24 March a detachment of sailors and Red Guards appeared in the Don Committee office, where the regional conference of Social Democrats was taking place, and the commander produced an order on behalf of Shamov, the Don republic [At the end of February 1918, when the Bolshevik troops defeated General Kaledin's cossacks and entered Rostov-na-Donu, they proclaimed the establishment of the Don republic. It lasted until May 1918.] people's commissar for the struggle with counterrevolution [Imitating the Bolsheviks in Moscow, who had called their government the Council of People's Commissars (CPC), local Bolsheviks in many cities formed their own CPCs. This led to chaos in local administration because local CPCs issued their own decrees. In addition to CPCs, various other Bolshevik organizations competed for power, such as Military Revolutionary Committees, military headquarters, ECs of soviets, presidiums of city and provincial soviets, and others. Here, people's commissar for the struggle with counterrevolution refers to a chief of the Cheka, Lenin's political police.], to the effect that the editorial board of *Rabochee Slovo* was to be liquidated. At the same time, they occupied the printing shop. On the following day, by a special decree of the Military Revolutionary Committee, all newspapers except those of the Bolsheviks and the Left SRs were closed. New periodicals could appear only with special permission of the Committee for the Press.

Some groups of [SD] party members submitted applications for permits to publish new newspapers: *Rabochaia Zhizn'* [Workers' Life] and *Rabochaia Mysl'* [Workers' Thought]. The Military Revolutionary Committee categorically refused. Sharp workers' protests at factories and plants did not succeed in breaking through the stone-hard brains of the highhanded "revolutionaries" who relied on bayonets. The Don Committee of the RSDWP attempted to publish leaflets, but their printers and distributors were terrorized. After the press was strangled, half of the total number of members in the soviet—the SDs, SRs, and those without party affiliation who did not support the Bolsheviks—were expelled from the soviet. Another special decree pronounced the SD and SR factions in the soviet as counterrevolutionary and outlawed them.

---

## DOCUMENT SIX

---

## "Underhandedly"

20 February 1918

Dear Comrade K. A.:

While I was in Petrograd, the soviet [the soviet in Izhevsk, Bolshevik-controlled before elections in February 1918] confiscated our printing shop [which belonged to the SR party]. When I came back, we started campaigning to return to the soviet. [The author most likely means they started an election campaign for the coming elections to the soviet.] At the elections to the soviet, we [SRs], the Mensheviks, and a considerable number of unaffiliated delegates who joined us received the majority. Seeing from our declaration that power was slipping from their hands, the Bolsheviks and the Maximalists [a faction or group identical with or part of the Left SR party organization] embarked on merciless revenge. First, they arrested our SR party committee and took away [their] arms. Then, however, on our announcement in the soviet about it, those arrested were released. On the next day, however, 17 February, as we were discussing with the Mensheviks candidacies for the Executive Committee [In elections to the soviet in the spring of 1918, the Mensheviks and the SRs formed a joint opposition

---

This letter to K. A. Brede, a Socialist Revolutionary and a member of the CEC in 1917, was written from Izhevsk, an industrial town in Vyatka province. The Izhevsk workers played a very special role in the history of the Russian Civil War. Although political conditions in Izhevsk were similar to other industrial towns, the Izhevsk plant produced handguns. When the workers rose against the Bolsheviks in August 1918, they armed themselves with the weapons they produced and overthrew the Bolshevik dictatorship and restored to power the Menshevik/SR-led soviet, which had been disbanded by the Bolsheviks. This letter first appeared in an SR newspaper, *Delo Naroda*, no. 6, 15 March 1918, p. 1, now a bibliographic rarity in the Hoover Institution Library.

bloc. After the elections, the new majority had to nominate the EC of the new soviet.], two powerful grenades were thrown into the room. The grenades' safety locks were released, but fortunately they did not explode.

This is not all, however. The Executive Committee was duly elected, the majority in it was ours [Menshevik-SR], and Sosulin, a member of the CEC of the first convocation, was elected chairman. When the newly elected Executive Committee was formed, its members, on their way home after an evening session, were ambushed. Apolon Sosulin, a Menshevik, was killed, and Stepan Nasledin, an SR, was seriously wounded. They were walking together at night, on 19 February. On 20 February, during the day, another newly elected member of the soviet, Vasilii Ivanovich Buzanov [A member of the PSR, Buzanov was elected chairman of the Izhevsk soviet at the election in May 1918, but that soviet was also disbanded by the Bolsheviks. After the successful uprising against the Bolsheviks in August 1918, Buzanov was restored to the chairmanship of the soviet.], member of the Constituent Assembly, was wounded at the very entrance to the plant. We were told that all our party activists should expect the fate of those killed on Saint Bartholomew's night. [References to Saint Bartholomew's night (*Varfalomeevskaia noch'*) were common in the press of many Russian cities in the spring of 1918. To stage a Saint Bartholomew's night in the Russian political context of that spring meant to settle accounts with the enemies of the Bolsheviks. In reality it meant that soldiers and sailors, or "Brotherhoods," as they called themselves, went on a rampage in a number of cities, sometimes on their own, at other times in conjunction with Bolshevik committees. It was most widespread in the south of Russia and in the Ukraine. The soldiers and sailors killed property owners, class enemies (*burzhui*), Jews, officers, and sometimes opposition politicians—Kadets, Socialist Revolutionaries, and Mensheviks. Well-known reprisals of this kind include the massacre of officers in Sebastopol, a rampage in Rostovna-Donu, and arbitrary killings in Kiev, Kharkov, and Samara in February and March 1918.]

Yours, . . . from IZHEVSK

## DOCUMENT SEVEN

### Among the Workers

Orekhovo-Zueyvo, April 1918

More than half a year has passed since Orekhovo-Zueyvo became a city. [In 1917, two villages, Orekhovo and Zueyvo, in Vladimir province were merged into one city.] The unity of Orekhovo and Zueyvo, though, is purely formal. Just as in the old days, these two, forcibly turned into one city, continue to live their separate lives. Orekhovo is the Manchester of Russia: factories, factories, and more factories. It is clean in the streets, in the yards, and in the soldiers' barracks. The school building is simply perfect. There is an excellent theater, where sometimes Chaliapin [Fyodor Ivanovich (1873–1938), a famous Russian opera singer] himself, Sobinov [ L. V. Sobinov (1872–1934), a well-known Russian tenor], and even Pavlova [Anna Pavlovna (1882–1931), a famous Russian ballet dancer] perform. A huge park where workers relax is in exemplary order. Such a park would be an honor to any provincial capital. There is also a workers' club and an employees' club. Everything about life in Orekhovo has the flavor of Europe with a taste of Nizhnii Novgorod [This is a paraphrase of a well-known passage from A. S. Griboedov's (1795–1829) play "Woe from Wit" that ridiculed high society's Westernized manners and language, which still had a large dose of Russianness à la Nizhnii Novgorod.], but this touch of "Russianness" does not prevent Orekhovo from being an exemplary industrial center. Here we have a workers' milieu—the soil for the growth of Socialist cadres.

Zueyvo is a Russian village: dirt, three cinemas, and a church. The population is well-off. The majority are home-owners who also have a plot of land. Their inclinations are petit bourgeois, and their behavior is "kulak-like" [kulak, literally, a fist, refers to a rich peasant in Russia]. In the old days the pubs were flourishing; then the taverns came selling drinks, also to take out; now it is the day of tea parlors. They serve homemade vodka. The Zueyvites' political attitudes are reactionary to the extreme. [From the Socialists' point of view, reactionary attitudes in 1918 could have meant anti-Semitism, promonarchist feelings, hostility to socialism, devout religiosity, or staunch defense of private property.]

---

This report first appeared under the title, "V rabochem kotle," in *Zaria Rossii* (Dawn of Russia) (24 May 1918, Petrograd), Hoover Institution Library.

The Orekhovites' earnings are enormous. Their pay has increased by 700 percent, on the average. The maximum increase has been 1000 percent, and the minimum, 400 percent. Simultaneously with the pay increase, though, productivity has decreased sharply, as was noted by the engineers at the Sava Morozov, Vikula Morozov, Zimin, and other factories. [The foregoing are textile mills employing thousands of workers. The Morozovs were well-known textile magnates in imperial Russia.] At the Sava Morozov factory, for example, labor productivity has decreased by 40–45 percent; at Vikula Morozov, by up to 50 percent. There are several reasons for such a sad state of affairs. The first of them is indolence and a negligent attitude to work, the second is a realization that one can get away with impunity for bad work, and, finally, the third reason is the shortening of the workday and the emergence of "bagman trade." [With the mounting difficulties over food supply in the spring of 1918, private traders, most of them former soldiers, appeared in increasing numbers on Russian railroads and rail stations. They usually carried just a bag of grain for sale, hence the name.] An engineer from Sava Morozov's factory said,

> Laziness is the main evil of factory life. They come to work twenty, thirty minutes late and leave half an hour early. One has to leave his office half an hour early or else run the risk of being locked in an empty building. It is impossible to demand anything from the workers; they would accuse you of captiousness. The workday has been cut to eight hours, as is well known. But in fact, it has been shortened to six and a half or seven hours.

Even the factory committee members complain about sloppy work: "Nobody wants to admit that bad work hurts production. They still think they harm somebody else." I heard from some workers, "What is it to us? Get rid of it, and that's all. It's all the same anyway, you've got no profit even if you work like five [workers]!"

"Yes, but now you work for yourselves. It is workers' power, is it not?" [These words were often used by the Bolsheviks. The official party line was that, after the October Revolution, the working class came to power and the workers worked for themselves because they lived in a workers' state.] "Hey man, try harder! We can't manage without the owner. It's a lot of trouble to run a business. We are workers, why should we push on to become owners?" "Our business is work." "Without the owner we can't make it." One hears such conversations all the time.

Before the October coup, there was never even any talk about transfer of factories to the workers. After the October "revolution," many began to talk about the socialization of factories, but shortly thereafter they had to

concede that "socialization had to wait." At the present time, no one raises
the question of socialization anymore.

[One unidentified worker said the following:]

> Enough making fools out of us! We've had it! We've got too many of all
> kinds of riffraff sitting on our backs already! The Bolsheviks shout,
> "Down with the owner!" But they have climbed on our backs instead of
> him! In the old days we did not know how the owners took advantage of
> us, but now we see how the new bosses rip us off.

A worker from the Vikula Morozov's factory said,

> It's turned out to be pretty bad. We have so many masters now that the
> devil himself would not be able to count them all. The Bolsheviks used to
> shout that the expenses for administration were too high, and now the
> expenses for all those damned committees have increased fivefold! So
> many masters you can't feed them all. They are singing sweet songs like
> angels but are sitting on our backs like devils!

During the first month of Socialist construction, the factory administration was looked on skeptically as the "servants of capital," but then the
workers noticed that they "could not manage without them." And now they
are saying straightforwardly, "You've got to give it in the neck to all these
committees! No good will come out of them!" As in the old days, the workers
now come with their problems and needs to the old factory administration.

"No, you'd better ask the committee," the engineers say. "What good
will it do me to go there, can't you help, somehow?"

"I can't. This is within the competence of the committee."

"Damn it, this committee invented all kinds of committees!"

In broad circles of Russian society and particularly among the Moscov-
ites, the conviction is widespread that the industrial centers are the strong-
holds of Soviet power. It used to be that they also thought so about
Orekhovo-Zueyvo. As evidence, they referred to the fact that the soviet
had a Bolshevik majority there. But . . . this was so long ago! The Bolsheviks have completely lost ground here. For awhile workers were putting up
with the Bolshevik soviet out of inertia: "It is there? OK! Let it be so."
Now the mood in the broad working masses is anti-Bolshevik. This was
revealed particularly clearly during the new elections to the soviet that
lasted for almost three months. Having observed the fruitlessness of the
soviet's work, the workers boycotted elections in February, and they had to
be postponed until March. But in March, the workers did not show up for
the ballot. (The workers' passive attitude to elections can be seen in the

following example: At one of the sections of the Sava Morozov factory, out of 2,000 workers, only 250 showed up to vote. To the Bolsheviks' dismay, even those 250 voted for non-Bolsheviks.) After long and laborious efforts, the elections finally took place. The results were pitiful for the ruling party. The majority of those elected were SRs [Socialist Revolutionaries], Mensheviks, or those without party affiliation. The Bolsheviks did not want to recognize their defeat, but it became obvious that new elections might produce even worse results; the matter was somehow settled.

In Orekhovo-Zueyvo only periodical literature loyal to Soviet power and the newspaper *Rannee Utro* [Early Morning] are available. Such newspapers as *Zaria Rossii* [The Dawn of Russia], *Svoboda Rossii* [Freedom of Russia], and *Nashe Slovo* [Our Word] [Menshevik and SR newspapers] are not sold here. What is worse, however, is that even subscribers often do not receive these journals by mail. Any "disloyal" newspapers that by some chance manage to get through cost ten kopeks more than *Rannee Utro*. Books have disappeared from the workers' lives, and they are sick of brochures. Reading Sherlock Holmes, Andrei Krechet, and what is generally called "Pinkerton-type stuff" is flourishing. There is also some demand for classical novels, but these are not available.

The theater, which used to be in such perfect order, now has been "democratized." It has become dirtier. On one side of the stage, for unknown reasons, hangs a portrait of Karl Marx. Apparently, the Orekhovo Democrats found it necessary to familiarize the German economist with Russian theatrical arts. Let him look at it, perhaps he'd like it. The theater is always full. Tickets are expensive. On the days when "celebrities" come, the first rows cost up to 25 rubles. By the way, nowadays it is no longer the bourgeoisie but the proletariat and its representatives who are "trudging to the first row." It is amazing how quickly the masses took from the bourgeoisie all its ostentatiousness, all that is negative: dressing beyond their means, garish stylishness, and squandering money. As a result, despite huge earnings, savings "for a rainy day" are insignificant and few.

Many speculate [sell on the black market] with cloth instead of wages from their factories. [Paper money, given the skyrocketing inflation, was worthless; moreover, the Bolshevik authorities were often not able to deliver paper money to the provincial cities. Thus workers were often paid with the products they manufactured.] The majority of speculators are women. Moral decay has reached unprecedented proportions. Marriages for a month or three are an everyday occurrence. Faithful couples are jeered at. To cheat, to dupe somebody, is considered up to the mark. Vulgarity, crassness, and rudeness are considered to be the top of the democratic heap. The girls try to "get a guy" as soon as possible. For the lack of local "fiancés," they "marry" prisoners of war en masse. The general mood is "loot the looted." [This Bolshevik slogan from the end of 1917, early 1918, tries to convey that the goods in possession of the bourgeoisie had been stolen from the people through exploitation. Now the time had come to settle old accounts and loot the looted.] No thought about the future: "Après *nous* le déluge." The close observation of workers' lives leaves a bitter aftertaste. People are at a dead end, and they do not see any way out.

One thing is encouraging though. During the last two months a certain sobering up has been noticeable, a change of attitude from destructiveness to [the end is missing].

A. Orlov

DOCUMENT EIGHT

## The Yaroslavl Proletariat in the Dock

April 1918

The Assembly of Workers' Representatives [*upolnomochennye*] from 22 factories and plants [These assemblies emerged in January 1918 in many Russian cities as organizations of workers free from government control. At first they were primarily concerned with the drastic deterioration of workers' economic situation, but by April 1918, they had become centers of the workers' protest movements against the Bolshevik dictatorship. These assemblies were banned and their national leaders arrested in July 1918.], railway workshops, and trade unions has entrusted me to tell the workers of Russia, on the pages of *Vpered* and by all other means, how on April 18 the Bolshevik authorities put on trial the Social Democrats, the Soviet of Workers' Deputies (which had been disbanded with the use of bayonets), and, with them, the overwhelming majority of the Yaroslavl

---

During the first six months of their rule, the Bolsheviks often resorted to trials of their political opponents. This document shows the attitudes of Bolsheviks and Mensheviks during a unique period in Soviet history, when opposition parties were still running in elections and, as in this case, winning them. First published in *Vpered* (24 April 1918, Moscow), p. 2. See also document 15.

proletariat, which had elected the Social Democrats to the soviet. This truly unprecedented affair officially charged the citizens Shleifer, Loktov Bogdanov, and Rostov with "counterrevolutionary agitation."

During February and March, enchantment with "communism" was rapidly fading in the minds of the Yaroslavl workers, and as time went on, ever larger masses of workers were going over to the side of the Social Democrats. The Bolshevik authorities relentlessly fought against the SDs. Their leader, Shleifer, was arrested three times. On March 22, an announcement appeared, signed by the Red Guard commander Rubtsov and the Fifth Detachment commissar Smirnov, to the effect that persons disseminating counterrevolutionary Menshevik and SR literature would be shot on the spot.

The workers set up the Central Bureau for New Elections to the Soviet. By April 9, three-fourths of the soviet delegates had been elected. Only the Kopen mill was silent because it was surrounded by vigilant Red Guard sentries. Although this mill sent delegates to the soviet, they were not elected at a general meeting, but delegated by its factory committee. [ This implies that the factory committee of that mill sent representatives to the city soviet in violation of electoral rules. These representatives were not elected on the factory floor, but handpicked by the factory committee itself.] On April 9, the new soviet assembled. The credentials commission (50 percent Bolshevik) approved of the mandates of 98 percent of the deputies. By party affiliation there were 47 SDs, 13 SRs, and 38 Bolsheviks. When the election of the new chairman took place, the vote count produced these impossible results: for a Menshevik, Shleifer, 60 votes, and for a Bolshevik candidate, 63! That would mean there must have been 123 voters, whereas the soviet consisted of only 98! As it turned out, the members of the provincial EC did the Bolsheviks a favor by casting votes for them. Some Bolshevik sympathizers in the audience took part in the voting as well. The cheats were driven out, but they did not seem discouraged. They took care of everything. The voting took place at midnight, but at 10 A.M. a note was delivered to the local *Izvestiia* saying that "the session of the Soviet did not take place!"

The chairman of the Military Revolutionary Committee [MRC], Voronin, announced that the soviet was dissolved and that comrades Shleifer, Bogdanov, Loktov, and Rostov were under arrest. The workers' deputies announced that they would not submit to coercion and that this was an infringement on the rights of the workers' soviet. The "Red" democrats burst in and began a despicable assault on the soviet. One by one, members of the soviet were grabbed, pulled away from the common circle, and thrown down the stairs. Petrov, a member of the Cheka, was among the first of the attackers. The circle of comrades holding each other arm in arm was finally broken. Several comrades were beaten up, among them Prigozhina, a woman printer, who fell down unconscious after the beating. Shleifer, Loktov, and Rostov were taken away to Korovniki (a hard labor prison), but Bogdanov, unnoticed, walked away.

In response to this banditlike assault on the soviet, the indignant Yaroslavl proletariat went on strike, accompanied by an outburst of protests. The strike started from below; with little coordination it spread to factories and plants, trade establishments, streetcars, printing shops, and the entire railway system. The railway workers in Rybinsk also went on strike. Vologda [workers] sent a telegram asking if they should join in the strike as well. Even some "loyal subjects" [ironic reference to the Left SRs who were still coalition partners of the Bolsheviks] became indignant. The Left SR paper *Novyi Put'* [New Path], no. 32, published the following letter to the editor entitled "Is It Not Time?"

> At present comrades, we face a struggle with authorities who dictate their will and trample on our rights of freedom of speech and inviolability of the deputy. For what comrades, have we fought for decades with the autocracy? And for what have we sacrificed the lives of many of our best comrades? It was definitely not to have dictators after we had won our freedom, dictators who decide our fate (without any right to do so) and the fate of the comrades we elected. Comrades! Don't you see to what extent your lawful rights—freedom of speech, freedom of assembly, freedom of the press, and freedom to strike—have been violated, in order to hide from you those shady deals that are going on behind the closed doors of our rulers? [The Bolsheviks feared that if they passed the files of the soviet over to the newly elected EC, certain facts would emerge that the Bolsheviks preferred to keep from public scrutiny.] Horrors perpetrated by criminal hands defile the ideas of the true fighters for liberty. [This is an explicit reference to some wrongdoing by the Bolshevik authorities.] It is time, comrades, to raise your voice in a powerful protest against those who lead us to ruin. In struggle we have won freedom, in struggle we shall strengthen it.

Under the impact of rising worker protest, the haughty authorities were forced to grant concessions. The railway workers' strike committee was set free. Comrade Rostov, who had gone on a hunger strike in prison, was released and exiled from Yaroslavl province. The new elections to the soviet were scheduled for 20–30 April. The hearing for Shleifer, Bogdanov, and Loktov was set for April 18.

In a few words, this is the background to "the case of counterrevolutionary agitation." On April 17, Comrade Naletov and I arrived in

Yaroslavl at the instruction of the regional party bureau [SD] to organize the defense of our Yaroslavl comrades. We went to the MRC and demanded access to the investigation files. The secretary said that Granovskii, the commissar of justice, had taken them. We went to the commissar. He emphatically assured us that he did not have the files and could not possibly have them because he, the commissar, was a witness in that case. We returned to the tribunal. The secretary showed us a receipt to the effect that the case files had been taken by Commissar Granovskii. As a result, we, the defense attorneys, could not familiarize ourselves with the case files before the trial.

On the evening of April 17, we were invited to attend a meeting of the Assembly of Workers' Representatives. The workers told us that by putting their comrades—Shleifer and others—in the dock, the authorities had in effect put on trial the Social Democratic party, the Yaroslavl soviet, and the entire Yaroslavl proletariat. In view of this, the Assembly of Workers' Representatives gave us the following warrant: "The assembly authorizes comrades Rybal'skii, Naletov, Meshkovskii, and workers' representatives Sokolov, Nizov, and Blokhin to act as defense attorneys for comrades Shleifer, Loktov, Rostov, and Bogdanov and by defending them, defend the honor of the Yaroslavl proletariat."

On April 18, at 9 A.M. workers began filling the local court. Only representatives of organizations and special delegates from factories and plants were admitted. There were so many delegates that no seats were left for those who came late, and they had to sit down on the floor. A great number of these delegates delivered their authorization for us to defend the accused on their behalf. Those not admitted to the courtroom filled up the corridors and thronged the street at the entrance to the court. The "defendants" were led in. The workers came up to them and greeted them on behalf of their workshops. The guards, embarrassed, moved away to the doors. In the office, defense attorneys were hurriedly studying the case. What they discovered would have made even Shcheglovitov's [I. G. Shcheglovitov (1861–1918) was the minister of justice from 1906 to 1915 in several imperial governments. In revolutionary circles, Shcheglovitov's name was associated with the trial of the SD faction in the Second State Duma.] hair stand on end.

There was no indictment of any kind to show who had initiated the legal proceedings and what exactly the charges against the defendants were. The "case" file started with the testimony of the witnesses—the Bolsheviks—and their testimony was recorded by . . . [Nothing is missing here. The author used ellipses to show his astonishment.] office clerks. None of the defendants was interrogated, none of the defendants was shown materials from the preliminary investigation, and none was asked what he could furnish in his own defense. Neither the conclusions of the investigative commission nor the indictment was in the "case" file. The entire file consisted only of Bolshevik "testimony," although it was not clear to whom it was given or on whose instruction. The name of Bogdanov, a member of the SD city committee and a member of the soviet, could be found only on the cover. None of the witnesses even mentioned his name. Nevertheless, he was also in the dock. About Comrade Rostov, a member of the SD regional committee, it was said that he spoke unfavorably about the "people's commissars" at a railway workers' rally, saying that they did nothing good for the workers. Also at that rally, Comrade Loktov, an SR, and Comrade Shleifer spoke approvingly about the Constituent Assembly and disapprovingly about "Soviet power" and urged the workers to come out with arms against the existing state order. After that rally, the railway workers "staged an armed uprising, having seized a rail car with weapons." Furthermore, on April 9, the day of the soviet's first session, Comrade Shleifer came to the 181st regiment, and in the course of his conversation with the deputy chairman of the regiment's committee,

> he was urging the soldiers to come out, if not against the entire soviet,
> then at least against some of its representatives, who, by their dedication
> to the cause of socialism and by their tireless and fruitful work for the
> benefit of the soviet, caused particular indignation and hostility of the
> anti-Soviet parties of the Mensheviks and Right SRs. [The Mensheviks
> and the SRs were often referred to as anti-Soviet parties in Communist
> literature. This is somewhat misleading; these parties maintained that
> state power had to belong to institutions elected on the basis of universal
> suffrage, above all to the Constituent Assembly. In this sense, the Menshe-
> viks and SRs were against the October transfer of power to the soviets.
> They were, however, represented in the soviets and winning majorities in
> elections to the soviets in the spring of 1918. Remaining soviet parties,
> they favored another constitutional order. The Bolsheviks identified their
> cause with Soviet power, but in fact disbanded the soviets, as in this case,
> when they lost elections to the opposition. In that sense, the Bolsheviks
> were an anti-Soviet party.]

Sometime after 10 A.M. the trial began. In violation of the decree stipulating that the judges of the military revolutionary tribunals had to be elected by the soviets, at the judges' desk we saw all the leaders of the Yaroslavl commune [In the spring of 1918, Bolshevik leaders in many Russian cities used the word *commune* to refer to their city government, in imitation of the Paris Commune.], who must have elected themselves. Not only was the chairman not elected by the soviet, he was not even a Communist from Yaroslavl. He had just arrived from Rybinsk together with the prosecutor, Nakhimson. [S. M. Nakhimson, an old Bolshevik, in 1917 was a member of the Petrograd Bolshevik party committee. In October 1917, Nakhimson was a member of the Military Revolutionary Committee of the 12th army and a member of the Central Executive Committee. In early 1918, he was appointed military commissar in Yaroslavl, and from 2 July 1918, chairman of the provincial EC. He was killed during the Yaroslavl uprising in July.] Several workers rose from their seats with warrants in their hands and declared that they had been authorized by their constituency to exercise the right to a binding vote in the court. [In their propaganda, the Bolsheviks repeated again and again that political power belonged to the working class. Workers often took these assertions seriously; in this case they apparently expected that their duly elected representatives would have a say in the decision of the court.] They were told that they would not have a binding vote. The workers who thought that they were going to get a binding vote grumbled, "And who gave you the right to judge? We have been sent here by workers and whom do you represent?" To safeguard "order" the Red Guard detachment was brought in. The judges began to examine the composition of the defense. And again, from all sides of the auditorium, workers asked for the floor and showed their defense warrants. The frightened prosecutor demanded that the number of defense attorneys be limited: this was not a political, but a criminal case(!) Furthermore, he proposed that the case of Comrade Rostov be treated separately because he was not present at the trial (he had been exiled from the Yaroslavl province). He also suggested that "the accused, Bogdanov, who had escaped arrest, be confined and isolated from communicating with the witnesses."

Sokolov, a worker who acted as a defense attorney for Comrade Rostov, demanded that Rostov's case be heard in his absence. I, as Bogdanov's defense attorney, explained that Bogdanov was not hiding from anyone and that there was no legally executed warrant issued for his arrest. As far as his isolation from the witnesses was concerned, it should be truly embarrassing for the Bolsheviks to talk about that in view of the fact that the commissar of justice and others—Bolshevik witnesses— entered the judges' room in open view before the proceedings began. The judge left the auditorium for consultations and on returning announced that Rostov's case would be considered separately and that not more than two persons could act as defense attorneys for each defendant. Nothing was said about confinement of Bogdanov. The chairman suggested that the secretary read the indictment. The defense was astonished—there had been no indictment in the case file. Where did it appear from? During the break we learned that the indictment . . . [ellipses in the text] had been brought from Rybinsk. Moreover, we discovered that it was not signed by anyone. The indictment narrated that the wily Menshevik CC [Central Committee] had come out with a slogan—Seize Power in Provincial Soviets! [There was no such slogan. The Menshevik CC decided to urge local organizations to end their walkouts and boycotts of the soviets and to compete instead with the Bolsheviks at the polls.] —that the SR CC was doing the same, and that the local organizations of these parties displayed considerable energy in this direction. Not a single name was mentioned in the indictment. It was only said that "they (the Mensheviks and SRs) had agitated for an armed uprising and that they were helping the counterrevolution." Here is one interesting detail. At the end of the indictment it was said in reference to the strike:

> The local bourgeoisie, the counterrevolutionary groups of merchants and landlords, as well as degraded officers, students, and other White Guard activists wholeheartedly welcomed and supported Menshevik and SR appeals. This was clearly seen during the first day of the railway workers' strike when the merchants closed down their shops hoping to create panic and bloody clashes. [During numerous strikes in the spring of 1918, the Bolsheviks resorted to violence, as attested by many of the documents in this volume.]

This is how the talented author of the indictment turned the workers' strike into "bloodthirsty merchants closing the shops." The chairman asked the defendants if they pleaded guilty to "counterrevolutionary agitation." One after another, the accused rose from their seats and declared that they were not counterrevolutionaries but Socialists duly elected to the soviet by the Yaroslavl proletariat and that it was not they who should be accused, but the Bolsheviks who were guilty of disbanding the soviet and of unprecedented violence to the achievements of the revolution. The defense demanded that a number of worker witnesses be summoned, and the tribunal admitted the testimony of these witnesses. The cross-examination lasted until 2 A.M. after a three-hour supper break. After the cross-examination, the deliberations began and lasted until the following morning. The request of the defense to postpone the deliberations until morning was rejected on the grounds that the prosecutor had to leave in the morning to attend to some party [Bolshevik] business. All workers sent by their enterprises to attend the trial remained in the auditorium until the end of the proceedings. Hungry and exhausted, they nevertheless listened to all the speeches with unabated interest and recorded all the testimony. The judges were not as assiduous. One of them left for the session of the EC, which astonished the defense: How could a judge pronounce a verdict, provided it had not been prepared in advance, if he had not listened to all the deliberations?

Long deliberations lasting many hours thwarted the prosecutor's clumsy attempts to find evidence pointing to the "counterrevolution" of the defendants. On the other hand, the hearing produced quantities of material for charging the Bolsheviks with insurrection (and an armed one at that) against the soviet. The workers unanimously testified that Comrade Shleifer and others fought the Bolsheviks by means of ideas not arms and that they always restrained the workers, who were sometimes ready for hot actions against those in power. For example, it was ascertained, even from the Bolshevik testimony, that Comrade Shleifer had gone to the regiment not to prepare an armed uprising but to invite the regiment's delegate to the session of the soviet and to find out whether the regiment was going to disband the newly elected soviet, as had been rumored. (There were only fifty people left in the regiment.) When the facts were checked, it turned out that the armed uprising of the railway workers amounted to workers' attempts to organize the defense of their neighborhoods against bandits, who had committed a number of robberies at the time, under the guise of requisitions. [In the months after October 1917, the Bolshevik authorities imposed so-called indemnities—requisitions of money, houses, furniture, and so forth—on the defeated bourgeoisie. The bandits mentioned here must have tried to pass for Bolshevik requisition detachments.] All the charges fell apart except the most important one: that the defendants were the leaders of the soviet and that the soviet was not controlled by the Bolsheviks.

I shall not cite speeches here. Of the prosecutors, only Nakhimson spoke. The other, a soldier, waved his hand and walked out. It was announced that he "felt ill." The workers were saying later that he really felt sick because of Bolshevik justice. Nakhimson's speech, which lasted two and a half hours, referred to the Riabushinskii [P. P. Riabushinskii, head of one of the largest industrial and banking houses in prerevolutionary Russia] house and to all sorts of other things, but not to anything that could be considered proof of the defendants' guilt in this case. The railway workers, present at the trial, learned from the prosecutor that the railway proletariat was the most "backward segment in the workers' movement" and that counterrevolution had always nested in its ranks. In the end, the prosecutor said that indeed there were not so many facts providing Bogdanov's and Loktov's guilt, but that a verdict expressing serious public reprimand "had to be passed against such a dangerous agitator as Shleifer for causing the strike." Both the defense and the accused went on the offensive at this point. A worker, Nisov, tried to read a workers' resolution, which was a much better indictment against Bolshevik authorities, but he was stopped.

All of us ended our speeches to loud applause from the whole audience, and the chairman, completely lost, threatened that he would order the auditorium cleared because of "noise." At 9 A.M. the tribunal withdrew for consultations and one hour later made public the following resolution: "In the name of the people, the Military Revolutionary Tribunal has resolved to acquit citizen Bogdanov and Loktov and to exile Citizen Shleifer, within twenty-four hours, from the Yaroslavl province for one year."

Having read the verdict, the judge hurriedly withdrew to the judges' room. Workers surrounded Comrade Shleifer and, coming into the streets with him, said [to the judges]: "You have passed a verdict today not just against Comrade Shleifer, but against all of us. At the new elections to the soviet on April 20–30, we will pass a verdict against you, the bosses!" [At these new elections, the Menshevik-SR bloc won by an even larger margin over the Bolsheviks. This newly elected soviet was disbanded as well. For election returns of the second elections, see, "Yaroslavl," *Vpered*, no. 80 (10 May 1918, Moscow).] This was the beginning of the election campaign in the good old city of Yaroslavl.

I. RYBAL'SKII

---

DOCUMENT NINE

---

## Disbanding the Tambov Soviet

April 1918

New elections to the city soviet ended in Tambov in the beginning of April. The Social Democrats and Socialist Revolutionaries won the majority of seats, not the Bolsheviks, who had held them before the elections. The Bolsheviks won only one-third of the seats in the soviet. The situation was unambiguous. Power in the city was slipping out of the Bolsheviks' hands. But it was not easy for the Bolsheviks to part with power, and they were ready to do anything to keep it despite the will of the Tambov work-

This report, "Razgon Tambovskogo Soveta," first appeared in the Social Democratic paper *Novaia Zhizn'*, no. 87 (1 May 1918), p. 4. Hoover Institution Library.

ers. At the session of the newly elected soviet, the Bolsheviks declared an ultimatum: either they be assigned seven out of twelve seats on the Executive Committee or they would consider themselves "free to act." This ultimatum was turned down, and the Bolsheviks left the session, which continued anyway. A new EC was elected, and a plan was drawn up for the soviet's work in the immediate future.

It is necessary to point out here that the new EC was elected on the basis of proportional representation, according to soviet regulations. Seats on the EC were left vacant for the Bolshevik representatives if they wished to take part in the work of the soviet. The Bolsheviks, of course, did not. Instead they immediately set out to implement their "freedom of action." First of all, the Bolsheviks who had been members of the old soviet [before the elections], organized a joint session with the EC of the Tambov province. At this session they found the excuse they needed to disband the newly elected city soviet. Ostensibly, the old soviet members had not been informed about campaign meetings during the elections. Therefore, the provincial EC resolved to consider that the elections had been held improperly, that their results should be annulled, and that new elections should be scheduled. For the time being, the pre-election city EC was to exercise "all authority accorded to the soviet." By the way, right there and then, the pre-election city EC and the provincial EC were merged into one, even though they had previously been hostile to one another. An official notification on these decisions, marked "to implement," was sent by the provincial and the city EC to the newly elected city EC of the Tambov soviet.

The next session of the newly elected soviet was scheduled for April 5. But when the members arrived for the session, all entrances to the city duma building, where the session was to take place, were blocked by armed militiamen and Red Guards. They would not let anyone enter the building. The members of the soviet were searched and their deputy cards taken away and destroyed. Some members of the soviet managed, however, to enter the building and open the session. Then, on Bolshevik orders, armed men began to pull members of the soviet out of the assembly hall by force. They threatened them with weapons and turned off the electricity. The members of the soviet had no choice but to comply. In the meantime, the provincial and the pre-election city EC announced that power over Tambov had been transferred from the soviet to the Bolsheviks and the Left SRs.

Those who assumed dictatorial power wanted to make sure that the legitimately elected soviet, which they had disbanded, would not assemble again. The next session of the disbanded soviet was scheduled for April 11 in the Naryshkinskaia reading room. When the members of the soviet came for the session, they saw the doors of the reading room locked and a poster on the wall signed by Commissar Gusev informing them that no meeting of any kind would be allowed there. The members of the soviet, however, remained at the entrance to the reading room, waiting for others to come. Then a Bolshevik commissar, Silin, called up the armed Red Guard unit by phone. Four of them arrived quickly.

The members of the soviet, headed by the Executive Committee, had to abandon the reading room; they then went to the Zemstvo board building, where the session of the soviet finally took place. Several commissions were elected: on economic matters, on cultural work, and an auditing commission to examine the files of the old EC. It was resolved that sessions would continue to be held. The Tambov city duma was disbanded almost simultaneously with the disbandment of the city soviet. The members of the city board [of the duma] who had followed the duma resolution and refused to hand over business to the new masters of the city were arrested. For several days, they were kept under arrest and then released. The city duma protested against Bolshevik coercion and resolved not to recognize that it had been liquidated.

---

DOCUMENT TEN

---

## Kovrov: Vladimir Province

March 1918

As is well known, Kovrov was the scene of outrageous and bloody events around March 20. A large rally of railway workers on March 12 demanded that new elections to the soviet take place immediately. After the rally, three comrades were arrested. Alarmed workers demanded that they be released immediately, but the authorities refused and declared that "any worker protest would be mercilessly suppressed by armed force." Then the workers decided to stage a peaceful procession. The general meeting of railway workers in Kovrov adopted a resolution: "An Appeal to Workers!"

This report first appeared in the journal of the Menshevik Central Committee, *Novaia Zaria* (New Dawn), no. 1 (22 April 1918, Moscow), pp. 41–42.

Freedom of the press, freedom of speech, freedom of assembly, and inviolability of person—none of these exists anymore. . . . Workers cannot merely observe how, in their own name, those who in fact do not express the will of the working people are preparing the ruin of the revolution. The present soviet acts against the interests of the working class, and it must be replaced by the true representatives of the working people. Comrades! Begin new elections of your deputies to the soviet immediately.

The Red Guards opened fire on the peaceful demonstration. Martial law was imposed and arrests began. At the demonstration, the workers were marching in tight lines and singing revolutionary songs amid the uninterrupted crackle of rifle and machine-gun fire from the Red Guards, who, retreating, at first were shooting over the heads of the demonstrators. The workers were carrying banners with the inscription, "We demand freedom for the arrested revolutionaries," which was the same banner the Bolsheviks marched with in July. [In July 1917, the Bolsheviks, then a party in opposition to the provisional government, staged a rally in Petrograd that was seen as an attempt to seize power. Several Bolsheviks were arrested. The demonstration demanding their release must have taken place in Kovrov.]

The secretary of our party organization [Menshevik] in Kovrov described the moment when the shooting began:

One could hear the workers' powerful singing: "Rise! Get up working people!" At the corner of Mostovaia and Moscow streets, the Red Guards ranged side by side in close order and began to shout: "Disperse! We will shoot!" A tall Red Guard led them. (They say he was a Bolshevik, the chairman of the factory committee from the Treumov factory.) [I. A. Treumov's factory was the biggest in Kovrov, producing paper and other related products.] He was waving his gun in front of the demonstrators. The crowd broke up in panic and flung out in different directions, particularly women and children. . . . The shots resounded. To save their lives, some grasped at the Red Guards' bayonets trying to take away their rifles. NOT A SINGLE SHOT [all caps in the original] came from the side of the demonstrators. Then a terrible thing happened. The tall Red Guard shot point-blank at the heads of two comrades and killed them and slightly wounded a third. For a moment a deathlike silence set in. The bodies of the dead comrades were carried to the Zemstvo hospital. One could hear shouts: "Let the earth be light for you, comrades!" and "Curse on you, murderers!" The demonstrators began to sing: "You have fallen in the fateful struggle . . ." and went to the workshops. Donations were collected for the funerals of the slain.

As it turned out those killed were Rybkin, a worker from the railway workshops, and I. I. Sten'kov, an electrician from the Treumov factory. The general meeting at the workshops decided to summon someone from the EC to give them an explanation. The EC responded that it considered the meeting illegal, that no EC member would give any explanation, that an order had been issued to encircle the place of the rally, and that the Red Guard units had been called up from Vladimir. More than five thousand people took part in this rally. These were the events of the first day.

At night, a wave of arrests began. Several members of the Menshevik organization were arrested. In its resolution of March 20, the Kovrov Menshevik party committee declared,

> All actions of the EC are truly counterrevolutionary. The usurpers of power proclaimed themselves a "workers' and peasants' government," but in fact act contrary to the will of the majority, contrary to the will of the people. By means of Red Terror [note that this term was used as early as March 1918], martial law, and other extraordinary measures from the times of Nicholas Romanov, they arrest revolutionary leaders and do not even balk at shooting workers and peasants. . . . We demand (1) immediate release of arrested Socialists, (2) immediate new elections to the soviet, (3) restoration of the democratic local self-government, (4) immediate reconvocation of the all-Russian Constituent Assembly.

The latest reports received by the regional party bureau include new arrests on the night of March 20. The Menshevik party committee in Kovrov was decimated by these arrests. Up to forty comrades were taken away. On the morning of March 21, a detachment of Red Guards was stationed at the machine gun factory. All over town, a declaration of martial law was posted. A truck from Vladimir with a machinegun and a detachment of armed Red Guards was patrolling the streets. At night they broke into the apartment of technician N. Maslennikov and raised havoc. At the end of the workday, the workers had to pass through the lines of Red Guards. Some were arrested. Throughout the night, shooting went on in town. At the workshops confusion reigned. "A threat that one could be shot paralyzes the intensiveness of activity"; with these words one of the survivors ended his report.

## DOCUMENT ELEVEN

## Around Russia: Roslavl Nightmares

May 1918, Smolensk province

Two weeks ago a piece of news—that the local population in Roslavl had disbanded the soviet and that a punitive expedition had pacified the town—went unnoticed in the press. Questioning the local inhabitants, I have found out the following: The local soviet was elected before demobilization [sometime at the end of 1917]. Because there were not many workers in town, soldiers played a key role in the soviet. About a month ago, however, the soviet decided that its term was over and scheduled new elections. [Usually the term of a soviet was six months, which would suggest that the previous elections took place in mid-October 1917.] These elections gave the majority to the opposition ("Mensheviks," as they say here). The soviet announced that the opponents of "Soviet power" [The Bolsheviks referred to the Mensheviks and the Social Revolutionaries as anti-Soviet parties (see document 8).] would not be admitted into its ranks. The Red Army was on the side of the soviet, and its composition remained unchanged.

Railway workers are a particularly active social group here. They were represented by the Bolsheviks in the old soviet, but now they have elected the Mensheviks. That their representatives were not admitted into the soviet increased their irritation with the authorities and the Red Army soldiers. Around April 20, they made an attempt at an uprising. The local population supported them. The brave Red Guards immediately surrendered and gave up their weapons: several machine-guns and seven hundred rifles. During the uprising only one man was killed—a worker from the railway shops. The next day reinforcements arrived to aid the soviet, and the railway workers surrendered. The conditions of surrender were full amnesty to all participants in the uprising, recognition of the new composition of the soviet, and the elimination of privileges for the Red Guards in the distribution of food.

At night, when the railway workers were on their way home, the Soviet detachments treacherously assaulted them, seized their arms, and made numerous arrests. When the railway workers sent a deputation that de-

---

Roslavl is a small town in Smolensk province. This report appeared in *Novaia Zhizn'*, no. 90 (15 May 1918, Petrograd), p. 4.

manded that the "conditions of the peace agreement" be observed, they were told that they should not worry. Certain inquiries would be made and then everyone would be released. Indeed the majority of those arrested were released. Before the holiday [Easter], the railway workers sent another deputation. They were told that those arrested had been sent to Moscow. On Monday, May 6, it turned out that this "Moscow" was in fact in heaven. During that day, four corpses were found buried in the sand on the riverbank and a fifth was caught in the river by fishermen. The corpses were delivered to the Zemstvo hospital. The medical examination showed that the victims had been tortured before death. In addition to shotgun wounds, there were also many bayonet wounds. Some victims had had their eyes put out. Yesterday it was rumored that several new corpses had been found. Now they have stationed a Red Guard sentry there and prohibited any further digging. Indignation and depression characterize the mood in town. They have cooled off to the idea of elections. As before, the demobilized soldiers from the local soviet are in control of everything.

A. RATNER

---

DOCUMENT TWELVE

---

## Around Russia: The Berezovskii Plant in the Urals

May 1918, Perm province

On May 9, the workers of the Berezovskii plant in Ekaterinburg *uezd* [part of a *guberniia* (province)] assembled for a general meeting. The meeting came to the conclusion that the present soviet and its EC were not

---

Berezovskii *zavod* (Berezov plant), a small mining town in the Urals, is one of the oldest and richest gold mines in European Russia. Situated twenty kilometers from Ekaterinburg (now Sverdlovsk), Berezovskii zavod was one in a chain of mining towns in the area. At the turn of the century, Ekaterinburg and environs had thirty-two steel and iron plants employing more than thirty-two thousand workers. In this industrial area large mines and plants were located in small towns that grew up around these plants. By the turn of the century, Berezovskii zavod employed more than twelve thousand workers. This report first appeared in *Novaia Zhizn'*, no. 105 (1 June 1918, Petrograd), p. 4.

fulfilling their duties and therefore new elections had to take place. It was ascertained at the meeting that some members of the soviet lived in excessive luxury. They appropriated the best houses in town [That the Bolshevik authorities requisitioned the best houses for their personal use was reported from numerous provincial towns. The top Bolsheviks were aware of this, for Grigorii Zinoviev said at the Eighth Party Congress in March 1919, "Here and there in the provinces and sometimes in large centers, the reform of living quarters distribution boiled down to the following: they took houses away from the bourgeoisie but did not give them to workers. Instead they gave them to Soviet functionaries. Sometimes they gave these houses not only to Soviet bureaucrats, but also to their grandmothers, mothers-in-law, and other relatives." (*Vos'moi S'zed RKP(b) Stenograficheskii otchet* [The Eighth Congress of the RKP(b). Minutes] (Moscow, 1959).], provided themselves with luxurious horse-drawn carriages, and spent public funds without giving any account. It was also established that 150,000 rubles, raised by imposing an indemnity on the bourgeoisie, had somehow disappeared without a trace. [See document 8. To impose indemnity on the bourgeoisie meant to extract funds from the propertied classes. According to Gukovskii, a Bolshevik deputy commissar of finance in March 1918, most of these funds never reached the treasury, but were used up by local Bolshevik authorities for their own needs. (*Protokoly VTslk chetvertogo sozyva* [The Protocols of the CEC of the Fourth Convocation] (Moscow: Gosizdat, 1920), p. 130.] Moreover, a commissar from Ekaterinburg escaped from the town with 53,000 rubles. He also somehow got hold of funds from the [Berezovskii] plant. All this alarmed the workers, and they decided to demand that the Soviet send at least several of its members to attend the meeting and clarify the circumstances of the above-mentioned events.

The workers' delegation returned with a response from the Soviet that its members were not going to attend any meeting that they considered illegal, that is, organized without the Soviet's knowledge and approval. Approximately ten minutes after the workers' delegation returned from the soviet, a detachment of Red Guards appeared at the general meeting. A drunken member of the Soviet was their leader. Without any warning they shot several volleys at the crowd. Fifteen completely innocent people lay dead on the spot. Others began to run away. But the salvos thundered one after another. Blood was shed. . . . Lying on the ground the wounded were writhing convulsively in pain. The drunken commander of the Red Guards ordered the capture and arrest of those running away from the bullets. Several people were seized and placed in a cell at the Soviet. In the evening the Soviet issued the following resolution and had it posted all over the plant:

In view of an open rebellion, which had as its aim the overthrow of the existing Soviet power, martial law is declared at the mines of the Berezovskii plant from this day onward. It is permitted to be on the streets from 6 A.M. to 7 P.M. only. Persons agitating against Soviet power, and those detained after 7 P.M. on the streets, will be shot without any mercy. [ This Bolshevik resolution is similar to other resolutions of the time. Bolshevik sources stress that armed rebellions of counterrevolutionaries against Soviet power were taking place, which is also what Soviet official historiography emphasizes. The point, however, is that in the case of the Berezovskii plant and in many similar cases, the so-called anti-Soviet rebellions were not rebellions at all and were not directed against the Soviets but against the Bolshevik dictators ruling in the name of the Soviets. A "rebellion" was in fact a demand to hold new elections, and "counterrevolutionaries" were the workers themselves.]

signed: THE SOVIET

That same evening a reinforced detachment of Red Guards was summoned from Ekaterinburg. In order to be even more intimidating, the Soviet executed three more innocent people who had been detained during the day. At night, indiscriminate searches began. They were looking for arms and for culprits. During the night, they arrested about fifty people. On the way to the Soviet those arrested were beaten with rifle butts. The campaign of terror intensified in the morning. They searched every passerby and shot aimlessly into the streets. Two men and one woman were killed by stray bullets. During the day of May 10, five more people of those arrested at night were executed in front of the Soviet. Among them were two heroes of the present German war [World War I]. On May 11, six people were executed, and on May 12, two. During these four days, the total number of victims who were executed rose to over thirty.

DOCUMENT THIRTEEN

# Brief Reports from the Provinces

June 1918

## *THE SHOOTING IN SORMOVO*

The details of the shooting are as follows: After the general meeting of workers at the Sormovo plant on June 26, a popular SD [Social Democratic] leader, Upovalov [See Upovalov's account of his activities in 1918 in "Kak my poteriali svobodu," *Zaria*, no. 2 (1923, Berlin), reprinted in Mikhail Bernshtam, *Nezavisimoe rabochee dvizhenie v 1918 godu. Dokumenty i materialy* [Independent Workers' Movement in 1918. Documents and Materials] (Paris: YMCA, 1981).], was arrested. On June 27, the workers of the iron casting shop where Upovalov worked found out about his arrest and went on strike in protest. They decided to summon a general meeting of the entire plant. They went to the electrical station to turn on the plant's whistle. On their approach, the Red Guards fired a volley. As a result, two persons were killed and ten wounded. The general meeting of the plant declared a strike until Saturday and delivered its demands to the EC: (1) to set free all political prisoners immediately, (2) to put on trial those guilty of the shooting, (3) to abolish all repressions against those who took part in the strike on June 18. The mood is very agitated.

## *IN SIMBIRSK*

A campaign of dreadful terror has begun in Simbirsk. Many public figures have been forced to go into hiding. Among them are the Social Democrats Cheboksarov and Krasnov. Krasnov's wife was told that her husband was sentenced to death and that she was going to be seized as a hostage [presumably until her husband returned], but she managed to escape.

---

These are newspaper clippings from the Menshevik newspaper *Iskra*, no. 4 (29 June 1918) in the Nicolaevsky Collection, series 279, box 664, folder 9. The material *Iskra* published was so critical of Bolshevik authorities that they shut down the paper after several days. This was the last paper legally published by the Menshevik Central Committee in Soviet Russia in 1918.

## ARRESTS, SEARCHES, AND THE CLOSING DOWN
## OF THE SD PAPER IN KOSTROMA

In connection with the growth of SD influence on local workers, the authorities have started a campaign against the Social Democrats. During June 22–23, members of the local SD committee, Diakonov, Vorob'ev, Borishanskii, and others were arrested. An SD leaflet about the workers' conference was used as a pretext for making the arrests. The Red Guards made a raid on the editorial office of *Nash Put'* [Our Path], the paper of the local SD organization. They confiscated books, personal correspondence, and diaries. The paper was shut down without any reason. An ambush was set up at the editor's apartment. They are waiting for comrade Nifontov's return, but he has left Kostroma. The situation is alarming.

OUR OWN CORRESPONDENT

# From Repression to Civil War
## *(June–October 1918)*

## DOCUMENT FOURTEEN

## Iu. O. Martov to A. N. Stein

16 June 1918

Dear Comrade . . . [ellipses in original]

I am writing to furnish you with as much material as possible about conditions in Russia for your useful work in making this information public. To a certain extent, we are informed of your efforts. I am writing immediately after a small Bolshevik coup d'état. On June 14, the All-Russian CEC, with the votes of the Bolsheviks against those of the Left SRs [Socialist Revolutionaries], decreed to expel the opposition, that is to say us [the Mensheviks] and the Socialist Revolutionaries, from the CEC and suggested that all other soviets do the same. The resolution was passed on the grounds that we were counterrevolutionaries and that we were taking part in the conspiracies and uprisings of the Czechoslovaks and so on.

As far as we are concerned, it is a consciously false accusation on the Bolsheviks' part because the numerous attempts to link our organizations with such actions have been laid bare quickly and clearly. Bolshevik investigators themselves could not succeed in implicating even one Menshevik in the conspiracy trials. (Some SRs were, though.) Lack of evidence for the decree, as far as we are concerned, was made up for by a proposition that our campaigning against Soviet power made possible the rise of the counterrevolution.

With our expulsion from the soviets, the very foundation of the Soviet constitution is destroyed because the soviets have ceased to represent all workers. In those places where we are in the majority, the soviets will be liquidated. This decree summarizes the process that has been going on *everywhere* during the last few months. Everywhere the workers demanded

This is a translation of a copy of this letter in German in the Nicolaevsky Collection, series 17, box 51, folder 4. Another version of this letter was published in Russian in *Sotsialisticheskii Vestnik* no. 7/8 (1926, Berlin), pp. 16–18. The German version is somewhat shorter and omits (1) a negative characterization of Larin in the beginning, (2) Martov's personal requests at the end, and (3) details on the murders of Bolsheviks by the insurgents in small towns. The German-language version is also milder in tone. A. N. Stein was one of the key links between Russian and German Social Democrats. A close associate of Martov, Stein was also a member of the German Independent Social Democratic party and a German citizen. He informed German Social Democrats about the latest developments in Russia and organized their visits to Russia in the summer of 1920.

new elections to those soviets that were elected before the October coup. The Soviets have stubbornly resisted this demand. As a result, struggle over this question often escalated to workers' strikes and the suppression of workers' demonstrations by armed forces (Tula, Yaroslavl, etc.). In some places the workers succeeded in forcing the authorities to hold new elections. Everywhere the returns from these elections either strengthened the opposition or brought a majority to the Mensheviks and SRs once again. In all these cases, by order of the MRCs [military revolutionary councils], the soviets were disbanded by armed force or the opposition delegates were *expelled* as "counterrevolutionaries" from the soviets.

The first method, that is, disbanding the soviet, was used in the following places: Zlatoust [an important industrial town in Ufa province], Yaroslavl [on events in Yaroslavl, see document 8], Sormovo [an industrial suburb near Nizhnii Novgorod where a locomotive plant was situated], Orel [province capital in the black-earth region south of Moscow], Vyatka [province capital in the Urals, where Izhevsk and Votkinsk plants were located; see document 7], Roslavl [see document 11], Tambov [see document 9], Gus-Mal'tsevo (the center of the textile industry in Vladimir province), Bogorodsk (the center of the leather industry in Nizhnii Novgorod province), and other places. During the last few days, this method has also been applied to the *uezd* congresses of peasant soviets. [In early June, the Bolshevik government embarked upon a policy of disbanding peasant soviets and replacing them with the "committees of the poor." See Peter Scheibert, *Lenin an der Macht: Das Russiche Volk in der Revolution, 1918–1922* [Lenin, in Power: The Russian People in the Revolution, 1918–1922] (Weinheim: acta humaniora, 1984), pp. 122–31.] For example, they disbanded the congresses in Rzhev, Novotozhsk (Tver province), Yegoryevsk (Ryazan province), and elsewhere.

The second method, that is, expulsion of the opposition from the soviets, took place in the following soviets: Rostov-na-Donu (before the German occupation), Saratov, Kronstadt, Kaluga, and in many smaller towns. The struggle for new elections has led to unending arrests of workers. Protest strikes against all kinds of violent acts perpetrated by the authorities took place repeatedly in Sormovo, Tula [province capital where two armaments plants were located], Yaroslavl, Lugansk [an important industrial town in Ekaterinoslav (Dnepropetrovsk) province (Donetsk area)], Sestroretsk [a suburb of Petrograd, where a large armaments plant was located], Kostroma [province capital in the Moscow industrial region where, in June, the Menshevik/Socialist Revolutionary bloc won elections to the soviet], Kolomna [Moscow province, central industrial region, with a large locomotive plant. The Mensheviks and Socialist Revolutionaries won elections to the soviet there in June, and the soviet was disbanded.],

Bogorodsk [a textile industry town in Moscow province], Kaluga, Kovrov [see document 10], Rybinsk, Arkhangelsk, Tver, Orekhovo-Zueyvo [a textile industry center in Vladimir province; see document 5], and at some factories in Moscow and Saint Petersburg. At present, a one-day strike has been declared simultaneously for June 18 in Nizhnii Novgorod and Vladimir provinces in protest against the disbanding of a workers' conference that assembled in Sormovo and represented forty thousand workers from those provinces. It is also a protest against the shooting of workers who had staged a rally in support of this conference (one worker was killed and four wounded). [The shooting of workers by Bolsheviks in Sormovo on 10 June 1918 was the subject of Menshevik interpellation in the CEC, just a few days, as it turned out, before they were expelled from this "legislative" institution. See *Protokoly VTsIK chetvertogo sozyva* [The Protocols of the CEC of the Fourth Convocation] (Moscow: Gosizdat, 1920), p. 398. For more information on the shooting in Sormovo on 10 June, see "Sprengung einer Arbeiterkonferenz," *Stimmen Aus Russland,* nos. 4–5 (15 August 1918, Stockholm), p. 18.] A general strike is scheduled for June 17 in Tula to protest the arrest of a number of workers there. [Specifically, the Tula workers protested the arrest of Aleksandrov, the chairman of the Tula Workers' Conference who was arrested on 13 June in Moscow while attending an intercity conference of independent workers' assemblies. The Bolsheviks ruthlessly suppressed the strike in Tula.] Yesterday, one factory (Gustav List's) was on strike in Moscow, and tomorrow there will be more strikes in protest of the arrest of the entire [intercity] workers' conference, where delegates from a number of factories had gathered in order to discuss the political and economic crisis. Saint Petersburg is in commotion because representatives of the Saint Petersburg workers took part in that conference as well.

Such "independent assemblies without party affiliation" have lately sprung up in all those places where Bolshevik Soviets do not permit new elections or where they disband the newly elected soviets. These assemblies are elected on the model of the soviets. They consist of delegates elected by all the workers, yet they oppose the "state bureaucratic soviets" because the latter, as institutions of the state, are subordinate to the CPC. (Since October 1917 an uninterrupted process of centralization has been going on that is increasingly robbing the local soviets of their independence.) These assemblies consider themselves "independent working class organizations" whose role is to defend the interests of the proletariat vis-à-vis the pseudoworkers' government. Already in January, such an assembly appeared in Saint Petersburg. Now it unites all the factories and the majority of workers so that the Saint Petersburg soviet is completely isolated from the masses right now.

The expulsion of the opposition from the soviets is going to speed up the expansion of the assemblies and strengthen the influence of their bureaus [The bureaus of workers' assemblies were elected at the general plenary sessions. They were the equivalents of Executive Committees.], whereas the soviets are turning into institutions of the Bolshevik party. That party is progressively acquiring the character of high- and low-ranking functionaries of the Bolshevik government. Because the process of centralization and bureaucratization of the state apparatus has gone a long way since October, this army of functionaries has turned into a machine ready to carry out any order of the central government. We hope that the formation of these assemblies, which are unconnected with the soviets, will make it possible to prevent the dispersion of the proletariat. Conditions are approaching when counterrevolution prevails, and we hope the assemblies will preserve for the proletariat revolutionary cadres capable of exerting influence on the development of political events when the pseudoproletarian dictatorship is liquidated (provided the revolutionary situation remains such that the existence of these organizations, expressing the will of the masses, is thinkable at all).

During all this struggle over the soviets, persecution of our party became much more relentless. They have shut down our newspapers almost everywhere. Our official newspapers, *Novyi Luch'* in Saint Petersburg and *Vpered* in Moscow, have been banned. In Moscow, we are allowed to publish only a "private" daily, *Nash Golos* [Our Voice]. ["Private" means that the newspaper did not represent the Menshevik Central Committee or any other official party organizations. *Nash Golos* was closed at the end of June as well, after several weeks of existence.] In the provinces, only five or six papers survived in some out-of-the-way places. The closing down of our newspapers caused political strikes as well (Tula, Ekaterinodar, Lugansk). Attempts to put the editorial boards of newspapers on trial [usually for discrediting Soviet power in the eyes of the masses] likewise brought about stormy protests and rallies (Novonikolaevsk in West Siberia, Kharkov, Odessa).

In Odessa, the trial of the editorial board of *Iuzhnyi Rabochii* [Southern Worker] (editors, Tuchapskii and Garvi) [Tuchapskii was involved in Social Democratic activity as a printer at the turn of the century. Petr Garvi was in the party from the very beginning as well. For a brief account of this trial, see Petr A. Garvi, *Zapiski Sotsial Demokrata (1906–1921)* [Notes of a Social Democrat (1906–1921)] (Newtonville, Mass.: Oriental Research Partners, 1982), pp. xxxvii–xli.] turned into a powerful demonstration of the entire proletariat. Workers' delegations from factories arrived in court with declarations of solidarity with the accused. The trial ended with an acquittal. In Kharkov, the trial of editors F. Kon and Ber [Feliks Kon and

B. N. Ber; for more information on trials involving the opposition press, see document 15] of *Sotsial Demokrat* [Social Democrat] did not materialize because the threatening posture of thousands of workers assembled there made the judges run away. After this the authorities decided not to try us anymore, but to close newspapers by administrative order. The trials here against me, Dan, Martynov, and other comrades remain unfinished. [In early April 1918 the Bolsheviks started two political trials against Menshevik leaders in Moscow. One was against Martov, who was accused by Stalin of slandering Stalin's revolutionary past. The other was against Dan and the editorial board of *Vpered* for publishing an article critical of the Brest treaty.]

They make arrests for "counterrevolutionary activity" or for "agitation against Soviet power" and the like. In Kolomna, Bogorodsk [Moscow province], and Tver, the workers succeeded by means of political strikes, forcing the Bolsheviks to release those who had been arrested. In Tyumen [Siberia] on the other hand, the general strike, which broke out when seventeen Social Democrats were arrested, remained fruitless. In Lugansk, a workers' political strike saved the life of A. Nesterov, formerly a workers' deputy in the Second Duma. He was sentenced to death without trial and had already been put up against the wall.

Many of our comrades were executed. A gang of Red Guards seized a miner, I. Tuliakov, formerly a deputy in the Fourth Duma, and executed him not far from Sulin (Taganrog area) [part of the Don Cossack territory]. This was before the Germans marched in. Just a few days ago in Bogorodsk (Nizhnii Novgorod province), they shot and killed Emel'ianov, a Menshevik, after disorders broke out in response to the Bolsheviks' disbanding the soviet. Four Bolshevik commissars were killed by the crowds. (According to the testimony of the Bolsheviks themselves, comrade Emel'ianov was shot in revenge. He was not accused of taking part in the disorders.) In Rostov-na-Donu, after their victory over Kaledin [General A. M. Kaledin; see document 2], the Bolsheviks shot an old Menshevik worker, Kalmykov, even though throughout Kaledin's rule in Rostov, the Menshevik party had selflessly protested against annihilation of the Bolsheviks by the cossacks.

These are only a few examples out of many. Now, in connection with our expulsion from the CEC, we expect that the terror against us will reach its highest degree. During the CEC session, the necessity of taking me, Dan, and other comrades as "hostages" has already been discussed. [The proposal to take Martov as a hostage was made as early as June 1918, two and a half months before the attempted assassination of Lenin, which brought about the Bolsheviks' official state policy of taking hostages as a method of struggle with their political opponents. This was also before the Civil War started in June–July 1918.] So far under arrest are two members of the Central Committee, Kuchin and Troianovskii; two members of the Moscow committee, Egorov and Malkin (workers); as well as Kamermakher, an influential worker from Saint Petersburg, a printer, and a number of party functionaries in the provinces.

I have listed all these facts to demonstrate the true relationship between the proletariat and the Bolshevik party. It should be added here that this government relies on the apparatus of factory committees, which likewise [like the Bolshevik Soviets] refuse to hold new elections and likewise have been turned into a hired bureaucracy. The factory committees hold the masses on the threat of hunger. They fire those who are recalcitrant (especially during curtailment of production). They impose fines on workers if they strike. They disband workers' meetings by armed force, prohibit the selling of opposition papers on the factory premises, and so on. This is what our Paraguayan communism looks like.

The workers' economic dependency on the state inhibits them from breaking with the Bolsheviks. Nevertheless, this process has made substantial headway. In big cities it advances under the slogan of the restoration of civil liberties and the Constituent Assembly, and in the provinces it takes on stormy forms. There the workers' masses are dissolved in the petit bourgeois masses whose frame of mind is either Orthodox Russian or bourgeois. In Saint Petersburg, Nizhnii Novgorod, Tula, Yaroslavl, the Bryansk-Mal'tsevo industrial region, as well as in large parts of Vladimir, Kostroma, and Moscow provinces, the workers have completely abandoned the Bolsheviks. In Kazan, Samara, and other areas on the Volga, the workers' movement away from the Bolsheviks is also very strong. In the Urals, a former bastion of bolshevism, one plant after another has turned its back on it. In the entire South (before the Germans marched in), except for a part of the Donets Basin, the masses have completely given up bolshevism. Generally speaking, at present bolshevism relies primarily on the lumpen proletariat, Latvian riflemen, detachments of prisoners of war [The Bolsheviks formed detachments of so-called Internationalists who fought on their side in the Civil War. Many of these Internationalists were World War I prisoners of war, former German, Austrian, and Hungarian soldiers.], and the Chinese. They also rely on some Red Army detachments insofar as those are not demoralized to such an extent as to pose a threat to the Bolsheviks themselves. [Martov is doubtlessly referring to several instances of Red Army soldiers' rebellions against the Bolsheviks in May and June 1918, such as in Saratov.] In other words, the Bolsheviks rely on a hired gendarmerie.

In the countryside the Bolsheviks have relied for a long time on soldiers returning home from the front. In the chaotic conditions prevailing during the elections to the village soviets, these soldiers seized the soviets, terrorized the peasants (small property holders), and became the privileged group in the countryside. Because summer was approaching, these ex-soldiers were returning to their original peasant way of life. Submitting to the "power of the land," their sansculotte communism was fading away. Now the Bolshevik government, in its fight for power, has taken a number of steps that will inevitably lead to a total break with the peasants. To feed the starving population in the cities, they began to preach a "crusade against the village" to take away grain from peasants by force. The peasants did not want to sell grain at the fixed price (which is, by the way, ridiculously low in view of the devaluation of paper money).

Aiming first and foremost at broadening their base in the Civil War, Lenin and his comrades have turned this crusade into a punitive expedition [*dragonada*]. They hire the lumpen proletarians and send them with unlimited authority into the villages to requisition grain. A number of bloody clashes have already taken place. At present, this measure is being supplemented by another. In addition to the village soviets, they will create "committees of the poor," whose task will be to take away any "surplus" grain from the well-to-do peasants and deliver part of it to urban detachments. The other part they can keep for themselves. One can easily imagine the kind of carnage that will break out because of this.

At the present moment, according to all indications, we find ourselves at a turning point. The Czechoslovak uprising [The Czechoslovak involvement in the Russian Civil War is complex; during World War I the Czechs, like the Hungarians and the Serbs, were taken prisoners as soldiers of the Austro-Hungarian Empire. Because the Czechs' loyalty was to the Allies and not to the Austrians, the Czech prisoners were armed in Russia. When Trotsky issued an order to disarm the Czechs, who were on their way to Vladivostok in May 1918 to be evacuated to France, they refused and disarmed the Bolsheviks instead. This was the beginning of their uprising against the Bolsheviks, which would involve them in the Russian Civil War on the anti-Bolshevik side for two years.], apparently endorsed by the Allies, has every chance of not being quickly suppressed by the Bolsheviks. Encouraged by this uprising, various social groups—the bourgeoisie, the petit bourgeois intelligentsia, and the active part of the middle peasantry—have begun to rally around on the Volga, in the Urals, and in Siberia. The convocation of the Constituent Assembly remains their slogan. For how long is hard to say. The danger is that a new government may be formed on Russian territory [This happened just as Martov was writing this letter. The Socialist Revolutionaries immediately formed a Committee of Members of the Constituent Assembly in Samara and attempted to organize a government that could act as an alternative to the Bolshevik CPC. The Allies did indeed support the Czechs and the Socialist Revolutionary government, and two months after this letter was written the Allied intervention began.], a government backed by the Allies and maybe even by the Japanese or some other expeditionary force. This danger will make the Germans either broaden their occupation [of Russia] or offer Lenin an "honest alliance" for the preservation of his power and suppression of enemies on the Volga and in Siberia. [In this case, too, Martov's analysis of the situation was close to the course of Soviet-German relations in the summer of 1918. There were two tendencies in the German government: one, those who wanted to overthrow the Bolsheviks and replace them with a government friendly to Germany, similar to Hetman Skoropadsky's regime in the Ukraine. Occupation of Petrograd and Moscow was considered. German ambassador Karl Helfferich, for example, favored such a course. The second tendency—those who felt that the Bolsheviks in power still continued to be useful to German interests—was reflected in the so-called additional clauses to the Brest Treaty, concluded in August 1918, indicating cooperation between the two governments. The Bolsheviks pressed the Germans to withdraw aid to White general [P. N.] Krasnov on the Don as compensation for their fighting the Allies. See Karl Helfferich, "Lenin Braucht Ludendorff's Divisionen," in Wilhelm Joost, ed., *Botschafter bei den Roten Tsaren: Die Deutschen Missionchefs in Moskau, 1918 bis 1941, nach geheimakten und personlichen Aufzeichnungen* [Ambassadors to the Red Czars: Chiefs of German Missions to Moscow, from 1918 to 1941, According to Secret Documents and Personal Papers] (Vienna: Fritz, 1967), pp. 69–99.] It is also possible that the Skoropadsky affair [installing in Russia a German puppet government like that of Hetman Skoropadsky in Kiev] will be replayed in Saint Petersburg and Moscow as well. Or a final "Bonapartism" of Lenin's dictatorship will take place if he decides to break with the ideology of "communism" in one stroke and to form a government of pro-German orientation as a counterpart to the democratic or Kadet-Octobrist government in the East [Siberia] with a pro-Allied orientation. . . .

Greetings to all friends,

your

L. Martov

DOCUMENT FIFTEEN

## The Working Class under the Bolshevik Dictatorship

[July 1918]

Dear Comrades:

News of what is really happening in Russia reaches Western Europe with great difficulty. This news is often incomplete and even distorted. The Bolshevik authorities have monopolized all means of communication and do everything they can to present to Western Europe, especially the international proletariat, the "Soviet Republic" as a flourishing Socialist oasis amid the desert of the world war, a country in which socialism has been half-realized and in which the working class has won political hegemony. That is why the European Socialist parties have seriously misjudged the situation in Russia. They perceive the Bolshevik rule in a way that has nothing to do with how this rule manifests itself within Russia.

Under these circumstances we consider it our debt of honor, dictated to us by our Socialist conscience, to bring to the attention of our West European comrades and brothers the true picture of what is happening in Russia. It is our duty to show how this supposedly Socialist government brings disgrace on the very word *socialism* and discredits the proletariat in whose name it performs its outrages and whose will it ostensibly fulfills. The international proletariat must be familiar with the true state of affairs in Russia both in the interests of its own struggle and in the interests of the Russian Revolution and the Russian working class.

This memorandum has as its goal familiarizing the world with the current situation in Bolshevik Russia not on the basis of theoretical reasoning and subjective judgments, but on the basis of verified facts. The material we offer has been drawn almost entirely from the trustworthy Socialist press. Our key sources were the main newspapers of the Russian Social Demo-

This handwritten document, prepared by the Menshevik Central Committee, is a report to the Second International and to Western Socialist parties based on information from local organizations. The report attempts to present a systematic summary of at least the major acts of violence and persecution of political opponents by the Bolshevik government during what now appears to be the most peaceful period, from October 1917 to July 1918. Because few provincial Russian newspapers were available in the West and because most non-Bolshevik press was shut down during the first few months, this report is one of the few testimonies on local politics and local opposition politicians in Bolshevik Russia in 1918. Nicolaevsky Collection, series no. 6, box 5, folder 26.

cratic Workers' party (Menshevik): *Luch* (*Novyi Luch, Nasha Gazeta*) [The titles in parentheses are the titles under which these periodicals resumed publication, usually after they had been shut down by the Bolshevik authorities.] in Petrograd and *Vpered* and *Iskra* in Moscow, edited by F. Dan and L. Martov, members of the Central Committee; the Petrograd and Moscow editions of the Social Democratic newspaper *Novaia Zhizn'*, published with the closest participation of Maxim Gorky; and *Novaia Zaria,* the weekly journal of the Central Committee and the Moscow organization. To a limited extent we have also used a Socialist paper of cooperatives, *Vlast' Naroda* (*Rodina*), published in Moscow, and one of the most reliable and respectable dailies of Russian liberalism, *Russkie Vedomosti* (*Svoboda Rossii*).

The material we present for the judgment of European Socialist public opinion is not all-embracing. The first reason is that to collect all the cases of Bolshevik repressive policy would require a thick volume that would have delayed publication for a long time. Second, difficulties in communications between the cities, a total break of communications in some areas, repressions against the press, and the slowness and unreliability of the postal service and railroad transportation, all these conditions prevailing in Russia have made it impossible to collect all the material. That is why we narrowed our task. We excluded all data in our possession concerning persecution of and violence against civil servants or the bourgeoisie, its political parties, and press. We have set ourselves a more modest task: to present the measures of Soviet power against the Socialist parties and the working class (and also against the peasantry and the institutions of local self-government). But even with these limits, our survey will be far from complete. We have hardly any data on entire regions of what used to be Russia—the Ukraine, Caucasia, Crimea, and Siberia—where Bolshevik authorities were just as ferocious as in central Russia. Our data on central Russia are somewhat better, particularly on the central industrial region and the Volga basin area. But it is important to keep in mind that far from all the facts were reported in the press in this area. Even if they were, provincial newspapers do not reach the capitals regularly. And finally, at certain periods, particularly recently, the independent press has been shut down everywhere and the majority of facts have not become public knowledge. Nevertheless, we believe that our report, although incomplete, presents enough of a picture to enable our West European comrades to get an idea about the nature of the Bolshevik regime and the methods of its rule. And this is exactly what our immediate goal is.

Our survey covers the period up to July 1, 1918, in a more or less systematic manner. After this date, we have included only the most important and vivid facts, omitting the secondary ones.

## INTRODUCTION

From the very first days of its rule, the Bolshevik party, which had seized power relying on army units stationed in the rear, began resorting to repressions against those who resisted or refused to recognize the new government. Initially, the Lenin-Trotsky government directed its main blows against the civil servants of the provisional government, that is, against the democratic intelligentsia (numbering in the thousands) who conscientiously and diligently served the political authority established by the February Revolution. Refusing to recognize the Bolshevik government, they went on a strike that lasted several months. (For this, the Bolsheviks labeled them "saboteurs.") In the course of its struggle with the civil servants, the Soviet government departed from democratic principles for the first time. It resorted to the arrest of strike leaders, depriving them of their rights, dissolving their organizations and trade unions, and forbidding them to assemble and convene congresses.

The Bolsheviks' other opponents at that time were the so-called White Guards, who tried to render armed resistance to the usurpers of power. The White Guards consisted of officers, cadets of military schools, students, and some not as yet demoralized detachments of the Russian army. These groups were mercilessly suppressed and executed by the Bolshevik party. At first, repressions were directed almost exclusively against these two groups of Russian society. On one hand, the Soviet government consolidated its position by breaking the resistance of the "saboteurs"; on the other, it generated sharp opposition of various segments of Russian society, civil organizations, and political parties.

As the Soviet government proceeded to engage itself in "normal" state activity, it increasingly adopted the approach of no compromise. Instead of responding favorably to the demands of democratic circles [In the Russian political context of late 1917, the term *democratic circles* identified those political organizations, groups, and parties—the Kadets, the SRs, and the Mensheviks—that had as a platform universal suffrage.], it went farther along the path of political adventurism and confronted democratic circles with a dilemma. Either they recognize Soviet power and submit unconditionally to its directives or they would be considered "counterrevolutionaries" for whom no laws apply and for whom no political rights or guarantees of security exist in the "Socialist Soviet Republic." Since Democracy [Democratic parties and organizations] for the most part did not want to and could not accept the first choice, which would have signified a break with all its revolutionary traditions [All Russian revolutionary parties, including the Bolsheviks, for decades advocated the introduction of universal suffrage and the convocation of the Constituent Assembly, which were accomplished by the leaders of the February Revolution. Only after the Bolsheviks saw that they would not have a majority in the Constituent Assembly did they publicly reverse their political stance. Other political parties (and, as indicated in Dan's letter, document 3, a third of the Bolshevik faction in the Constituent Assembly) remained loyal to the principle of universal suffrage. For these political parties the disbanding amounted to a "break with all revolutionary traditions."], the Bolsheviks declared that the entire Democracy, other than their own party, was "counterrevolutionary" and began to struggle with it.

Step by step, they began to liquidate all the social and political achievements of the February Revolution, in the process setting themselves against all classes and groups of the population, one after another. Because local self-government was in many cases the main center of organized resistance, the Bolsheviks started with an attack on the city dumas and the zemstvos [provincial councils], which had all been elected by general, equal, direct, and secret ballot by both sexes on the basis of proportional representation according to the law passed by the provisional government. Destruction of local self-government was slow but sure and ended only in the spring of 1918. The Soviet government only did away with it when it found sufficient forces to replace, at least visibly, the abolished local self-government. The Bolshevik municipal departments in the soviets were absolutely incapable of coping with the tasks of local economy, which fell into total decay, as did much of the entire economic and social life in Russia as a result of Soviet government actions.

Having embarked on the destruction of local self-government, the Lenin-Trotsky regime reached a point where disbanding the Constituent Assembly was unavoidable even though it had been elected on the basis of the most democratic electoral law and even though nine-tenths of its deputies were members of Socialist parties. This institution was incompatible with the dictatorship of the Bolshevik party, and on January 5, 1918, the Constituent Assembly was impudently disbanded by a detachment of armed sailors. Everything has its logic, however. A war on Democracy and on its institutions forced Soviet power to open fire on those political parties and social organizations that embodied the will of Democracy. That, in turn, signified struggle with the press and violation of personal inviolability, freedom of assembly, and freedom of association. This struggle gradually acquired proportions that Russia did not experience even under the czarist autocracy. Tyranny and arbitrary rule in the Soviet republic exceeds by far the tyranny and violence of the government of Nicholas Romanov.

The workers reacted passively to the Bolshevik seizure of power and even favored it because they expected the realization of demagogical promises: immediate conclusion of peace, solution to the food supply crisis, and liquidation of exploitation. At that time the Bolshevik party could still assert with a certain validity that the Socialist parties struggling against Soviet power did not have support among the broad popular masses. And the Bolsheviks could justify repressions against them. But the picture changed drastically over several months. In the minds of the deceived masses, Bolshevik rule revealed itself as a dictatorship over the entire country against the will of the majority of the population. The Brest Treaty destroyed the independence of Russia. The "socialization" [in quotation marks to indicate its lack of correspondence to reality] of factories and the nationalization of banks and trade, instead of leading to a planned Socialist economy and liberation of the working class, have led to the total destruction of Russian industry, to cessation of trade, and to unheard-of unemployment. As a result, the workers have stopped regarding the Bolshevik government as *their* government and little by little are beginning to get disillusioned with Bolshevik "Socialist" experiments.

As time goes on, the working class is turning its back on the new regime and demanding that civil liberties and institutions of local self-government be restored and that the disbanded Constituent Assembly be reconvened. As the working class frees itself from the tutelage of the Bolsheviks, they [the Bolsheviks] label it [the working class] counterrevolutionary and begin struggling with it. They employ the same methods as the autocracy and the Lenin-Trotsky government itself did in the beginning against Socialist intelligentsia and some groups of workers who supposedly sided with the "bourgeoisie." Masses of workers are being arrested, and their organizations, both professional and cultural, are being disbanded and persecuted because they do not recognize "Soviet power" and openly come out against it. Workers' demonstrations and workers' conferences [Independent Workers' Assemblies; see document 14] are being shot at. Workers' meetings are being disbanded by armed force.

The Bolsheviks respond to the workers' economic struggle in the same fashion. Because private enterprise has been abolished and because the "Socialist" government now acts as sole entrepreneur, it employs the same means against the workers that were at the disposal of the capitalists and the bourgeois governments, including lockouts, dismissals en masse, and strike breaking. During the last few months (beginning in the spring of 1918), the working class has been the main opponent of Soviet power. All means at the Bolsheviks' disposal are directed against it. The Soviet authorities do not balk at disbanding the soviets of workers' deputies if these organizations come out against the Bolsheviks, even though, formally, the soviets are the basis on which the Lenin-Trotsky government rests.

The position of the peasantry is analogous. Bolshevik agrarian policy has caused civil war in the countryside between various strata of peasants. By taking the side of one or another strata, the Soviet authorities generate hatred toward themselves on the part of all others. The extent to which the majority of the peasantry hates the new regime is demonstrated by recurrent cases of savage carnage and lynching of authorities, as well as by outbreaks, evermore frequent, of real peasant uprisings, now an everyday occurence. The Bolsheviks respond to this by sending punitive expeditions into the countryside to pacify rebellious peasants.

The Bolshevik food supply policy, combined with their foreign policy, doomed all of northern and central Russia, including the capitals, to famine. This gave the Bolsheviks the idea of organizing a crusade against the countryside. Detachments of armed workers would requisition grain from peasants. This measure caused a new outburst of hatred in the countryside of the cities and of Soviet power in particular. Peasant uprisings have blazed up more and more frequently, and the number of Soviet officials annihilated by peasants is increasing.

We see, therefore, that the so-called dictatorship of the proletariat and of the poorest peasantry is in fact, at the present time, directed against the will of the majority of the population in Russia and against the workers and peasants. Furthermore, the punitive measures fall hardest on those classes. The dictatorship of the Lenin-Trotsky government is turning more and more into a dictatorship of like-minded party functionaries who rely on a well-paid bureaucracy and on bayonets, machine guns, and artillery of the "Red Socialist Army," specifically created for struggle with the "internal enemy." In fact, the Red Army recruits come not so much from the ranks of the proletariat as from its scum and from other vagabond elements replenished with déclassé elements of the demoralized old army. These recruits do their job for the sake of good pay and a full stomach at a time of general unemployment and famine. The more acutely the Soviet officials feel that their position is shaky and that the end of their rule is inevitable, the harder they will try to hold on to power, at least for awhile, resorting to unheard-of repressions, employing methods of terror that make the terror of the great French revolution and the terror of the czarist regime pale in comparison. The slightest manifestation of opposition, in particular workers' independent action, causes a reaction in both central and local authorities the likes of which Russia has not experienced in the darkest epochs of its history.

## STRUGGLE WITH THE SOCIALIST AND WORKERS' PRESS

A free and independent press is the main enemy of any despotic government that does not enjoy the support of the majority of the population. Criticism in the press further undermines confidence in, and the authority of, such a government and contributes to the rise of opposition movements. That is why all autocratic governments have always directed their repressions against the press. As long as the Soviet government enjoyed the support of the not-yet-demobilized soldiers and the passive support of workers who believed Bolshevik demagogic promises, it was quite liberal in dealing with the press. The press remained free, and the government resorted to repression only in exceptional cases. The situation changed drastically in December 1917 when the composition of the Constituent Assembly [The elections to the Constituent Assembly started on 12 November 1917, three weeks after the Bolsheviks seized power, and went on for several weeks. The returns from the provinces came in slowly.] was becoming clear and when the struggle around its convocation [Even the Bolshevik party was divided on the legitimacy of disbanding the Constituent Assembly; thus Lenin had to overcome the opposition of all political parties and a part of his own party. For a detailed description of the Bolsheviks' thorough preparations for disbanding the Constituent Assembly, see Peter Scheibert, *Lenin an der Macht: Das Russische Volk in der Revolution, 1918–1922* [Lenin in Power: The Russian People in the Revolution, 1918–1922] (Weinheim: acta humaniora, 1984), pp. 16–22.] began to unite the forces of Democracy, shattered as they were. [This refers to the internal crises of the Menshevik and SR parties that were rooted in deep divisions over policy. In the Menshevik Central Committee the two factions came to a stalemate—ten to eleven—and no binding policy could be adopted until the party congress in December 1917. On the formal breakup of the SR party, see Oliver Radkey, *The Sickle under the Hammer: The Russian Socialist Revolutionaries in the Early Months of Soviet Rule* (New York: Columbia University Press), pp. 95–163, and on the Mensheviks, Vladimir Brovkin, *The Mensheviks after October: Socialist Opposition and the Rise of the Bolshevik Dictatorship* (Ithaca, N.Y.: Cornell University Press, 1987), prologue.] From this point onward, persecution of the press began. This persecution has been more or less systematic, but not always consistent. The struggle between the government and the press is going on, with ups and downs in intensity, up to the present time. And now the Soviet government can proudly say that it has surpassed the record of the czarist autocracy, which never succeeded in exterminating the entire nongovernment press to the extent the Lenin-Trotsky government has done.

In the beginning the Soviet authorities showed signs of vacillating in their treatment of the press. They fined the newspapers, they introduced censorship and then abolished it, they closed newspapers and then allowed them to resume publication, sometimes under the same or a slightly altered name. They summoned the newspaper editors to court hearings or simply arrested them by government order. Sometimes they confiscated separate issues of a paper. They also confiscated supplies of paper. The nationalization of large publishing houses made it impossible for some newspapers to come out. They prohibited newspaper salesmen and street vendors from selling opposition papers. They undermined the retail trade on which most papers depended.

The appetite grows with eating, and little by little the Soviet government began to systematize its measures against the "subversive" press, surpassing in its ardor even the autocracy. Now they demand that the newspapers be registered and have a permit for publication. If in the beginning the Soviet authorities attempted to weaken the influence of the non-Bolshevik press, now [by July 1918] they do everything in their power to destroy it. In this, they are successful. Now we turn to materials from the Russian Socialist press for the period from November 1917 to July 1918.

The first cases of persecution were registered in November. In Saint Petersburg, several Socialist papers of diverse political views—*Novaia Zhizn', Volia Naroda, Den',* and *Delo Naroda*—were closed for a short time. During the fighting in Moscow [In Moscow, the Bolsheviks encountered serious resistance when they tried to seize power. The fighting between the supporters of the city duma and the Bolsheviks went on for several days in early November 1917. The Russian original uses the words *civil war* here. I have avoided this term because it connotes a larger historical period than the first few days of fighting in November 1917.] all Socialist papers were temporarily closed. A much greater number of newspapers were closed in December. On December 10, in Moscow, censorship of the press was introduced (later abolished). For not complying with it, some bourgeois and all Socialist papers were temporarily closed. Many Socialist papers were subjected to systematic confiscation of separate issues, which were burnt in makeshift fires right in front of the printing shops by the Red Guards. The same was done with leaflets of various Socialist parties and groups. Those who tried to disseminate them were subjected to arrests, beatings, threats of execution, and so on. In Yaroslavl one boy was shot for selling an SR [Socialist Revolutionary] paper.

In January, the number of closed newspapers was particularly high. This was the month of the disbanding of the Constituent Assembly. On the eve of its opening, all Socialist newspapers were closed in Petrograd and Moscow, some temporarily, some forever. On January 2, an SR paper, *Volia Naroda,* was closed. It had been published with the close involvement of Breshko-Breshkovskaia, the famous "grandmother of the Russian Revolution." [E. K. Breshko-Breshkovskaia (1844–1934) was a Socialist Revolutionary, who, during her long career in the party, took part in major campaigns and activities of the Populists and later of the Socialist Revolutionaries. She knew Petr Lavrov and Mikhail Bakunin and was among those who went to the people in 1874. Tried in the famous trial of 193 in 1878, she was also one of the founders of the party of Socialist Revolutionaries at the turn of the century, making her the oldest and most experienced revolutionary and a link between the generations, hence, the "grandmother of the Russian Revolution."] The premises were searched, and many members of the editorial staff were arrested, among them Argunov, the editor and one of the founders of the SR party and a member of the SR Central Committee, P. Sorokin, and E. Stalinskii. The latter two spent over a month in prison. Zaslavskii and Klivanskii, the editors of the newspaper *Den',* were also confined for a month. During the wrangling with the Red Guards who were conducting the search, Klivanskii was wounded in the arm and another editor, Gulis, in his side by a bayonet. The authorities requisitioned a printing shop owned by the People's Socialist party. Almost simultaneously with the assault on the Petrograd press, the rout took place in Moscow and in many provincial cities. And finally, during January, the entire army press at the front, which did not share Bolshevik views, was liquidated.

In February, the repressions subsided somewhat, especially at the end of the month. The Socialist press in the capitals continued to exist, except for short intervals. In the beginning of the month, however, we witnessed a new fit of Bolshevik administrative zeal. On February 2, the "provisional rules for the press" were published. These rules are just as reactionary as the rules of the czarist government were. The rules penalized editors and owners of newspapers for published materials and prescribed that a copy of every paper be sent to the Commissariat of the Press. One by one, seven dailies were closed in Petrograd. Some of them could not resume publication later. In Moscow, the Menshevik *Vpered* was banned but continued to come out, as in the old days, underground, despite the ban. In Kiev, the printing shop of a Socialist paper with the largest circulation, *Kievskaia Mysl',* was requisitioned, and the paper ceased to come out for some time. As a matter of fact, under the czarist regime, Trotsky and Lunacharskii, now commissars, were permanent correspondents of this paper abroad. In Yaroslavl, all local Socialist papers were closed and the sale of Socialist papers published in the capitals prohibited.

According to *Ponedel'nik,* a Moscow weekly, during March, the Soviet authorities closed forty-seven newspapers, imposed fines on seventeen periodicals for a total of 278,000 rubles, requisitioned twenty-two printing shops, confiscated printing presses, typesetting, and paper supplies in nineteen printing shops, put the editors and staff of fourteen dailies on trial, and arrested the editors of six newspapers. Socialist papers were closed in Saratov, Samara, Rostov-na-Donu, Novonikolaevsk, Ekaterinoslav, Irkutsk, and Odessa. In Saratov, they also destroyed the lists with addresses of all the subscribers to non-Bolshevik papers in the capitals. In Odessa, they put the editorial board of *Iuzhnyi Rabochii* on trial for appeals to overthrow Soviet power. Because the paper was published by the Odessa Menshevik party committee, all of its fifteen members were put on trial. All of them were longtime members and revolutionaries, and some of them were workers.

In April, repressions against the press continued and even intensified as the opposition movement against the Bolsheviks and Soviet power grew. In Moscow, Soviet authorities closed *Vlast' Naroda* and its sequel, *Rodina*. They also started court proceedings against *Vpered*, which had become the main paper of the RSDWP. [*Vpered* (Forward) was the newspaper of the Moscow Mensheviks in 1917. After Moscow became the Soviet capital in March 1918, *Vpered* became the paper of the Menshevik Central Committee.] These proceedings, however, never culminated in a trial because the Bolsheviks feared it would end in a scandalous fiasco. At first, one of the editors of *Vpered*, L. Martov, was accused of making a disrespectful comment about People's Commissar Stalin. [People's commissar replaced the term *minister* in Lenin's government, which was officially called Council of People's Commissars (CPC).] Then they brought up charges against F. Dan, S. Kats, and staff member Kaplan. At that point the party CC, the Moscow regional bureau, and the Moscow city committee declared that they bore collective responsibility for the material in the paper. The authorities issued an order to the effect that these three party organizations were liable to be put on trial. In response, quite a number of provincial party organizations expressed their solidarity with the accused and requested that they be put on trial as well. At the same time the workers at numerous factories in Moscow expressed their solidarity with them.

In Petrograd, seveal dailies were closed. In Kostroma, Kaluga, and Yaroslavl, the local authorities levied a special tax on the sale of all non-Bolshevik newspapers (from three to five rubles for each copy). In Sormovo (a suburb of Nizhnii Novgorod), a paper of the local soviet (mostly Mensheviks and SRs) is published clandestinely despite the ban. All Socialist papers in Nizhnii Novgorod were closed. In Kineshma (Kostroma province) the authorities prohibited the sale of all bourgeois and "pseudo-Socialist papers." In Kolomna (Moscow province), the authorities made it obligatory for all owners of taverns, canteens, and other establishments as well as home owners to subscribe to official Soviet periodicals. Socialist newspapers were closed in Tula, Tomsk, Smolensk, Ryazan, Armavir, Orenburg, Samara, Voronezh, and Tver.

In May and June, repressions may appear to be diminishing, but this can be explained by the fact that almost the entire Socialist press in the provinces and a part of it in the capitals has been irrevocably liquidated. There is nothing left that could be closed. In Petrograd, the authorities closed the Menshevik *Novyi Luch* and *Novyi Den'* and an SR paper, *Delo Naroda*, for publishing the resolution of the SR party congress on foreign policy. With this the existence of the SR press in Petrograd came to an end. Of all the Socialist papers, only *Novaia Zhizn'* remained and not for long. In Moscow, the case of *Vpered* was reopened, but the paper was closed forever. In Orel, a ten-thousand-ruble fine was levied on the only remaining non-Bolshevik paper, *Slovo Naroda*. Socialist dailies were also closed in Arkhangel'sk, Tambov, Tomsk, Kazan, Voronezh, Kronstadt, and Astrakhan.

At present, as we write this report (end of June), not a single Socialist paper comes out in Moscow. Only the government-controlled press is permitted. In Petrograd, too, all Socialist papers have been closed. It goes without saying that in the provinces the situation is not any better. The working class and Democracy do not have a single periodical of their own, whereas before the Bolshevik coup, their number reached several hundred. Under these conditions, party organizations began to resort to an old method (well tried under czarism), publishing underground. But the authorities immediately confiscated declarations and appeals published underground and made short shrift of those who disseminated them. In this fashion, the Soviet authorities have destroyed the cornerstone of democracy and liberty, freedom of the press. At present, not more than two or three Socialist papers come out (and in small towns at that) in all of Soviet Russia. (After the assassination of Count Mirbach, a great majority of Left SR papers were closed as well.) [Count Wilhelm Mirbach (1871–1918) was the German ambassador to Soviet Russia in 1918. On 6 July 1918, Mirbach was assassinated by two terrorists who arrived in the German embassy with valid Cheka documents. Until recently it has been accepted that Count Mirbach was killed by the Left Socialist Revolutionaries to invalidate the Brest Treaty. Yurii Felshtinsky, however, argues that because of their political commitments the Left Socialist Revolutionaries had no choice but to accept the responsibility for an assassination they did not engineer (Felshtinsky, *Bol'sheviki i Levye Esery: oktiabr' 1917–ilul' 1918. Na puti k odnopartiinoi diktature* [The Bolsheviks and the Left SRs: October 1917– July 1918. On the Way to a One-Party Dictatorship] (Paris: YMCA, 1985).

Who sent the assassins to kill Mirbach? What was the role of Lenin's secret police? These questions have been reopened.]

## PERSECUTION OF THE LEADERS OF THE SOCIALIST PARTIES AND LABOR MOVEMENT: ARRESTS AND EXILES

Once the Soviet government embarked on the course of repressions, it started to persecute individual political leaders, those "dangerous" to the "existing order." Like any despotic government, it preferred to rely on summary reprisals by executive order rather than on judicial procedure. It retained the "Revolutionary Tribunal" [For a discussion of the revolutionary tribunals, see Peter Kenez, "Lenin and the Freedom of the Press," in Abbot Gleason, Peter Kenez, and Richard Stites, eds., *Bolshevik Culture* (Bloomington: Indiana University Press, 1985), pp. 131–50.] primarily to deal with cases of real and imaginary "conspiracies" against Soviet power, speculation, violation of countless Bolshevik decrees, and other abuses such as theft by government bureaucrats, whose number is incomparably higher now than under the czarist regime.

It is simply impossible to count and list all the individuals who have suffered from persecution, both judicial and summary. Suffice it to say that their number is in the tens of thousands. Just as before the revolution of 1917, the prisons in the capitals and even more so in the provinces are overflowing with members of Socialist parties. At present, in the Butyrki jail in Moscow alone, more than one thousand workers and peasants are imprisoned. Most of them have been arrested, just as in the last days of Robespierre's dictatorship, on charges of counterrevolution. Moreover, the number of those arrested from among the "bourgeoisie" is many times smaller than the number of arrested Socialists. This is because the monarchists or even the Kadets are by far less dangerous at present than the Socialists, who are gaining influence and popularity among the workers and broad democratic circles with every passing day.

We have deliberately omitted from our survey all data on persecution during the first month and a half of Communist party rule because it was directed primarily against civil servants of the overthrown provisional government. Their number would probably be several thousand. Among them were, for example, Socialist ministers in the provisional government Maliantovich, and Liverovskii—seized by the Bolsheviks on the night of October 25—Nikitin, Gvozdev, Salazkin, Maslov, and a commissar of the provisional government, Voitinskii, a Social Democrat [SD] who had been sentenced to four years of hard labor under the old regime. Simarily, we omit here data on the mass arrests among officers, the clergy, students, monarchists, and members of bourgeois parties. We have limited our survey to Bolshevik reprisals against the Socialists only. But here again our survey is not complete.

Arrests of Socialists began more or less systematically in December 1917. As early as November, however, Ravich (an editor of an SD paper) and Diushen (a member of the city duma), Menshevik candidates for the Constituent Assembly, were arrested in Yaroslavl for refusing to obey the orders of Soviet power. On December 16, they arrested in Petrograd the entire council of supervisors [*starosty*] at the Tube plant because the workers there adopted a resolution against the Bolsheviks. They also searched the office of the Committee in Defense of the Constituent Assembly [a forerunner of the Workers' Assemblies, independent workers' organizations opposing the Bolshevik dictatorship] and the Committee of the Democratic Parties and Organizations. Everyone who happened to be there, about forty people, was detained. Of those, sixteen were imprisoned in Peter and Paul Fortress and kept there without any formal charges for five weeks (Vainshtein, Ermolaev, Bogdanov, Bramson). The prisoners sent an open letter in protest against their unlawful detention. At many factories and plants, resolutions in support of the prisoners were adopted. During December, members of the Union in Defense of the Constituent Assembly (mostly workers) were repeatedly subjected to temporary detention for disseminating declarations of that union and for organizing rallies. The number of arrests in December was so high that prisoners in the basement of Smolny protested in an open letter against unbearable overcrowding and unsanitary conditions.

The number of arrests in January was even higher than in December. In connection with the disbanding of the Constituent Assembly, an order was issued in Petrograd to arrest the entire CC of the SR party. CC members went into hiding. At the same time, members of the Peasant Union [a powerful organization led by the Socialist Revolutionaries. During December 1917 and January 1918 intense political struggle for control of the Peasant Union was going on between the Bolsheviks, the Socialist Revolutionaries, and the Left Socialist Revolutionaries. See Scheibert, *Lenin an der Macht,* pp. 117–22.], I. Sorokin and Shmelev, were arrested. On January 12, the CC of the People's Socialist party was searched and a secretary arrested. A worker at the Maxwell factory, Shchekunov, was arrested for collecting signatures on a declaration of protest against the shooting during the demonstration in defense of the Constituent Assembly. On January 23, sailors searched the Nevsky shipbuilding plant to find and arrest Avdeev, a local SR worker, but the workers at the plant did not give him away and he was able to escape. A great many workers were arrested in January as they were distributing proclamations at the rallies. According to the chairman of the investigative commission, out of twelve hundred persons under arrest in Petrograd by January 20, at least 25 percent had been arrested for political offenses.

In Moscow on January 5, a group of SDs headed by Teitel'baum were arrested at a rally in defense of the Constituent Assembly. They were beaten up in the commissariat, subjected to all kinds of derision, and threatened with a revolver. An SD paper, *Vpered,* received a letter from the Butyrki jail from one of those arrested, a women printer, Ulanova. She wrote,

> We are in a dungeon where in the old days the autocracy made short work of us workers and Socialists. And now we are thrown behind bars by the Bolsheviks. And they do it in the name of a workers' organization—the Soviet of Workers' Deputies . . . . Comrade workers! A crime is being committed. In our name they perpetrate violence upon us. Just as in the last days of czarism, they shoot with bullets at a demonstration in honor of the Constituent Assembly. . . . Demand from the Bolsheviks, who have deceived the workers [The Bolsheviks, before they seized power, had pledged to convene the Constituent Assembly.], demand from them the freedom that they have stolen from the People.

NOVGOROD: After the rally in defense of the Constituent Assembly, more than seventy people were arrested.

SIMBIRSK: Social Democrats Cheboksarov and Krasnov (the chairman of the city duma) were arrested.

SORMOVO (Nizhnii Novgorod province): Bykhovskii, the secretary of the Mutual Aid Fund and a member of the SD committee, was searched and put on trial by the Revolutionary Tribunal.

BOGORODSK (Nizhnii Novgorod province): At a workers' rally, SD workers Surikov and Gladkov were arrested.

EKATERINBURG: On January 15, the SR party committee premises were searched, and two members, Zhelezkov and Kashcheev, arrested.

During February there were considerably fewer arrests than in January and December. This is partly because of a relative "pacification" in the wake of the disbanding of the Constituent Assembly and partly a result of a circular sent throughout Russia by the commissar of justice, Steinberg [Isaac Steinberg was a people's commissar of justice from mid-December 1917 to 6 March 1918. On that day, the Left Socialist Revolutionaries resigned from the coalition government to protest the Brest Treaty.], who recommended resorting to arrests and other repressive measures only in cases of "extreme necessity" because "suppression of counterrevolutionary activity must be conducted within the bounds of revolutionary legal order."

NIZHNII NOVGOROD: Naletov, Zakhoder, and Gofman, the leaders of the SD party committee and members of the city duma, were arrested and sentenced to exile from Nizhnii Novgorod. They went on a hunger strike in prison.

BOGORODSK (Nizhnii Novgorod province): Eight leaders of the local SR, SD, and Bund organizations were arrested.

MINSK: Persecution of Socialists reached such proportions that they had to go underground, just like under czarism.

PETROGRAD: In early March, the Red Guards arrested Kuz'min, an SD worker, for a disrespectful comment about them at the cartridge plant. They beat him up with rifle butts, wounded him in his side with a bayonet, and threatened to finish him off. Thanks only to the intervention of Riazanov, an influential Bolshevik and a member of the CEC, was Kuz'min saved and released.

MOSCOW: Chirkin, a railway worker, was arrested when he arrived to give a lecture.

BOGORODSK: Mass arrests among the SRs and SDs took place for "agitation against Soviet power."

KHARKOV: SDs Tkachenko, Kaloshin, and Bondarenko, workers of the locomotive plant, were arrested.

ZLATOUST: After the Bolsheviks lost elections to the local soviet, thirteen workers, Mensheviks, and SRs were arrested.

SARATOV: The authorities issued an order to arrest SRs Altovskii and Betlin.

IVANOVO VOZNESENSK: For publishing a proclamation in defense of the Constituent Assembly, SR party committee members were arrested.

PERM: An order was issued to conduct a search and to arrest influential SD party members and workers Emel'ianov, Zhandarmov, Iakubov, Iakimov, and others.

SULIN (the Don cossacks area): Among those arrested were a distinguished figure in the local trade union movement, Tuliakov, a Menshevik, formerly a member of the Fourth State Duma, and Mesluev, a student. They were put on trial, but Mesluev was executed before the trial. At the trial, the prosecutor demanded the death penalty for Tuliakov. The workers from the local plant had always elected Tuliakov to numerous offices, including that of the state duma. Under their pressure, the defendants were acquitted. Tuliakov, however, did not escape a bloody end; several months later he was treacherously killed (see below).

KOVROV (Vladimir province): After the shooting at a workers' demonstration, up to forty Social Democrats were arrested.

KINESHMA (Kostroma province): The local soviet declared a state of siege and imposed a tax of one thousand to three thousand rubles on the Mensheviks and SRs for permits to hold public lectures.

KALUGA: The Kaluga SD committee telegraphed to Moscow: "A trial of the Menshevik leaders of trade unions and Menshevik members of the soviet is going on. They took them all to prison even before the verdict was determined. We appeal to political parties, trade unions, and social organizations to defend the accused. signed: THE MENSHEVIK FACTION OF THE SOVIET."

For April we have very meager data. By that time Russia had broken into pieces, and all communications were coming to an end. [By April 1918, the Bolsheviks had been overthrown or prevented from coming to power in the Ukraine, Caucasia, and parts of Siberia.] Moreover, in parts of Russia still under Soviet rule, a considerable part of the independent press had been liquidated. News from the provinces was reaching the capital in ever-diminishing volume.

MOSCOW: On April 20 a Menshevik, Ioffe, was arrested at a workers' rally. For speeches in the Moscow soviet, Kipen and Alekseev were put on trial by the Revolutionary Tribunal.

YAROSLAVL: Members of the SD party committee, Shleifer and Bogdanov, and an SR, Loktov, were arrested. On April 18, they were put on trial. [This trial took place after the Menshevik/Socialist Revolutionary bloc had won elections to the city soviet and after Shleifer had been elected chairman of the new soviet (see document 8).]

RYBINSK (Yaroslavl province): Members of the city duma—Mikhailov, Vitalin, Levin, and Karasnikov, Social Democrats—were arrested.

KURSK: The chairman of the city duma, Vasil'ev, an SR, was arrested.

SMOLENSK: At the Congress of Soviets of Western Provinces, a *Bolshevik* [underlined in the original], Sevastianov, was arrested for suggesting that freedom of speech at the congress be granted to the Mensheviks.

ROSLAVL (Smolensk province): In connection with disorders at the end of the month caused by food supply problems, mass arrests of workers (several dozen) took place. [For details, see document 11. In this report on the events in Roslavl, only arrests, not executions, are mentioned.]

TAMBOV: On the eve of May 1, the chairman of the local Menshevik organization, Orlov, was arrested. This caused a protest of railway workers.

YEGORYEVSK (Ryazan province): For speeches at a peasant congress, Social Democrats Belov and Lezhneva were sentenced to a three-months' imprisonment by administrative order.

LOSVENSKII PLANT (the Urals): For distributing a leaflet on the occasion

of the centenary of Karl Marx's birth, the secretary of the SD committee
was arrested on May 24.

The magnitude of repressions during June exceeded any other. Threatened on all sides, Soviet authorities lost all restraint and virtually declared
war on the working class.

PETROGRAD: In connection with the assassination of Commissar
Volodarskii [V. Volodarskii was assassinated on 20 June 1918 in Petrograd,
most likely by a Social Revolutionary terrorist group acting independently
of its Central Committee.] (who committed it is unknown), mass searches
and arrests were made among the workers of the Nevskii district. Among
others, they arrested an SR worker from Obukhov plant, Eremeev, as a
suspect. In response, the Obukhov plant workers (about five thousand)
went on strike and demanded that he be released immediately. The sailors
of the mine squadron, stationed near the plant, supported the strikers.
Under the sailors' pressure and threats [They pointed guns at the local
soviet and presented their demands.], Eremeev was set free. After this,
though, the sailors were disarmed and all Obukhov workers dismissed.
[For details of this incident, see "Zakrytie Obukhovskogo zavoda," *Novaia
Zhizn'*, no. 122 (24 June 1918, Petrograd).] In fact, the plant is still [at the
end of July 1918] not in operation.

Moscow: The extent of repressions here is particularly high. After the
rally at Shrader's factory, SDs Rashkovskii and Senderovich, as well as the
delegate of the Petrograd workers' assembly, Krakovskii, were arrested.
[This was on 9 June in Moscow. At the end of May, the Petrograd Workers'
Assembly sent a delegation to Moscow to establish contact with the Moscow workers and to promote the workers' assembly there. Krakovskii was
killed by the Cheka later in the summer (see document 16).] Almost at the
same time [13 June 1918], all the Moscow factory and plant representatives
("Workers' Conference") [This meeting also included delegates from Tula,
Sormovo, and other industrial cities. It assembled to prepare a convocation
of the All-Russian Workers' Congress.] were arrested (forty-five people).
Among them are Menshevik CC members Kuchin and Troianovskii. The
latter two are still in jail; the majority were released.

On June 14, the Bolsheviks expelled members of the Social Democratic and Socialist Revolutionary parties from the CEC. As they were
leaving the session, Disler, an SR, was arrested. When his family inquired
about his status, they were told that he was going to be held "as a hostage."
[A similar action was considered in regard to Martov (see document 14).
This was the first case of the Bolsheviks' taking hostage a member of the
legislative institution.] On June 17, a sixteen-year-old youth, Ratatovskii,
was arrested for posting declarations of the workers' assembly in the

streets. During a search at the Riabushinskii printing shops, proclamations were discovered on the person of a typesetter, Ruzhkov. He was arrested. On June 10, a member of the Petrograd delegation of the workers' assembly, Kuz'min, was arrested at a workers' meeting preparing a convocation of the Moscow Workers' Assembly.

PETROGRAD: On June 11, the offices of the SR Central Committee and the SR publishing house were closed and sealed. The same was repeated in Moscow in July. Several party members were arrested.

KOLOMNA (Moscow province): SD committee members Moskvin, Elenin, and Rozen were arrested. In response, workers of the Kolomna machine-building plant went on strike, and all those arrested were released.

SARATOV: Fifteen Social Democrats (the entire SD committee) were put on trial by the Revolutionary Tribunal. Many of them are workers. They were charged with criticizing Soviet power. At the session of the tribunal, the audience greeted them with an ovation. The tribunal found the defendants guilty and resolved to expel them from the workers' milieu.

TULA: An SD worker, Upovalov, was arrested. Several days later five more workers were arrested at the cartridge plant. Then several members of the strike committee at the armament plant were arrested in connection with the political strike protesting worker repression. [On 17 June 1918, Tula went on a general strike, partly in response to the arrest of Tula representatives at the intercity conference of workers' assemblies.] On June 13, the chairman of the Tula Workers' Assembly, Aleksandrov, and the secretary of the SD committee, Kogan, were arrested on the street.

ARKHANGEL'SK: Members of the SD and SR factions in the city duma were arrested and brought to Moscow. In response, the Arkhangel'sk SD party committee issued a declaration in protest. As a result, all of its members were also arrested on June 25 and brought to Moscow.

MOTOVILIKHA [an important industrial town not far from Perm in the Urals; see document 7] AND IZHEVSK (the Urals): After the new elections to the local soviet ended unfavorably for the Bolsheviks, they made mass arrests among the workers of these plants (up to seventy people). Crowds of people assembled to protest these arrests. They were disbanded by the Red Guards, who beat the workers with rifle butts and shot into the air to disperse them.

TYUMEN: On June 2, nineteen SDs and SRs (all members of the city duma, sixteen of them workers) were arrested. Local workers went on strike in protest. Red Guards opened fire on workers' crowds.

OREL: The Soviet of Workers' Deputies was disbanded, and workers Glukhov (SD) and Volobuev [Other sources spell the name *Volubaev.*] (SR) were arrested.

VIAZNIKI (Vladimir province): The local SD organization was completely decimated by arrests, made in response to the success of the SDs in the elections to the soviet.

RYEZHITSA (Orel province): Local authorities issued a decree [It was not uncommon in 1918 for local authorities to issue decrees on their own, in imitation of Lenin's people's commissars.] that read "Persons of anti-Soviet power [*litsa antisovetskoi vlasti,* illiterate formulation; what is meant is persons of anti-Soviet convictions] (monarchists, bureaucrats, underlings of the old regime, officers, the bourgeoisie, speculators, marauders, Right Socialist Revolutionaries, Mensheviks, People's Socialists, and Kadets) will be persecuted [*budut presledovat'sia*]."

During the month of July, repressions continued without interruption both in the capitals and in the provinces. The absence of opposition party press or, for that matter, any other press independent of the authorities means that we cannot provide much factual data. We shall point out, therefore, only the most well-known cases.

PETROGRAD: The entire board of the Printers' Union was arrested for taking part in preparations for the general strike on July 2.

MOSCOW: On July 17, the premises of the Central Committee of the SD party were searched, and CC member Iugov and Moscow committee members A. and B. Malkins and a typist, Vera Gronshkevich, were arrested. On July 23, all the participants in the Congress of Workers' Assemblies were arrested in Moscow. These delegates from Petrograd, Moscow, Kolomna, Sormovo, Nizhni Novgorod, Tula, Bryansk, Kulebaki, Tver, Vologda, and Orel were elected by many thousands of workers at factories and plants. They assembled to prepare an All-Russian Workers' Congress. The Bolshevik government denounced this attempt, labeled it a "counter-revolutionary conspiracy," and decreed that those arrested would be tried by the Supreme Tribunal, well-known for its death penalties. Among those arrested are well-known leaders of the workers' movement, such as members of the Central Committee of the SD party; R. Abramovich, whom many leaders of European Social Democracy know personally (particularly in Austria and Switzerland); Al'ter, a member of the Bund CC; V. Chirkin, a former chairman of the Metalists' Union; union leaders Ia. Smirnov, I. Volkov, and D. Zakharov; a well-known worker metalist, N. Glebov [leader of the workers' opposition at the Putilov plant]; as well as Boris-enko, Berg [E. Berg, Socialist Revolutionary and chairman of the Petro-grad Workers' Assembly], and others.

We have already pointed out that in many cities, Socialist party organizations had to go underground because of repression. We have left out the repressions against cooperatives, although these have intensified in the last two to three months. All this information is on the pages of the periodicals of the cooperatives. Likewise we have not listed all the data in our possession on cases of persecution of trade unions that do not support Soviet power. Finally, we are singling out under a separate heading the Bolshevik government's struggle with its favorite form of workers' organization—the Soviets of Workers' Deputies—because these are getting out of control and are increasingly against the Communist government.

What we have said so far, however, is enough to ascertain that the government referring to itself as "Socialist" and "Communist" has managed to destroy, in a short time, freedom of association, freedom of the press, and inviolability of person. Below we shall show how it did away with freedom of assembly. With all these measures, the Soviet government has returned Russia to prerevolutionary times, having surpassed the record of the Romanov's autocracy. [The manuscript ends here. Unfortunately, no section dealing with Bolshevik reprisals against the Soviets has been found. For a discussion of the elections in the spring of 1918, see Vladimir Brovkin, *The Mensheviks after October: Socialist Opposition and the Rise of the Bolshevik Dictatorship* (Ithaca, N.Y.: Cornell University Press, 1987), chap. 5.]

CENTRAL COMMITTEE OF THE RSDWP

---

DOCUMENT SIXTEEN

---

## Iu. O. Martov to A. N. Stein

25 October 1918

Dear Aleksandr Nikolaevich:

It has been a long time since I had a convenient opportunity to send you a letter. Neither have I received anything from you. The latest news was brought to us by Comrade Guterman, who saw you before you left Berlin. During the last three months so much water has flowed under the bridge here that I would have had to write volumes to share with you

Nicolaevsky Collection, series 17, box 51, folder 4.

everything of interest. Therefore I shall familiarize you with only the most important.

1. The general situation for our party has become unbearable. All outward manifestations of its existence have been annihilated in Soviet Russia. Everything is destroyed: the press, the organizations, and so forth. Unlike czarist times, it is impossible to "go underground" to do any fruitful work because not only do the gendarmes, street sweepers, and the like keep an eye out for unreliability, but a segment of ordinary citizens (Communists and those with vested interest in the Soviet regime) regard denunciation, surveillance, and shadowing not only as proper but as the fulfillment of their supreme duty. Therefore, thinking about a somewhat regular functioning of underground organizations is out of the question. A lot of Mensheviks have been arrested. After the participants (Abramovich, A. N. Smirnov, and many others) in the Workers' Congress [This congress never took place. A preparatory meeting of workers' representatives was called for 22 July 1918. The delegates arrived in Moscow, but were arrested at the second session by the Cheka and imprisoned. Their protest declaration was published in numerous periodicals and books at the time. See, for example, *The Case of Russian Labor Against Bolshevism* (New York: Russian Information Service, 1919).] had been arrested (twenty-four of them are still in prison here in Saint Petersburg and in the provinces), they arrested more people. Some, however, managed to escape arrest. That is why we maintain communications only minimally and with great difficulty.

But all this would not have been so hard had this fit of terror against us not revealed the internal weakness of our movement. By the spring of 1918 our movement had begun to acquire impressive proportions, embracing the masses in almost all workers' centers. But by that time, the collapse of industry, which had been delayed by artificial means, was in full swing. Three-fourths of the factories and plants closed down. The hungry masses began to realize that the paltry doles [*podachka*. Martov is using an expression that was common at the time in the political vocabulary of opposition-minded workers. There had been four categories of food rations, with the lowest for the "bourgeoisie." A new food ration for workers was introduced at the end of May in Petrograd in connection with workers' unrest there that raised the workers' ration at the expense of other groups of the population. The workers' assembly then passed a resolution condemning the "paltry dole." The text of the resolution is in Mikhail Bernstam, ed., *Nezavisimoe rabochee dvizhenie v 1918 godu. Dokumenty i materialy* [Independent Workers Movement in 1918, Documents and Materials] (Paris: YMCA, 1981), p. 165.] from the state would not flow endlessly and began leaving for the countryside. The *workers'* movement seemed to disappear.

The masses of workers who remained at the factories lost hope that industry could be saved, turned their backs on the "opposition," which had previously expressed their discontent, and threw themselves into total apoliticism and unending indifference.

As a result our hope disappeared that bolshevism could be overcome by the forces of the working class now that it has been cured of utopias. We also lost hope that it would be possible to avoid the liquidation of the Bolshevik utopia by the forces of counterrevolution. Also by that time [at the end of the summer of 1918] the situation had become clearer in those areas where there were no Bolsheviks. It turned out that the weak, petit bourgeois Democracy was incapable of channeling its struggle with bolshevism into the stream of struggle for the revolution. In the East and in the North, it is hopelessly pulling toward a "national" alliance, that is, a coalition with the clearly counterrevolutionary bourgeoisie. As a result, it is steadily losing credibility in the eyes of the working masses after the Bolsheviks had been chased away with the approval or even with the help of these same masses. This factor explains, to a considerable extent, the Bolsheviks' quick successes at retaking Simbirsk, Kazan, and Samara. [Bolshevik forces retook these cities in September 1918 after they defeated the forces of the Socialist Revolutionary–led government of the Committee of the Constituent Assembly in Samara. Martov points to two parallel political developments in the summer of 1918. On one hand, the Socialist Revolutionary forces, allied with the Czechs, were quickly able to establish their authority in a large area on the Volga and the Urals in June–July 1918 because of persistent peasant and worker uprisings against the Bolsheviks. On the other hand, the Socialist Revolutionary government was helpless vis-à-vis officers' organizations that sprang up after the Bolsheviks were gone. These organizations struck indiscriminately at leftists of all persuasions.]

This is getting worse and worse because an ever-greater role in the anti-Bolshevik struggle is being played by all sorts of officers' and cadets' units, with sympathies ranging from Kornilovite at best to monarchist at worst. They are becoming a more decisive factor in the "national" coalition than the Committee of the Constituent Assembly and similar elements. Furthermore, it is likely that, with [President Woodrow] Wilson's victory [in World War I], the division among the propertied classes on the question of orientation [In the spring and summer of 1918, Russian non-Socialist political parties, organizations, and leaders were divided into two camps: those who supported the Allies and expected help from them in their anti-Bolshevik struggle and those who, for the same ends, relied on Germany.] will disappear and they will all become Allied supporters. In such conditions, the "Thermidor" [counterrevolution] to which our Robespierres are leading will acquire an all the more ominous, restorationist, and Black

Hundred–like [Black Hundreds were Russian fascists who staged Jewish pogroms.] character. As long as the war with Germany was still going on, the Allies were inclined, in the interests of the war, to shift the political center of anti-Bolshevik forces to the left. They supported the SRs [Socialist Revolutionaries] against the Kadets and the Right. But if the war is going to draw to a close and if the Ukrainian, Don, and other reactionary forces join the Allies, the latter would most probably abandon the SRs, the Constituent Assembly, and so forth, whose cause would then be lost.

All this caused a great turmoil in the party. At first, our right elements, adjusting to the emerging situation, took the next step and openly identified themselves with the foreign occupation [The Right Mensheviks publicly endorsed the Allied landing in Arkhangel'sk, Murmansk, and Vladivostok.] and with the struggle against the Bolsheviks as part of a "coalition." [The Right Mensheviks likewise supported the coalition with the Kadets in their struggle against bolshevism.] They proclaimed it to be a "national task" to restore capitalist order. Headed by Liber, they organized the Committee for Active Struggle for the Regeneration of Russia. [Not to be confused with the Union of Regeneration, which was also founded in summer of 1918 and which was a multiparty organization including primarily the Kadets, the Right Mensheviks, and the SRs, the committee mentioned here was a part of the Social Democratic party.] This created a de facto split in the party, which did not become de jure only because terror put such pressure on all of us that any public debate in the party or a convocation of a conference or congress to judge rebellious elements became impossible.

On the other hand, another part of the party, by way of reaction to this "activism," has begun to "wobble," especially under the influence of reports of the Bolsheviks' growing popularity in Europe. There is talk that the Socialist world revolution is "bypassing democracy" and instead taking the Bolshevik road, that it is dangerous doctrinairism to oppose this process, and that one must look for some kind of a "bridge" to bolshevism. Actually, of course, no bridge is possible, except an outright surrender, because bolshevism does not admit the idea of an opposition party, even if it is ultraloyal and accepts the Soviet form of government. The only "reconciliation" they admit is for members of this or that opposition party to join them as individual guests.

In such a hopeless situation, hesitant elements cannot help but think of creating some new group, and the more decisive, more demoralized among them are going over to the Bolsheviks *avec les armes et bagages*. Throughout the entire history of bolshevism we have not had so many defections. From our resolutions you will see how the CC is responding to this process: trying to reformulate the party's position on the problems of revolution and eliminating the ambiguity and discrepancies that had been there because we had to reckon with our right faction and guard our internal unity. By formulating our position more clearly and by dotting our i's, we hope to calm down our public somewhat. The appearance of [Karl] Kautsky's brochure [*Demokratie oder Diktatur*] brought us great satisfaction and strengthened us in our key views.

2. About the events in the country during the last months, I must say that the reports about the "Red Terror" as they appeared in the *Frankfurter Zeitung* and *Berliner Tagesblat* do correspond to reality. Better to say that they are less than reality because they do not give a detailed picture of what took place in Petrograd and in the provinces. This wave of terror has not arisen from any tangible pressure from the masses or been a result of mob rule. The most that the Bolsheviks can say in their own defense is that their party periphery threatened to take the law into their own hands if the center did not order them to.

Ostensibly under the influence of this threat, Zinoviev began inciting murder in the districts [of Petrograd] and directly ordered the Kronstadt sailors to execute three hundred officers kept there (a most innocent bunch). According to the statement of the Petrograd Cheka itself, they executed eight hundred people. Then followed the order of Pokrovskii [commissar of internal affairs] about the obligatory taking of hostages, and executions rolled across the provinces. The overall number undoubtedly exceeds ten thousand people. As a general rule, Socialists were not executed, but cases of executions of our people, most often Socialist Revolutionaries, were registered in some places. Among our people, a worker from the Sestroretsk plant in Petrograd, Krakovskii (an Internationalist), who had been released from the Moscow prison at the demand of his entire plant, was executed. The local Cheka [*chrezvychaika*] seized him on the street and immediately shot him before the city Bolsheviks had a chance to interfere. They are all terribly depressed because Krakovskii enjoyed popularity and had good relations with many Bolsheviks.

In Rybinsk, as the Cheka itself admitted, they shot two of our men: Romanov and Levin (secretary of the Council of Trade Unions). According to our data, two others were shot as well. There was no charge of any "conspiracy" there; neither was there any popular movement. They were simply shot in cold blood as dangerous people. Even before that, two workers, Social Democrats, were executed in Vitebsk; one Social Democrat (Rapillo) [was executed] in Vologda and one in Nizhnii Novgorod (secretary of the party committee, Ridnek). [Ridnesk in original; all other sources, however, refer to Ridnek.] All were shot without any foundation. One can surmise that in the more out-of-the-way localities, there were many executions of inconspicuous party workers. The prisons are overflowing with our party members. Still in prison in Moscow are members of the

Central Committee: Iugov, Iakhontov, Troianovskii, G. Kuchin (Oranskii), in addition to Abramovich and those taken with him. [Rafail
Abramovich described his experience in prison in his letter "Ein Offener
Brief Aus dem Moskauer Gefaengnis," *Stimmen Aus Russland,* nos. 5–6
(15 October 1918, Stockholm):43–48.] Troianovskii and Kuchin have been
in prison for more than four months already. Also in prison are Aleksei and
Boris Malkin (brothers); a former officer, Stoilov; a former Geneva student, Kogan; an economist, G. Kipen; a former officer, I. Kushin (a secretary of the CC); a former American emigrant, Ravich [When M. Ravich
returned to Russia from the United States in 1917, he became secretary of
the Yaroslavl Menshevik organization and the editor of the *Trud i Bor'ba*
newspaper.]; the well-known P. N. Kolokol'nikov (who was arrested after
his speech at the Congress of Cooperatives where he had criticized Bolshevik policy on cooperatives); and others.

Among those arrested together with Abramovich in connection with
the Workers' Congress was a member of the Latvian CC [of the Socialist
Democratic party], Vetskaln, a personal friend of F. Platten [Fritz Platten,
secretary of the Swiss Socialist party during World War I and member of
the Zimmerwald group, was a close associate of Lenin and acted as an
intermediary in arranging Lenin's return to Russia through Germany in
1917.] and a former chairman of one of the carpenters' unions in Switzerland. He is in prison to this very day. In Saint Petersburg, an old
Menshevik, Nozar'ev; a cooperatives' worker, Breido; a worker, Panin;
and still other workers are in prison. In Nizhnii Novgorod, Perm, and other
provincial centers, all well-known party workers who had not gone into
hiding were arrested. In Moscow, the pattern of such arrests has been as
follows: after a long time we would succeed in transferring the cases to the
judicial authorities [from the Cheka], who would conclude that there was
no material for a trial. And then, as it used to be in the times of the
gendarmes [under the czarist regime], the accused would be "on the list of
the Cheka" [In 1918 that meant that the Cheka had exclusive control over
the life and death of those prisoners.] as they say. They could be kept
endlessly there unless the Cheka [in the original *chrezvychaika,* a pejora-
tive name for the Cheka] succeeded in having its idea approved that all
political opponents be sent to "concentration camps," that is, into new
prisons where, occasionally, the Cheka would execute hostages. [The official policy of taking hostages from among the "bourgeoisie" was adopted in
early September 1918 during the Red Terror campaign. In numerous cases
hostages were executed.]

3. As far as the general situation of the Soviet republic is concerned, it
is important to note that, in addition to a growing danger from the South, it
is rapidly moving toward financial bankruptcy. According to estimates for

the second half of 1918, the revenue is two and a half billion, the expenses are thirty-seven billion, and the annual deficit is about forty billion. That means that there will be unavoidable famine combined with the fuel supply catastrophy in both capitals. Industry is disappearing, and, to the extent that it is disappearing, an ever-larger number of Communists have to be placed in all kinds of offices. As a result, Soviet power is experiencing a bureaucratic flood, which it is trying in vain to contain. This flood completely paralyzes organizational work in economic and social spheres. The Bolsheviks themselves are trying to fight another very special ailment, the hypertrophy of the police apparatus. Its has become a force in its own right, suppressing other institutions of power. This may cause a split someday between our Robespierres and our Herbertists [followers of Jacques Rene Herbert during the French Revolution who were also called *enrage* for their violent and abusive attacks against the Girondists and against Robespierre.], the representatives of pure *Lumpenstvo* [from the German *Lumpen,* in other words, the epitome of mob rule].

We are following the German events with the utmost attention. Kautsky's brochure confirmed my fears that events there may produce manifestations of bolshevism in Germany as well in that the [German] revolution will develop against the background of a decay of economic forces, the simplification of economic functions in a society at war, and the role of the movement of soldiery and of the *Ungeschulten Massen* [unschooled masses] generally. What is Liebknecht's [Karl Liebknecht, a well-known left-wing German Social Democrat and an outspoken opponent of war, was in prison from May 1916 to October 1918 for his antiwar activities. When the German revolution broke out, Liebknecht founded the Spartakus group; after an unsuccessful uprising in January 1919, Liebknecht was killed.] mood like? And what is going on with the *Unabhaengigen?* The Moscow committee, the Central Committee, and the comrades in prison send greetings to Liebknecht. Because we are deprived of the telegraph (censors will not allow messages from our party, which has been "outlawed"), we are sending greetings by mail. Please tell him this, just in case. Maybe the censors intercept mail as well. To him, to Haase, and to Kautsky, convey our greetings. All our comrades are sending them to you.

I shake your hand warmly. If you know someone traveling here, please send new books. For example, we do not have here a posthumous book of Eckstein's [Gustav Eckstein, who died in 1916, was an Austrian Social Democrat and a journalist who wrote for leading Social Democratic journals—*Vorwarts, Kampf, Neue Zeit,* and others— in Germany and Austria. Most likely, Martov was requesting his brochure *Kapitalismus und Sozialismus. Gespraeche zur Einfuerung in die Grundbegriffe des Wissen-*

*schaftlichen Sozialismus.*], a collection of articles by F. Adler [Friedrich Adler, one of the leaders of the Austrian Social Democrats, was imprisoned during World War I for the assassination of the Austrian prime minister in 1916. For European Internationalists like Martov, Adler's name was a symbol of opposition to war. After the 1918 revolution, Adler and Otto Bauer were among Martov's closest associates in creating what became known as the Vienna International, which tried to steer a middle course between Lenin's Comintern and the old Second International. Apparently Martov requested Otto Bauer's brochure *Die Russische Revolution und das Europaeische Proletariat,* published in Vienna in 1917, which Bauer wrote after he returned from Russia where he had been a prisoner of war. Of all the European Social Democrats, Bauer was, perhaps, the closest politically to Martov. The text of this brochure is reprinted in Otto Bauer, *Werkausgabe* vol. 2, pp. 39–89.], or Otto Bauer's articles on Russia; these materials may be useful.

Greetings

Iu. Tsederbaum

If you send your letter with someone traveling here, you can send him to the address that the deliverer of this letter will give.

---

DOCUMENT SEVENTEEN

---

## Concerning the Situation in Russia and in the RSDWP

October 1918

Dear Comrades:
On behalf of Comrade Martov and other members of the Central Committee of the Social Democratic party of the Russian Socialist Federal

---

In Russian the title of this document is "O polozhenii v Rossii i v RSDRP"; the text, however, is in German, typewritten on poor-quality paper. Nicolaevsky Collection, series no. 6, box 5, folder 27.

Soviet Republic, I should inform you about the general situation in Russia, about the position of the Social Democratic party, and about the latest decisions of its Central Committee. The Central Committee has not been able to inform you regularly because the Bolsheviks have completely monopolized every means of communication with Europe.

Within the working class, the movement against bolshevism started as early as January 1918. On January 5 and 9, the first victims fell in Saint Petersburg and Moscow. The Bolsheviks emerged victorious from the struggle with the Constituent Assembly. The workers' soviets, to which all political authority was supposed to belong, gradually lost the trust of the broad masses and a large part of the proletariat. In February–March [1918] a strong movement for new elections to the soviets was already gaining momentum everywhere. In January, one of the largest plants in Russia (Sormovo, where eighteen thousand workers were employed) went on strike and demanded new elections and a transfer of state power to the Constituent Assembly. This movement was led primarily by the Social Democrats, and it grew stronger with every passing day. The government was reluctant to undertake new elections because the general political situation was unfavorable to it (due to the Brest peace treaty, the civil war with the Ukraine [On 3 December 1917, the Bolshevik government recognized Ukrainian independence and at the same time put forward several demands to the Ukrainian Rada (government). When these were rejected, the Bolshevik offensive on Kiev began, referred to here as civil war. At the end of January 1918 the Bolshevik troops entered Kiev, although not for long. The German troops shortly replaced them.], and the onset of famine partly caused by it). The government hoped that the situation would change and postponed new elections [to the soviets], under various pretexts, as long as possible. In April and May, however, the situation could no longer be kept under control. In many localities, workers took the matter of new elections into their own hands. The Social Democrats demanded that the Constituent Assembly be reconvened and that democratically elected local self-government be restored. The Bolsheviks demanded that the "dictatorship of the proletariat" be preserved.

Despite unequal conditions (we had almost no press and were not allowed to campaign freely anywhere), the Social Democrats won overwhelming majorities in the workers' soviets in almost every province where elections actually took place. This was the electoral result in Sormovo, Tver, Tula, Kaluga, Kolomna, Bryansk, Yaroslavl, Rybinsk, Vologda, Tsaritsyn, Vitebsk, Ryazan, and in many other places. At some big plants, the Bolsheviks could not get even a single candidate elected. These election returns threatened to lead to a total collapse of bolshevism from within. Then, however, those in power set to work. They launched a campaign of malicious lies, dreadful terror, and, finally, falsification of election returns. Opposition speakers were systematically arrested. These were their favorite means.

Particularly noteworthy is what happened during the elections in Saint Petersburg and Moscow. In Moscow, the Bolsheviks decided that there would be no secret ballot. For the most part, elections at the factories took place in the presence of armed Red Guards and under conditions of unheard-of and unprecedented pressure. One of their favorite tricks, used on numerous occasions, was the following: They would tell the workers, "If you elect the Mensheviks and Socialist Revolutionaries, we will shut down the plant." In places where this threat did not work, other means were used. For example, a meeting was called for the election of representatives [to the soviet] from the post office employees (ca. six thousand). About five thousand were present. When it became clear that the audience was unfriendly, Commissar Podbel'skii declared that no elections were going to take place that day. Most people left the meeting, and then, when only about a thousand people remained, all of a sudden elections were carried out. It was useless to protest to the Election Commission because the Bolsheviks had a majority in it. The decisions they made were, for example, that the newly elected Bolsheviks become members of the soviet, whereas representatives of the opposition, elected at that very same meeting, were not admitted. This is how the majority was secured in Moscow. In Saint Petersburg the matter was resolved more easily. The [Bolshevik] majority was assured from the very beginning by means of a system of artificial representation, [although] the big factories voted overwhelmingly for representatives of the opposition.

Contrary to the laws governing the status of the soviets, the opposition-led soviets were not recognized as legitimate by the government or by the old pre-election ECs of soviets. Moreover, the Bolsheviks did not dispute the fact that these soviets were elected in the proper manner. Nevertheless, they assaulted opposition soviets without hesitation. Lenin proclaimed the dictatorship of the conscious (?) proletariat. In place of the soviets, disbanded by force, commissars were appointed and extraordinary commissions [Chekas] were set up. To implement the dictatorship of the conscious proletariat, the entire opposition was thrown out of the Central Executive Committee of Soviets. The provinces followed this example shortly thereafter. Only the Bolsheviks and the Left SRs were to remain in the soviets.

The workers, however, were not going to take it anymore. Bloody clashes broke out in many cities (Sormovo, Tver, Yaroslavl, and others). Many old-time party members could not wait to join the Czechoslovaks [that is, to join the Czechoslovak detachments in the Volga-Urals area]. The official party leadership, however, rejected this kind of a solution to the problem, feeling that it was necessary to organize the proletariat outside the soviets. Workers' conferences, properly elected, sprang up in many cities. This was in July. Almost the entire working class supported these nonparty conferences [nonparty because they did not want to be affiliated with any political party, even though many individual workers who participated in these conferences belonged to political parties]. At that time, the Social Democrats had an enormous influence on the masses. The primary tasks of these conferences were, first and foremost, to improve the workers' economic position and to try to alleviate the hardships caused by famine. Out of separate local conferences, an All-Russian Workers' Congress would come into being. The government saw the danger coming and took appropriate measures. Never before, not even during the darkest days of czarism, was the proletariat subjected to such an attack as in July–August 1918. Several examples should illustrate what was going on.

In Nizhnii Novgorod and partly in Vladimir province, where more than 100,000 metal workers are employed, a [workers'] conference was summoned on the initiative of Sormovo representatives. The workers raised the necessary funds. The Bolsheviks campaigned everywhere against it. They argued that it was a counterrevolutionary undertaking. Despite enormous difficulties, two hundred representatives of 100,000 workers arrived in Sormovo. Then all hell broke loose. A state of siege was declared. The Red Guards, already drunk, kept all public buildings under surveillance. Despite this, workers' delegates managed to open the conference, thanks to the support of thousands of workers. Trying to occupy the auditorium, the Red Guards began to shoot. This failed to stop those assembled there and bound them even more closely together. The Red Guards waited until the break, and when the delegates left the auditorium, they pursued the crowds into the streets. Then the Red Guards went on a rampage in the workers' neighborhoods. This was only the beginning. They then opened fire on people in the streets. (It was Sunday. It is important to note that only workers live in Sormovo.) The result was that two [The text is illegible here. It could mean two, or three, or eight.] were killed, nine wounded, and several dozen lightly wounded. On the next day, however, the conference assembled again and decided to call a strike. Never before was there a strike with such worker response. Everything stood still.

This was the beginning of a powerful wave of strikes that rolled across almost all of central Russia. Sparked originally by economic difficulties, the strikes acquired an explicitly political character. It was a workers' movement that, because of the bloody repressions, merged with the peasant movement and with the movement of Czechoslovaks. In some places armed uprisings broke out. Everywhere there were shootings (Moscow, Tver, Kaluga, Bryansk). Hundreds were shot, thousands were arrested.

Among them were members of the CC [Central Committee]: Abramovich, Troianovskii, Kuchin, Smirnov, Chirkin, Alter, Kipen, and others. Most of them are still in prison at the present time, October 12, the day of my departure. Martov, Dan, and others had to go into hiding. Every passing day brought escalating terror. Social Democratic organizations were destroyed. Their leaders were exiled, arrested, or shot and killed (like Comrade Ridnek, the secretary of the Nizhnii Novgorod organization). The Bolshevik victory was complete. The proletariat and its party ceased to exist. Most workers left their place of residence [The flight of workers from Petrograd was not always voluntary. Many workers of the Obukhov plant had to leave after Bolshevik authorities shut down their plant. Many locked-out workers went to the Urals, hoping to find employment there.] and migrated to the countryside. Industry is paralyzed. A dictatorship has been imposed on the proletariat.

The peasants are not willing to put up with requisitioning. They sought, where it was possible, to join the Czechoslovaks; where it was not possible they left their households, organized themselves in detachments, and started a peasant war against the Bolsheviks. This war is raging to this very day. The bourgeoisie fled to the Ukraine because famine was getting worse and worse. The class food rations do not make any difference anymore because, be it the first or the fourth category, one does not get anything anyway. A pound of bread costs 12 to 14 rubles in Moscow, and a pound of butter, 75 or 100 rubles.

The bourgeoisie set its hopes on the Czechoslovak movement, which was truly democratic in the beginning. In the course of time, though, right-wing elements began to acquire more and more influence. Certain tensions developed between separate regional governments. The Samara government [the Socialist Revolutionary–led government of the Committee of the Members of the Constituent Assembly] is democratic and enjoys the workers' and peasants' support, whereas the provisional government of Siberia is reactionary at this time. The Social Democratic party, or at least an overwhelming majority of it, and its Central Committee did not join this movement. Comrade Maiskii joined the Samara government without the knowledge of the party leadership. [I. Maiskii was a member of the Menshevik CC, who, along with Liber and others, disagreed with Martov's policy, which repudiated armed struggle against bolshevism. Maiskii crossed the front line and on arriving in Samara became a minister of labor in the Socialist Revolutionary–led government.] The CC sent several authorized representatives to collect information in Samara and Siberia. [Boris Nicolaevsky was one of those representatives. His account of the situation under the Whites shaped Social Democratic party policy to a considerable extent in regard to the Whites.] Part of the right wing within the CC did not want to accept this political course of the majority. They founded the Union of Regeneration of Russia [The full name of this factional grouping within the Menshevik party was the Committee of Active Struggle for the Regeneration of Russia. See document 16.] and, together with the SRs, declared the struggle against the Bolsheviks to be legitimate, even with the help of the Entente [Allies: British, American, French, Czech] troops; they published a declaration against the neutral policy of the Central Committee. [This policy of Martov's in the summer of 1918 was neutral in the war between the Bolshevik government controlling the central Russian provinces and the Socialist Revolutionary government controlling the provinces on the Volga and the Urals. Martov chose neutrality because he could not, and the majority of Mensheviks would not, support the Bolsheviks in their struggle against the Socialist Revolutionaries. Neither could Martov bring himself to side with the Socialist Revolutionaries, who were in open rebellion against the Bolsheviks. Many other Mensheviks did, which brought about a de facto split in Menshevik ranks.] In turn the CC responded that as soon as the founders of the union start implementing their decisions, they will cease to be members of the party. The right wing is led by Liber, Kolokol'nikov, Potresov, Levitskii, and others. Nevertheless, nowhere did it come to an open confrontation between factions. This was the situation in the party at the end of August. Currently, the situation may have changed considerably, but there is no definite news about it.

After the attempted assassination of Lenin, which our party disapproved of, a new wave of political terror reached gigantic proportions. Almost all party comrades who had been in any way known for their political activity had to flee or go into hiding. Even the optimists no longer believed that it was possible to coexist with the Bolsheviks. The destruction of industry was almost complete. Suffice it to say that the population of Moscow, of 2.5 million in April 1918, sank to 800,000 by September. In Petrograd the situation is much worse. At present (October 12) the situation is as follows:

1. Workers' soviets do not exist anymore anywhere.
2. New elections are not allowed under any circumstances.
3. The opposition soviets have been replaced by appointed commissars.
4. The opposition parties have been expelled from the soviets.
5. In the provinces, the plenary sessions of the Bolshevik Soviets are almost never convened, and in the capitals they are only a rubber stamp.
6. The working class is totally decimated.
7. Civil liberties do not exist anymore; boundless terror reigns instead.

8. Peasants are set against the Bolsheviks.
9. An attempt to establish committees of the poor in the countryside has failed.
10. The government maintains itself in power by the forces of the Red Guards only. To be sure, opposition is appearing in their ranks as well.
11. Famine reigns in the highest degree.
12. The government is de facto in the hands of the Military Council and the Cheka.

In regard to domestic policy, the SD party demands that the Constituent Assembly be reconvened. The Constituent Assembly may be able to unite Russia and should include representatives from all parts of Russia, provided the population in these areas is not opposed to participating in an all-Russian constituent assembly. The party also demands that local self-government be restored. These are our old demands. In regard to foreign policy, the party demands that the troops of the Entente be withdrawn from Russia. The party rejects any interference by the Allies into Russian affairs.

This was the political platform of the party before the German revolution. What the position of the party is now, I do not know. In any case it was the explicit wish of the Central Committee to establish contact with the Independents [the Independent Social Democratic party of Germany].

Unfortunately, Comrade Menders' departure came up unexpectedly, and I could not use all of the available material. I would like to apologize for the composition of this letter and remain available for additional information,

M. GUREWITSCH

# New Course and New Repressions
## *(December 1918–September 1919)*

## New Course in Soviet Russia
## (letters from Russia)

February 1919

Dear Comrades:

During the last two months [December 1918, January 1919], Soviet power has clearly been trying to embark on the path of reforms in its domestic policy. A whole series of factors have played a role in this sudden change. It seems that the experience of carrying through the policy of Red Terror to its logical end had the most direct effect on this turnaround in attitude. When "up there" they found out how local authorities in the provinces (including the former capital, now Zinoviev's patrimony) applied directives from the center on summary justice in regard to "counterrevolutionaries" and on taking hostages, even the fearless people's commissars were embarrassed. In addition, they must have learned from the reports of Rakovskii, Ioffe, and other diplomatic representatives what indignation this bloody bacchanalia caused among the working masses abroad.

In the atmosphere of bloody fumes, the weeds of the Soviet secret police began to bloom. The Cheka [*chrezvychaiki*] had been called upon to save the Soviet fatherland. And, as all saviors do, they began to turn into sovereigns, in accordance with age-old customs [in Russian, *spasiteli, poveliteli*]. By the time of the anniversary of the October Revolution, the civil and military bureaucracy had succeeded in devouring "All Power to the Soviets." This bureaucracy saw in turn that its power was being usurped by the autocrats from Lubyanka [the address of the Cheka in Moscow]. The expropriators are being expropriated. [This expression was used in Marxist literature in Russia for two ideas. The first was a Marxist concept that the capitalist class, that is, those who expropriate the surplus value from the workers, must be expropriated and that the means of production should be taken over by the dictatorship of the proletariat over the bourgeoisie. The second was more ironic in regard to Bolshevik expropriations, namely, bank robberies after 1905. Here Martov uses this expression sarcastically, for now the Bolsheviks' power is expropriated by their own political police, the Cheka.] From the Constituent Assembly to the soviets, from

---

This letter was published in a Social Democratic journal in Kharkov, *Mysl'*, nos. 1–2 (February 1919), now a bibliographic rarity. Hoover Institution Library.

the soviets to the commissars, from the commissars to the Cheka—this is the constitutional evolution of Soviet Russia during the last year. The situation was becoming dangerous for Soviet power itself. The "class self-consciousness" of the Cheka began to reach monumental proportions. The *Courier of the Extraordinary Commissions* openly argued that the destruction of the bourgeois order must be the mission of the revolutionary police. The dictatorship of the Cheka was defended without the slightest embarrassment. The question as to whether torture was useful was debated as easily as if the editors of this periodical were ancient Persians or Chinese.

At one of the private banquets celebrating the October anniversary, one important functionary exclaimed in his excitement, as I was told the other day: "I can do anything. If I please I can put horses into the Arts theater." This supreme achievement that excites the imagination of some Soviet bureaucrats was in fact surpassed in reality by the functionaries of the Cheka. "If we so please," a Cheka agent openly said, "*we can shoot even the Communists.*" Yes indeed, there were cases when they did just that. In several places, primarily at the front, even members of the ruling party experienced the horror of summary justice. Terror began to effect the terrorizers, which necessarily caused an instinctive and protective reaction.

Bolshevik slang reflects the new thinking by referring to the extraordinary commissions [*chrezvychaiki*] as excessively extraordinary commissions [*cherezchurki*]. But the man in the street finds the morbid humor of this pun extraordinarily stale. In Moscow the fateful letters Ve-Che-Ka (the All-Russian Extraordinary Commission) are deciphered as [*Vek Cheloveka Korotok* in Russian] "The Life of a Man Is Short." These letters glitter in lights over the "house of sighs," as it is called on the Grand Lubyanka street, over the building of a former insurance company, Anchor.

The beginning of the revolution in Germany was the second factor that induced Soviet power to steer the course of its policy a little bit to the right. The very necessity of appearing in the international arena in the role of not only the enemy of the old order but also as an ally of new Germany, new Austria, and so on compels the Soviets to "wash up" and wash some stains off their hands. Not without reason did K. Radek argue in the CEC that the expulsion of the Mensheviks had to be rescinded, that this measure would pull the rug out from under the feet of the Ebert-Hasse government, which would not be able to argue that only a part of the entire proletariat it was in power in Soviet Russia. Not without reason, another Bolshevik, L. Sosnovskii, pointed out in his interview to the newspaper *Vooruzhennyi Narod* [Armed People] that the names of Abramovich, Dan, and Martov are known in Europe as the names of Socialists and that therefore it was necessary to give amnesty to the party to which these people belong. Not without reason did Lenin himself finally, in his address to the Communists on November 27, cite from a letter of Friedrich Adler, who found it impossible to write to Lenin about anything else but about the necessity of freeing the arrested Mensheviks from prison. This speech of Lenin's became a kind of program for the new course.

The third cause for the turnabout in domestic policy was the clear and unequivocal bankruptcy of Left Communist policy, which had been based on the committees of the poor and a "crusade" against the countryside. As a result of this policy, grain deliveries ceased almost completely, and widespread and bitter peasant rebellions embraced about sixty *uezd* in the following provinces: Tver, Yaroslavl, Kostroma, Vladimir, Kazan, Penza, Moscow, Tula, Voronezh, Ryazan, Kaluga, Vitebsk, Smolensk, and Tambov. Moreover, draft into the Red Army in the countryside proved to be absolutely impossible because of the overall [*pogolovnaia*] hostility of the rural population. It was then that serious doubts arose in the Bolshevik ranks about the feasibility of proceeding in the chosen direction. On top of all this, a serious crisis with fuel and food supply reached such proportions by the beginning of winter that no doubts were left about the closeness of the catastrophe. And, finally, an external danger loomed on the horizon. An international punitive expedition, which was being prepared by the French and the British, was acquiring evermore ominous contours. That is why, at the time of the first anniversary of the Soviet republic, we were witnessing an unheard-of phenomenon—a liberal current in bolshevism.

## REFORMIST TENDENCIES IN POLITICS

On the occasion of the October anniversary, the CEC announced an amnesty. It served as a herald of Bolshevik reforms. The amnesty itself, however, does not belong to those acts of legislative creativity that can make Soviet power proud. Composed in deliberately vague and ambiguous language, it was full of all kinds of "tricks" that gave local authorities vast possibilities for interpretation. As could be expected, its implementation immediately ran into resistance of the almighty bureaucracy. Even in Moscow, the resourceful Krylenko tried to withhold its application to the case of R. Abramovich, A. Smirnov, and others in the workers' congress case. [On 24 July representatives of workers' assemblies were arrested in Moscow during a preparatory meeting for a workers' congress. See document 16.] It is quite likely that the whole business of amnesty was conceived as a way to close this case "decently."

Nevertheless, in Moscow, Social Democrats were freed as a general rule. (Today, Beliankin from Vologda and Voronov from Smolensk are still in prison.) They have also freed Berg, Feit, Disler, and Iliashevich. [These are all well-known Socialist Revolutionary politicians: E. Berg, chairman of the Petrograd Workers' Assembly, and Disler, a member of the Socialist Revolutionaries faction in the Central Executive Committee, were taken hostage by the Bolsheviks on 14 June 1918 when the opposition parties were expelled from the committee.] But they did not free Aleksinskii [G. A. Aleksinskii was an old Social Democrat and a supporter of the Plekhanov group, Edinstvo, in 1918] and Rudneva [The husband of Rudneva, V. V. Rudnev, was a member of the Party of Socialist Revolutionaries and the chairman of the city duma in Moscow in 1917.], even though both are ill. (She was arrested as a "hostage" for her absent husband.) Beyond Moscow, the amnesty is applied rather tightly. The local Chekas do not want to release their captives. Apparently they reckon that this will not anger their superiors that much. In Saratov, the amnesty has not been applied at all. In Petrograd, we managed to set free Comrade M. Nazar'ev, a member of our committee, with great difficulty. He was arrested when they shut down the *Rabochii Internatsional* [Workers' International]. Likewise, an old Social Democrat, Tessler, a participant in the first party congress, has not been freed.

The "unloading of prisons," as they say here, and the release of prisoners seized by the Cheka "for nothing," those thousands of "politicals" [that is, political prisoners] unaffiliated with any party, are taking place very slowly. And sometimes it is only the epidemic of typhus that accelerates the "unloading." It is likely that the main objective of the authors of the amnesty was to curtail the epidemic. The amnesty is proceeding slowly despite the fact that the vice-chairman of the Moscow Revolutionary Tribunal, Diakonov, published a colorful article in *Izvestiia,* full of indignation and sincerity, entitled "At the Cemetery of the Living." He described the horrible conditions in undoubtedly one of the best of Moscow's prisons (Taganskaia jail). As a result of the amnesty, however, Mariia Spiridonova and Sablin (the case of the Left SRs) have been freed, after they had been convicted [in the so-called Left SR uprising on 6 July 1918].

The next step along the lines of reform was a change in attitude toward the oppositional Socialist parties, primarily toward the Social Democrats. The decree that had expelled the Mensheviks from the CEC was rescinded. A French proverb says, when they need to kill a dog, they call it mad. It works the other way around too, though. At first, when they wanted to expel the Mensheviks, Bolshevik leaders saw a "Menshevik" hand in all "White Guard" conspiracies. At that time, neither the explicit decisions of the May party conference nor the expulsion from the party of the Yaroslavl insurgents [During the anti-Bolshevik uprising in Yaroslavl in July 1918, a group of workers led by SDs joined the insurgents and fought the Bolsheviks. The Menshevik CC expelled them from the party because it opposed armed struggle with the Bolsheviks.] were considered adequate evidence against enlisting the party in the ranks of counterrevolution. Now, on the other hand, they are looking for new "accents" in resolutions of our CC that would make it possible to grant the party legitimacy on this side of the barricade. In a word, the Mensheviks are described as an almost loyal party now. Here in Moscow the authorities do not put obstacles in the way of our meetings and lectures, and, finally, they issued a permit for publication of a newspaper [*Vsegda Vpered,* which was closed after fourteen issues].

This is not freedom of the press yet. This is not freedom of assembly and association either. This is only an exception from the overall lack of freedom. But at the same time, this is a breach in the solid wall of silence in effect since June [In June 1918, most of the remaining non-Bolshevik press was shut down. For details, see document 15.]. Obviously, the Bolsheviks use this "exception" for their own purposes. For example, the Mensheviks organized a rally on the occasion of the German revolution. The next day, "Rosta" [Russian Telegraph Agency] informed Russia and Europe that the Menshevik speakers at that rally supposedly appealed to support "Soviet power." What really happened was that the Bolsheviks came to the rally to "derange" it and made a stormy scandal when it was pronounced that the Constituent Assembly must be reconvened. The next day, they wrote in the papers that the Mensheviks failed their loyalty test and did not deserve amnesty.

Our relative well-being in Moscow does not extend to the provinces, however. In Petrograd, our Karl Marx club, the only auditorium where our comrades could meet, was closed and sealed after the beginning of the "new era." They would not even discuss the question of unsealing it or granting a permit for a newspaper. In Vitebsk, Abramovich was allowed to give a lecture, but in Smolensk they found it dangerous and did not allow it. Only in Tula, during the campaign of new elections to the soviet, did they grant our party freedom of campaigning, but did not allow us to resume publication of our party paper. In many provincial capitals and *uezd* towns the party continues to be expelled from the soviets. Another manifestation of the "new trends" is a piece of news, just received, that in Minsk, on the entry of Soviet troops there, Radek and Rakovskii organized a rally of Social Democrats, the [Jewish] Bund, Socialist Revolutionaries, and Paoley Tsion [a Jewish religious party]. All these parties were also allowed to publish newspapers.

The reformers have shown the greatest decisiveness, however, on the question of the status of the Cheka. The danger of this police for Soviet order has become very acute. The Bolsheviks, of course, did not raise the prospect of abolishing this shameful institution and replacing it with foundations of rule of law and independent courts. The matter boiled down to curbing the prerogatives of the Cheka in the dispensing of the lives and property of Soviet citizens and to establishing control over the Cheka. A few tangible things have been accomplished in this regard. A particularly hard blow for the Cheka was the introduction of "habeas corpus" for Soviet employees, specialists, and technicians. The Cheka was prohibited from arresting them without the consent of a corresponding hierarchy. Where there is an urgent need to make an arrest, the Cheka is obliged to provide proof of this to the hierarchy (an economic department, for example) within forty-eight hours. The same decree empowers the presidiums of the soviets, trade unions, and Communist party organizations to free persons arrested by the Cheka and place them under their trusteeship.

This idea is exactly what one would expect from the minds of bureaucrats. They want to guard from police arbitrariness not all citizens, but only those who are particularly useful for the economy and the state machine. This decree was precipitated by the fact that the Cheka had decimated, by arrests, an expedition ready to set out for Turkistan to save cotton production there. Of course there were members in the expedition who belonged to "counterrevolutionary" parties. It is a sign of the times that the decree was promulgated and that one can already sense it in undisguised distrust of the Cheka. It is unlikely that the Cheka is going to resign itself to this, although they ceased publishing their scandalous journal. They are trying to preserve the terrorist regime in all respects.

In its struggle against "liberalism" at the top, the Cheka can count on the numerous Soviet bureaucrats because the government's reformist pangs have caused great alarm within the bureaucracy about the security of their warm places and the admissibility of practicing their uncontrollable dictatorship over the common folk. Lenin and Zinoviev are compelled to defend the policy of compromise at the meetings of Communists. The Soviet bureaucracy in the provinces simply ignores "liberal" directives from the center. It seems that, other than in Tula, nowhere have they fulfilled the decree on returning the Mensheviks to the soviets. The liberal gestures of Rakovskii and Radek in Belorussia have caused indignation on the part of bureaucrats returning there from Smolensk and Vitebsk, where they have been sitting with nothing to do during the German occupation [of Belorussia]. These people intend to make sure that the re-establishment of "Soviet power" in Belorussia is not accompanied by a rejection of requisitions, indemnities [on bourgeoisie], "nationalizations" of a certain kind, and Red Terror, which had been flourishing there before the arrival of the Germans.

## ECONOMIC REFORMS

Economic reforms are likely to encounter no less vigorous resistance. One of the most important of these reforms was the actual abolition of the committees of the poor. The government made the decision to rely on middle peasants instead. The local authorities were ordered not to refer to them as "kulaks" anymore. The dictatorship of committees of the poor has fed the personal needs of all kinds of societal dregs and bureaucrats, and it is therefore unlikely that they will abandon their position without a fight. Nonetheless, the rejection of the committees of the poor is in principle of utmost importance because it must lead to the rejection of the goal to "build socialism immediately." For who would doubt that a reconciliation with the peasantry is possible only if the inviolability of individual economy is guaranteed. In a country like Russia the nature of the peasant economy determines the general character of the national economy. It is not accidental that, simultaneously with the abolition of the committees of the poor, the Commissariat of Agriculture abolished the "agricultural communes," those helpless associations of negligent peasants with whose help they hoped to squeeze out individual farming and to implant "socialism" in the countryside. Instead of these communes, they are now creating "state estates" to save the most profitable land from partition. They will be run by managers appointed by the commissariat. It is widely known that Lenin has demanded that experienced agricultural specialists who know how to manage these estates be cherished as the apple of his eye.

A radical change in food supply policy, adopted on December 12, will no doubt also encounter considerable opposition. Workers' organizations and trade unions are now allowed to purchase nonrationed food items freely and on a broad scale. It was decided to include fat and meat in the nonrationed category. Free trade with these products has been allowed to private individuals, and antiprofiteer detachments have been removed. The fact that these steps have been taken attests to the bankruptcy of the entire food supply system. Therefore, the so-called speculation, that is, trade with food products, is permitted again (with certain guarantees against real speculation). Trade capital is allowed to circulate freely. But most important, the Communist ideal of a state—where the state as a sole monopoly delivers everything (all items of consumption) to its citizens—is now recognized as unrealizable. And this is even though virtually yesterday it was still proclaimed that all internal trade was nationalized and the "naturalization" of wages was put on the agenda. One cannot demand a better testimony to the bankruptcy of the entire economic policy. There cannot be any doubt that this breach in [Communist] policy will not be filled.

The new course signifies a heavy blow to Soviet bureaucrats, whose very existence is linked to the Arakcheev-type pseudo-socialism and who will try to paralyze this policy. This will be all the easier for them because the leaders of Soviet Russia have not yet grasped the idea that in food supply and in peasant questions one cannot simply pour new wine into old barrels. Even while altering the course of their policy under the pressure of insurmountable difficulties, they do not consider changing their Jacobin bureaucratic methods. It is out of the question for them to put the new policy on the tracks of independent activity by the society. They still want to conduct all the reforms by state authority [*vlast'*], magnanimous and well-wishing. That is why simultaneously with the introduction of reforms, they continue with the destruction of free societal organizations.

For example, because of the bankruptcy of the state food supply agencies, the workers' consumer cooperatives and public consumer cooperatives must now carry almost the entire burden of regularly functioning food supply for the population. And instead of supporting these cooperatives, they have subordinated workers' cooperatives to the Food Supply Commissariat. And they have told public consumer cooperatives that these would not be disbanded if two-thirds of the seats on their managerial boards would be reserved for the Communists. All this is done at a time when Lenin is making "liberal" speeches about the unavoidable necessity of finding an "agreement with the cooperatives" because they are the representatives of the "petite bourgeoisie." They want to use the apparatus of these associations to fulfill functions that the bureaucratic machine was incapable of. In the process, they bureaucratize this apparatus and destroy its very soul—freedom and independence from state patronage. With one hand they are trying to broaden the social base of Soviet power, but with the other hand they continue their efforts to undermine democratic forces that should have been components in that broadened base. At a time when a debate at the top of Soviet hierarchy is beginning on whether the trade unions should regain their independence from state power, other workers' organizations, and no less important ones like the mutual insurance boards, are practically liquidated because all their functions have been transferred to the incompetent Social Security Commissariat.

This fundamental contradiction, unless it is resolved by an internal crisis within the Communist party itself [The crisis within the Communist party over trade unions broke out in the winter of 1920–1921.], makes all the reformist attempts doomed in advance. A part of the Communist party has to be ready to reconsider the very foundations of its party program.

There are no signs of such a crisis yet. Nevertheless, this does not deprive the new course of great significance as a symptom. The very fact that the Bolshevik regime is looking for ways to reform itself is additional evidence that not everything is lost for the Russian Revolution and that there may still be a way out other than capitulation to domestic and external counter-revolution and stagnation in the kingdom of utopia.

L. MARTOV

---

## DOCUMENT NINETEEN

---

## News from Russia

[This report has no date; from the contents, however, it is clear that it was written in the beginning of 1919, most likely in February.]

Dear Comrades:

The external and internal situation of Russia is much more favorable now than ever before. It is not clear, however, whether there are internal forces in Russia capable of taking advantage of this favorable situation [the defeat of Germany in the war and the ebbing of Red Terror by the end of 1918]. It is hard to give an affirmative answer to this question now. Russia's internal forces are melting away. They are exhausted, and the population in big cities is decreasing. The last factories are grinding to a halt, and the proletariat is withering away. Transport is getting worse every day. Economic decay worries the ruling circles more than anything else now. The tone of Soviet press, far from exultant, is rather serious and prone to self-flagellation. In government circles there was a struggle between two currents at one time, but the upper hand was gained by the moderates. A leading role among them is played by L. B. Krasin, the chief of Red Army supplies and a people's commissar for trade and industry.

In foreign policy the moderates' victory was manifested by Chicherin's note to the Allies confirming the Soviet government's acceptance of the

---

It is not indicated to whom this report was addressed. Yet it is clear that it was intended for a foreign audience. Nicolaevsky Collection, series no. 6, box 5, folder 30.

invitation to Prinkipo Island. [The conference at Prinkipo Island was to begin on 15 February 1919. The Allies invited all belligerent parties in the Russian Civil War to take part. General Denikin and Admiral Kolchak, counting on a military solution, refused to participate in any talks with the Bolsheviks. The Bolsheviks accepted the invitation on the condition that the Allies withdraw their troops from Russia before the conference.] In domestic policy the moderates scored a major victory when the nationalizations and socializations were abandoned in favor of engaging private enterprise. For example, at the end of December [1918], a concession was granted for the use of the North Arctic route and a special decree permitted private entrepreneurship in the timber industry. In mid-January, the CEC adopted a new plan for food supply that essentially boils down to the following: The state monopoly in food supply embraces procurement of bread, sugar, salt, oils, meat, and fish. All other commodities are declared free. [What is meant is that trade with other food commodities was legalized.] Requisitions of all nonmonopoly commodities are strictly forbidden. All fixed prices on nonmonopoly commodities have been abolished. Cooperatives are temporarily allowed to procure meat and fish. They will not be hampered in their activity, and special commissars will be appointed to protect them from the arbitrariness of local soviets. Obviously, under the weight of need, the policy of the Soviet government toward cooperatives has changed. It used to treat them with suspicion and to persecute them; now it is trying to protect and help them.

Among the opposition parties of Soviet Russia, the Social Democrat Mensheviks and Socialist Revolutionaries display some activity. The dominant current among the Mensheviks is the one led by Martov. They regard conspiracies and armed struggle against the Bolsheviks as inadmissible. At the same time, however, they want to organize mass working-class struggle against the ruling Bolsheviks by means customary to Social Democrats, that is, by systematic campaigning and worker organizing. That is why the Mensheviks are so categorically opposed to Allied interference in Russian affairs. They also oppose those Russian parties and societal groups who cherish hopes of defeating bolshevism by relying on the might of the Allies. The Mensheviks expect that the collapse of bolshevism will come about as a result of disillusionment among the broad workers' masses. The Mensheviks value the soviets as workers' organizations, and they participate in them at present in order to campaign for their program and to expose the wrongdoings of Soviet authorities.

The Menshevik point of view has gained acceptance among the Socialist Revolutionaries. A delegation of Constituent Assembly members arrived in Moscow from the Urals and published a declaration in the official Bolshevik paper, *Izvestiia*. (There are no non-Bolshevik papers in Moscow.

Only at the beginning of February did a Menshevik paper, *Vsegda Vpered,* begin to come out.) This declaration recognizes that it is imperative to struggle against Allied intervention and against those Russian social forces that are supported by the Allies [the Whites]. All reports to the effect that some kind of an agreement was reached between the Bolsheviks, Mensheviks, and SRs are fictitious and do not in any way correspond to reality. [The Bolsheviks used the partial legalization of the Mensheviks and SRs described by Martov (document 18) for propaganda abroad. They tried to create an impression that a multiparty, united front had formed against the Whites. In fact, as many documents attest, this legalization was short-lived and never went further than the toleration of one newspaper in one city for several weeks.] Up to the present day, the Bolsheviks have ruled Russia alone, and they have no intention of sharing power with any other political parties.

---

DOCUMENT TWENTY

---

## Brief Notes from Local SD Organizations

February 1919

### COMMUNISTS IN KOZLOV AND
### THE LEGALIZATION OF THE SD PARTY

The following is a response of the Communists in the town of Kozlov to the request of the Social Democrats that their party be legalized in accordance with the decree of the CEC of December 1918.

To the Initiative Group of the SDs in Kozlov, Tambov Province

Comrade Vainer:
In view of the fact that the Social Democratic party in Kozlov *uezd* has not sufficiently displayed complete loyalty to Soviet power and because its

---

*Vsegda Vpered,* no. 15 (25 February 1919, Moscow), p. 2.

composition is dangerous for the planned activity of the soviet, the Executive Committee refuses to legalize the party at present.

signed: Chairman
Secretary

## FREEDOM OF ASSEMBLY, KOLOMNA
### (BY TELEGRAPH FROM OUR CORRESPONDENT)
[*Vsegda Vpered,* no. 4 (11 February 1919, Moscow), p. 2.]

Local authorities prohibit lectures and meetings, and refuse permits for office space. In case of noncompliance they threaten with arrests. Help! Bring it to the knowledge of the CEC.

Kolomna Organization of the RSDWP

## TRADE UNIONS AS PUNITIVE INSTITUTIONS, MOSCOW
[*Vsegda Vpered,* no. 9 (18 February 1919, Moscow), p. 1.]

At the rally of the Moscow trade union of the rubber industry on February 3, this year, Comrade Al'brekhov delivered a report on a strike that took place at the Bogatyr rubber factory. The trade union resolved,

> Taking into account that the strike was caused by the agitation of all kinds of counterrevolutionary elements (this is their old song about instigators [author's comment]) who undermine the work of Soviet power in this entire industry, and by the demands of workers from various workshops to increase wages, the trade union resolves to close down the factory.

### RALLIES AND MEETINGS

On January 22, Wednesday, a huge workers' rally took place in the Lefortovo-Blagushinskii club. The main topic was The Current Moment. There were workers from Gnom factory and from other enterprises. Mariia Spiridonova [As the leader of the Left SR party, she was released from prison in the spirit of "liberalization" and resumed political activity. In February 1919, however, she was arrested again.] was the main speaker. Her speech lasted two hours. She gave very rich material about the activities of various commissars and punitive expeditions to the countryside. She cited examples of how peasants were harnessed instead of horses to the commissar's carriage, of ferocious executions, and so on. [The examples mentioned here were included in a remarkable document, *An Open Letter to the Bolshevik CC,* which Spiridonova and the Left Socialist Revolutionary Central Committee sent to the Bolshevik government. The letter was published in a small edition in January 1919 by the Left SRs (Hoover Institution Library). In that letter Spiridonova cited extensively from the letters she had received from peasants about the atrocities of local Communist authorities. It was a matter not only of brutal confiscations and requisitions, but also of the unrestrained arbitrariness and cruelty of Communist agents, whom the peasants compared to an old *barin* (master) from the times of serfdom.] From the Social Democrats, Comrade Shleifer spoke. [This is the same I. I. Shleifer who was elected chairman of the city soviet in Yaroslavl in April 1918, when the Menshevik/SR bloc won elections to the city soviet. After elections, the soviet was immediately disbanded. See document 8.]

### IN SOVIET RUSSIA; SAVAGES, OREL (BY TELEPHONE FROM OUR CORRESPONDENT) [*Vsegda Vpered,* no. 3 (6 February 1919, Moscow).]

*Izvestiia* of the Orel soviet on January 31 published the following information on the collection of the extraordinary tax in the village of Stepanovka, in the Orel *uezd:*

There were cases when those who failed to pay the tax were led outside into the frost naked. Then they were laid down on the snow, covered with snow, and two rifles were put on their shoulders. They were also kept in cold, moist basements for several hours on end, naked and hungry. Then they were beaten with ramrods.

## DOCUMENT TWENTY-ONE

## Around the Bryansk Region

January 1919

Dear Comrades:

Elections to the city soviet took place around December 20 [1918] in Bezhitsa. Seventeen Mensheviks, twenty-three Communists, and eight Left SRs were elected. The Right SRs were not able to take part in the elections. For all those familiar with the mood of workers in Bezhitsa in the not-too-distant past, these results are somewhat unexpected.

From December 1917 to the period of Red Terror [fall 1918], the Bolsheviks and Left SRs had been getting an absolutely insignificant number of votes in all elections. As a result, even the authorities in the capitals were seriously alarmed by the continued existence of this island of democracy. On August 17, last year, they "corrected" the "imperfections" of elections with the help of the Iron Detachment [a military unit]. One should add that the elections had been conducted in strict accordance with the Soviet constitution. The Bolsheviks disbanded the newly elected soviet and appointed the "revolutionary city soviet" consisting only of Communists, who had been so diligently falling flat in all the previous elections. At the same time they started strangling all political parties and unleashed terror against the population. All civil liberties were abrogated at once. The Mensheviks and SRs were compelled to cease all political activity. Some politicians had to leave the area.

When the discontented workers put forward their demands, they received a very cynical answer. For example, at one rally workers expressed their dissatisfaction with the lack of food. The chairman of the revolutionary soviet took the floor and addressed the workers with these words: "Who said there's too little bread? Come on out here! We still have Romanov's hotels [prisons], two of them right here. And those who still find it ain't enough, well then, we'll put those against the wall [execute them]." The Bolsheviks resort to threats of throwing workers in jail [*katalazhka*] (the cold room), right and left, over the most trivial things. Even children playing in the streets do not escape this.

It is not surprising that in these conditions there was no campaigning other than by the Communists before the new elections to the soviets. The

*Vsegda Vpered* no.2 (29 January 1919, Moscow) p. 4.

returns, indicated above, have been obtained in conditions of unheard-of voter absenteeism, intimidation of workers, and boycott of elections by the SRs. The spirit of the Bolshevik spring [a short-lived policy to tolerate opposition parties in the spring of 1919] did not affect the Communists in Bezhitsa. They tirelessly repeat the rudiments once learned, that every-thing non-Communist is counterrevolutionary. The Mensheviks, who con-stitute 35 percent of the soviet now, were not admitted, not one of them, to membership in the Executive Committee. In connection with the latest party conference [Menshevik party conference of December 1918–January 1919], there is a noticeable livening up among the Social Democrats. After a long silence they plan to hold several public lectures in the coming days on the current situation.

The situation in neighboring Bryansk is approximately the same. At the meeting of the cooperatives' employees, a Communist, Morozov, is-sued an order that only the Communists should be elected to the manage-ment board. He shouted, "Whoever is going to vote against this, I'll shoot at once!" Nevertheless, during the last few days, some Communists have begun to come to their senses.

On January 9 [1919] a meeting of RSDWP activists took place. Reports on the party conference were delivered, and a resolution was accepted that stated that the party policy adopted at the party conference was the only correct one at present. Therefore, the Bryansk organization of the RSDWP will devote all its energy to implementing these decisions right away and will start campaigning for party policy among the workers. Unfortunately, it is almost impossible to find an auditorium for a meeting in the city because they are all being used for the Red Army soldiers' daily cinemas and dances.

At the latest elections to the Bryansk city soviet, the Mensheviks re-ceived seven seats without any campaigning whatsoever. A considerable number of Red Army soldiers voted for the Mensheviks.

V. RIKMAN

---

## DOCUMENT TWENTY-TWO

---

## A Strike for Food (Viazniki, Vladimir province)

January 1919

Dear Comrades:

At the end of December and the beginning of January, a strike broke out in Viazniki because of famine conditions. Under the influence of our comrades, Social Democrats, the workers resumed work on the condition that they would get a definite answer within three days about whether they were going to receive the bread ration they were entitled to. A delegation was elected to negotiate with the authorities. Because no response was forthcoming, Demidov's factory stopped work again on December 30. (Two thousand workers are employed there, in the village of Iartsevo.) At the general meeting on December 31, a Social Democrat speaker tried to convince the workers to resume work so as not to harm the people's economy. He proposed a resolution that called up workers to stop the strike and called on the authorities to obtain deliveries of food from the center immediately.

At this time a member of the local Cheka, with a detachment of Red soldiers, arrived at the meeting. He started threatening the workers and achieved nothing. The workers did not resume work, but they did not reject our comrade's resolution either. On the next day the following factories stopped work: Beldev factory (1,200 workers), Demidov factory (1,100), Senkov factory (2,400), Poroshin (120), and Koshatin (90). The strike spread to all forty factories in the entire *uezd*. At the general meetings and conferences that took place throughout the province, our comrades, the Social Democrats, pointed out that the strike was caused by the policies of the authorities. They criticized these policies, but they did not encourage the workers to stay on strike in view of the extremely dangerous counterrevolutionary mood among the majority of workers. [The Social Democrats must have been afraid of a hunger riot, for according to official data, there were dozens of such riots, particularly in the small industrial towns of central Russia. The counterrevolutionary mood of the majority of workers was expressed in most cases in slogans like "Down with the Commissars" or "Down with the Commissars and Jews!"]

Nevertheless, the authorities arrested a member of the SD organization, Khokhlov, at the Viazniki railway station, just as he was going to depart for

---

Newspaper clipping from *Vsegda Vpered*, no. 2 (29 January 1919, Moscow), p. 4.

Moscow, as a representative of strikers, to negotiate with the central authorities. Comrade Savostink was arrested at the same time. The EC of the Viazniki soviet sent the following ultimatum to our SD organization:

> The Executive Committee of the Viazniki soviet and the Party Committee of the Bolsheviks hereby present an ultimatum to the local committee of the Menshevik party. The purpose of the ultimatum is to reveal the behavior of the party in general and in regard to the strike in particular. In case of an answer that is not in accord with the CEC decree on the Menshevik party legalization, or in case the strike is not condemned, the party committee and the party itself will be dissolved. In case of a positive answer, the Menshevik party will have to expel from its ranks all its members who took part in the strike in any way whatsoever.

The Viazniki committee of the RSDWP appealed to the Central Committee to attain the liberation of those arrested and to protect the organization from destruction.

---

DOCUMENT TWENTY-THREE

---

## Resolution of the Motovilikha Plant Workers (Perm province)

December 1918

One of the workers of the Motovilikha plant in Perm has delivered a document to our editorial board depicting the position of workers in this Bolshevik paradise and their attitudes to the Communist authorities. We are publishing this document in its entirety.

---

The Motovilikha metallurgical plant, located not far from the city of Perm, was one of the largest industrial centers in the Urals. This resolution was adopted in December 1918, only a few weeks before Perm was taken by the White Army advancing from the eastern Urals and Siberia (see introduction). The text published here is from the Siberian newspaper *Nasha Zaria* [Our Dawn], no. 185 (26 August 1919, Omsk). Newspapers from the White-held territory are a great bibliographic rarity. This issue, one of the very few, is in the Nicolaevsky Collection.

## THE PROTOCOL
### AGENDA

1. About food supply. We, the hungry workers, demand an increase in our ration of bread, not the kind that even pigs would not eat, but bread made of flour, in accordance with the [regulations for food supply] categories [The Bolshevik government instituted several categories of rations. The highest category was for Red Army soldiers and some highly skilled workers; the lowest category was for what were called the "bourgeoisie." In practice, as is clear from this resolution, the Communist functionaries enjoyed food supply privileges]: the first category—10 pounds for one person, 20 pounds for two, 30 pounds for three—as well as additional food products, such as meat, cereals, potatoes, and other foods. As of December [1918], we demand an increase of food rations, and if they are not going to be increased, we will be compelled to stop work.

2. We demand that leather jackets [This is a reference to agents of the Cheka, who were very fond of leather jackets and adopted them as a kind of unofficial uniform. Grigorii Zinoviev, the Petrograd party boss, was explicit about workers' attitudes to them in his speech at the Eighth Communist party Congress in March 1919: "Truly we cannot hide from ourselves the fact that in some places the word commissar has become a swear word. A man in a leather jacket (a Chekist) has become hateful, as they say now in Perm. To hide this would be laughable. We must face the truth." (*Vos'moi S'ezd RKP(b) stenograficheskii otchet*, p. 220.) Zinoviev's comments also suggest that the Communist leaders were well aware of the attitudes of workers in the Urals toward the Communists.] and caps be immediately taken away from the commissars and be used to manufacture shoes.

3. We demand the speediest possible acquisition of felt boots and warm clothes and their distribution to citizens.

4. We demand that the commissars and the employees of Soviet insti tutions receive the same food rations as the workers and that there be no privileges for bureaucrats.

---

In August 1919 Omsk was under the rule of the White forces of Admiral Kolchak. Many workers from the Urals, especially from Izhevsk, Votkinsk, and Motovilikha, retreated from their native towns with the White forces, fearing capture by the Reds. This explains why a worker from Motovilikha was in Omsk. Demand number 5, that power had to belong to the soviets and not to the Cheka, reflected the political position of the Mensheviks and the SRs.

5. We demand that threatening the workers with pistols at the meetings be abolished, that arrests be abolished too, and that there be freedom of speech and assembly, so that there will be true power of the soviets of peasants' and workers' deputies and not of the Chekas.

6. We demand that the taking away of food and flour from the hungry workers, their wives, and children be abolished, as well as imposing fines on those peasants who sell [foodstuffs], who deliver [food to cities], or who let [workers] stay overnight [in the countryside], and we demand freedom to bring up to one and a half *pud* [an old measure of weight in Russia] of food. [This is the quantity of food private citizens were allowed to bring into a city by the Bolshevik authorities. Private trade was banned, and those who tried to bring food into the cities were often fined, arrested, or even shot. Yet many workers traveled to the countryside, as is clear from this resolution, to buy food from peasants. They demand that they be allowed to bring at least the allowable quantity from the countryside.]

7. We demand that the Province Department of Food Supply, if it cannot provision the population with food, pass that authority over to the Motovilikha [plant] Department of Food Supply so that it can work independently.

8. We demand the convocation of the all-plant general meeting, to take place on 5 December at noon, with the participation of the Regional Department of Food Supply.

9. We demand that all appointees be removed [from their posts] and that those elected by the people take their place.

10. We demand pay for the time we spend at meetings if they take place in work time.

11. We demand that fines be abolished for the time workers spend in search of food.

12. We demand that commissars' taking rides on horses and also in automobiles be abolished.

13. We demand that the death penalty without trial and investigation be abolished.

14. We demand that the commissars be for the people and not the people for the commissars. (Electric workshop) [resolution]

All fourteen paragraphs have been adopted unanimously.

Chairman: LUCHNIKOV
Secretary: VESELIPOV
Assistant to the Secretary: ZERTIK

---

## DOCUMENT TWENTY-FOUR

---

## What Is Happening in Tula?

[March 1919]

Despite continued retreat of our [White] Army from the Reds recently, Red Army soldiers and officers keep crossing over to our side. Most of them are from Ryazan and Tula provinces because the Red Army units deployed on our front were formed in the Ryazan and Tula provinces. At least that is the case with the 35th Red division.

Given the predominance of workers in Tula's population, one would expect Tula to be "Bolshevik," but in fact this is not so. Moreover, a truly anti-Bolshevik movement, both in Tula itself and in Tula province, has been growing and continues to grow, just as in other provinces if not stronger. Perhaps this is so, at least in part, because Tula has been drinking from the bitter cup of Soviet life since October 1917, and its population, including the workers, have had enough of the commissars' Communist paradise and would rather have, at last, the conditions of a normal and lawful situation. [The workers' account follows.]

Conditions in the Soviet republic are so intolerable even for the workers that, almost every month, "troubles" occur among railway workers and factory workers. By the way, railway workers hold themselves autonomous vis-à-vis the Soviets and, in regard to other workers, apart from them. They have fixed up their food supply situation much better than other workers and diligently avoid admitting Communists to their organizations. When indignation over the policies of the Soviets would begin to boil over, and when the workers could no longer take commissars' taunts, workers' unrest would break out. Sometimes, unrest was the result of provocations set up by the Soviet itself.

The beginning of February (this year) [1919] was marked in Tula by worker unrest at the armaments' plant. Bolshevik newspapers and Soviet power holders claimed that this movement was caused by the "counterrevolutionary" work of the Right SRs, and they sacked a lot of workers from

---

The author of this report, a Tula worker, was an eyewitness to the events described. Drafted into the Red Army and enlisted in the 35th division, which was formed from the recruits of the Tula and Ryazan provinces, the author was either taken prisoner of war by the Whites or crossed the lines voluntarily. At any rate, he delivered this account to a Siberian paper in Omsk. "Chto delaetsia v Tule," *Nasha Zaria*, no. 185 (12 August 1919, Omsk).

the plant. "Ringleaders" (workers) were arrested and deported somewhere, and when the workers demanded that they be returned, they closed down the plant altogether. A few days later, they announced at the plant, on behalf of the Soviet, that the hiring of new workers would begin, but "unreliable" workers were not hired. As a matter of fact, in their worker policy, the Soviets strictly follow the practice of their czarist predecessors: they have blacklists of "unreliables," they have reinstituted spying on workers, and the workers' milieu is thoroughly corrupted by agents provocateurs. Politically conscious workers explain this by saying that the great majority of Soviets are former provocateurs of the czarist secret police [Okhrana], and honest workers do not want to be in the Soviet.

Scared and intimidated, workers endured until March, when the movement started again at all plants in Tula, even though the more experienced workers urged caution. This time the movement began because of hunger in the workers' families. The thing is that food rations were given only to workers, not to workers' families. This, of course, could not but worry the workers, who saw the pain of hunger in their families. The workers' March movement put forward a demand that food rations be given to workers' families as well. A huge workers' rally took place at the People's House, and workers suggested that the chairman of the Tula soviet, Kaminskii (a Jew), come there for negotiations. He got really frightened and refused to come, saying that he was ill. Then the workers sent two deputies [of the Soviet] in an automobile with instructions to bring him by force and if he would not come, then drag him in "by the scruff of his neck."

The workers were very agitated. Kaminskii was brought over. In his speech he promised to fulfill all the workers' demands, and at the end of the speech he even burst into tears. The workers believed him and went calmly home from the rally. That same night, however, two hundred workers were arrested and, under the guard of the Chinese [Before the revolution, Chinese were mostly migrant workers; under the Bolsheviks, many Chinese worked for the Cheka.], were transferred to the Butyrki jail in Moscow. By the way, at that rally, there were speeches about [the convocation of] the Constituent Assembly, and workers called for the struggle for the Constituent Assembly and for the overthrow of Soviet power.

After these arrests the Tula workers' movement did not quiet down for some time. They did begin giving food rations to workers' families, though, but only to those who were admitted to work after rehiring. They did rehiring through a filter, rejecting those considered to be "unreliable" workers, in other words, enemies of Soviet power. Another workers' economic demand—to keep their land plots in the surrounding countryside—was turned down by the Soviet. A great many workers, therefore, were left without any means, and, in conditions of a terribly expensive cost of living, they felt compelled to abandon Tula and returned to their native villages.

At approximately the same time, a powerful uprising of workers at the Bryansk plants in Orel province was going on. The Tula workers have ties with the Bryansk workers. The Bryansk workers started an armed insurrection together with the local peasants. This movement frightened Moscow because it went on for a long time and because the Red Army troops, dispatched to suppress it, were going over—entire regiments—to the side of the insurgents. The Bolsheviks managed to suppress this workers' insurrection only when, with the help of propagandists, they succeeded in sowing discord among the workers, who were tired of hunger and continued struggle. In any case, one can be quite certain that the Tula and Bryansk workers have a definitely negative attitude to bolshevism and to Soviet power. Now, at a time when the volunteer army of Denikin is approaching this area, it is particularly important to know that, in the Tula and Orel provinces, bolshevism has been overcome and that there, as everywhere, the population will meet Denikin as a liberator from the bloody nightmare of Soviet power. The Orel and the Tula workers, with rifles in their hands, will be able to get even with the Reds for all the taunts they have endured, just as the workers from Izhevsk and Votkinsk have done.

---

## DOCUMENT TWENTY-FIVE

---

## Leaflet of the Menshevik Central Committee

April 1919

*RUSSIAN SOCIAL DEMOCRATIC WORKERS' PARTY*
*PROLETARIANS OF ALL COUNTRIES, UNITE!*

Comrades:
Late at night, on March 30, the all-Russian Cheka began its chase after the Socialists. Dozens of Social Democrats, Socialist Revolutionaries, work-

---

This newspaper-sized leaflet is printed on one side only. Nicolaevsky Collection, series no. 6, box 6, folder 7.

ers, and intelligentsia filled up the prisons. These old-time inmates of czarist jails, fighters for the workers' cause, have proven their dedication to the workers' cause throughout their entire lives. Many of those arrested are members of the Central Committee and of the Moscow committee.

Last year, in November, the Communist party solemnly declared that the policy adopted by our party made it possible to recognize its right to exist legally in Soviet Russia. The Communist party promised to stop the infamous police persecution of which our party had hitherto been a victim. Now it has treacherously broken its promise. Nothing has changed in the SD party policy since November. It still maintains that, in the given internal and international situation, any attempts to overthrow the ruling party could play into the hands of Russian and international counterrevolution.

Just as in November, the SD party pursues only one goal: to organize workers and peasants in order to achieve, first and foremost, an honest implementation of the Soviet constitution so that the soviets express the true will of the laboring masses once again. Just as in November, the SD party aims to influence the working masses by means of the ascendancy of its ideas. Because of mistakes and crimes on the part of the ruling party, the working masses are driven into the camp of counterrevolution. [In January 1919, a small White Army force overran Perm province, a fall made possible by a serious anti-Bolshevik insurgency in the Urals. Some insurgents openly joined the Whites. It is incidents like these that are an example of the working masses being driven to the side of counterrevolution.] Just as in November, the SD party remains in opposition to the existing regime and hopes that the principles of democracy and political freedom will triumph through the will of the working classes after the defeat of domestic and international counterrevolution. The genuine power of the laboring classes is unthinkable, in our opinion, without the implementation of these principles. Salvation of the country from ruin and the revolution from defeat is unthinkable without an economic policy free from utopianism. [This reference to Bolshevik "utopian" policy in the countryside is utopian from the Menshevik point of view because it ran contrary to the market relations in the countryside and was based on the forced collection of grain.]

A system of terror that has already lasted for half a year has corrupted the ruling party to such an extent that it is no longer able to tolerate any independent political force. Even though the ruling party has a multibillion-ruble budget at its disposal, a monopoly on education, hundreds of periodicals, printing shops, paper, and buildings suitable for mass meetings, it was frightened to death when the masses had an opportunity to read, in the course of three weeks [in January and early February 1919 when, for the last time, a Menshevik paper was legally published in Soviet Russia], a two-page oppositional Socialist newspaper that was coming out with difficulty. Frightened that, at the factories and plants in Moscow, the Mensheviks could speak at rallies and campaign in a number of unions for their candidates to the executive boards, the ruling party decided to put an end to observing the law in regard to the Socialist parties and return to the system of terror. It has thus recognized its total powerlessness in the struggle for ideas with the, in its words, "pitiful group of Mensheviks."

In search of a pretext for resuming repressions, the Bolshevik party began to hold the RSDWP responsible for a number of workers' and soldiers' disturbances [In January, February, and March 1919 several workers' strikes broke out in Petrograd, Tula, Astrakhan, Orel, and other cities. In Orel, the disturbances escalated into a rebellion of Red Army soldiers as well (see introduction).] that were ignited by spontaneous discontent. It was easy for our Central Committee to prove by documentary evidence that allegations imputing the RSDWP with taking part in events in Petrograd, Tula, and Bryansk were false. The informers were compelled to fall silent, embarrassed. The latest insinuation, that the Mensheviks supposedly caused the strike at the Aleksandrovskii rail workshops, likewise broke down under the weight of the facts. [The strike at the Aleksandrovskii workshops in Moscow was one of many in the spring of 1919. For limited coverage of this strike, see, "Sobytiia v Aleksandrovskikh masterskikh," *Izvestiia VTsIK,* no. 74 (15 April 1919, Moscow), p. 3.] But even when exposed as liars, the Bolsheviks do not cease to assert daily that facts compromising the Menshevik party and proving its underhanded plotting are present. The slanderers, however, have not been able to put forward any concrete and verified facts.

There are none and cannot be any. For who among the Bolshevik leaders would seriously believe that a party that has always decisively rejected adventurism and rebelliousness in the political and economic struggle now, all of a sudden, would disorganize transport and cause further deterioration of conditions for the working people to make them embittered and in this way overthrow Soviet power? Nevertheless, these are the ridiculous accusations against the SD party.

Even under the provisional government of Kerensky, when the economic ruin was not as terrible as it is now, the SD party cautioned workers against excessively resorting to strikes, which the Bolsheviks had then encouraged. At present, given the catastrophic condition of the economy, the party would have degraded itself if, following the Bolshevik example [of 1917], it decided to prod the desperate masses along the path of strikes. No! The RSDWP indignantly rejects that kind of double-dealing. This is a Bolshevik practice. In Russia they denounce every strike as state treason; in Germany, where the conditions are no less catastrophic, they incite workers to uninterrupted strikes as a means of wrecking the Constituent Assembly and establishing a [Communist] party dictatorship. In Russia they call on the workers to raise the productivity of labor and observe labor discipline; in Germany they state proudly that the productivity of labor is falling due to Communist agitation.

Similarly, one has to be a liar or a madman to suppose that the RSDWP regards rebellions, refusals to go to the front, and other cases of disintegration in the Red Army as something allowing for political gain or something the party may have any sympathy to. From the very first days of the Red Army's creation, Social Democracy has welcomed everything that promotes its conversion into a genuine people's militia and everything that promotes the establishment of strict democratic discipline and eradicates those habits of licentiousness and parasitism that the present ruling party so unscrupulously propagated in the old army during the entire year [of 1917] in pursuit of its demagogical goals. [The Bolsheviks were charged with deliberately undermining discipline in the old army in 1917 for political reasons, something the Mensheviks did not want to do in 1919.]

We repeat once more: Even the accusers themselves do not believe any of the charges against us. And precisely because they do not believe them, all their actions in regard to RSDWP are inane and contradictory. First they close down our paper [The newspaper *Vsegda Vpered* was closed on 25 February after three weeks of existence. A permit for another SD paper, *Rabochii Internatsional,* was granted. Yet this paper was closed after only one issue.], then they inform us that the closing is not irreversible and that we may be granted a new permit for publication if we promise not to "undermine the strength of Soviet Russia's resistance" to its enemies. [This incident served as a pretext for closing *Vsegda Vpered.* In number 9 in February, A. Pleskov, a member of the CC published the lead article, "Stop the Civil War!" wherein he criticized the new spirit of militarism in the Bolshevik party. Pleskov implied that certain Bolsheviks thrived in the conditions of civil war, hence the call to stop it and return to normality. The Bolshevik press assailed Pleskov and the Mensheviks for their treason of "Soviet" Russia, surrounded by "enemies" and "armed to the teeth."] They seal our offices, then unseal them, and then seal them again. Then they arrest us under the guise of verification of documents and immediately announce in the press that five deserters were discovered among us. But then they release us with apologies and arrest us again a week later. In the meantime, the presidium of the Moscow soviet has announced that we are a legal party and that we may enjoy all the rights of a legal party. Yet a few days later that same Moscow soviet denounces us as enemies of the working class and publishes a resolution endorsing mass arrests of our party members and the baiting of us in the official press. The moral powerlessness of the ruling party has never been exposed so vividly before. Never before has the government, which calls itself a revolutionary and workers' government, resorted to the worst methods of a Black Hundred–type [The Black Hundreds were a reactionary, anti-Semitic organization under the old regime and thus became a metaphor for reactionary governments.] government to such an extent.

Masses of people, hungry and exhausted as they are, express their discontent by spontaneous outbursts of protests. Instead of trying to understand the deep roots of this discontent and instead of recognizing the necessity to change a senseless policy that is worsening the already difficult situation for working people, the ruling party is trying to distract the attention of hungry workers by reference to an "internal enemy." It is trying to impress on the workers that famine, the breakdown of transport, and other calamities are a result of underhanded plotting by malicious Mensheviks, SRs, and so on who have ostensibly set themselves the goal of driving the people to despair. Although the charges, used as a pretext for persecution of the RSDWP, are lies, it is a sad fact that the Bolshevik party does not want to tolerate any other party within the working class. This means that the party of [Red] Terror deprives workers and peasants of any right to free choice between the programs of different political parties. This means that it denies the workers a right to elect those whom they trust to the soviets. This means that it intends to retain the soviets, the factory committees, and other institutions for itself *at any cost,* even against the will of the majority of workers.

This is the true nature of the "power of laborers" or "power of the Soviets" in whose name the Bolshevik government speaks. The Bolshevik party clearly says to the masses, "the Soviet state is me" [a reference to the famous statement of Louis XIV, "L'état c'est moi"]. Any Socialist party aiming to gain influence in the soviets by means of ideas will be destroyed. This is clear. The working masses can draw their own conclusions. The RSDWP will draw its own as well.

The first period of terror was not without some hard lessons for us. When we were able to communicate with the working people again [when the decree, adopted in December 1918, on expulsion of the Mensheviks from the soviets was lifted], they drew themselves avidly toward us. In the eyes of the masses, persecution created an aura of glory around the Social Democrats for their unselfish defense of the workers' true interests. And this new wave of repressions will have the same effect. The working people will be convinced even more that the Bolshevik government, fearless vis-à-vis Clemenceau and Wilson, is morally powerless vis-à-vis a so-called petty group of Mensheviks who dare to tell the people the whole truth and nothing but the truth amid a reign of terror.

The Central Committee is calling on comrades to tighten their ranks in view of the coming repressions and wait calmly for the moment when the senselessness of Bolshevik terrorist policy will appear again in the guise of defeats and bankruptcies to which this policy will inevitably lead. Whatever conditions local organizations may face, their political behavior should not diverge a whit from the line adopted at the December party conference. [At the end of December 1918, the SDs convened a party conference, the first since May 1918. The decisions adopted reflected the Mensheviks' commitment to remain a nonbelligerent and noninsurrectionist party within the Soviet system.] At this difficult moment the Central Committee calls on all party members to remain at their posts and expresses its firm belief that the steadfast and dignified behavior of Social Democracy will make it possible for the party to come out of the impending ordeal, strengthened this time as well by new sympathies of the working people, although at a cost of hard sacrifices for individual members.

If the ruling party continues to persist in its terrorist policy of one-party dictatorship and if it continues to suppress any expression of freedom within the working class, it will have to take upon itself the burden of responsibility for the inevitable, in this case supremacy of counterrevolution, inevitable because the atomized masses will lose hope of being able to defend their rights. As a result, they will be driven to the camp of counterrevolution. The RSDWP declines all responsibility for the triumph of counterrevolution.

The demagogues and jailers of White and Red Terror, alternately taking power from each other, come and go. The Revolutionary Social Democracy, expressing the proletariat's permanent rights and wisdom, remains! The future belongs to it and only to it!

THE CENTRAL COMMITTEE OF THE RSDWP

## DOCUMENT TWENTY-SIX

### Letter from a Comrade Who Left Russia at the Beginning of April 1919

At the beginning of April, Dzerzhinskii arrested all the Central Committee and Moscow committee members of the Social Democrats who were in Moscow at the time, except Cherevanin and Zorin. [Document 25 describes these events in more detail.] Dan and Gorev were arrested, together with their wives; Martov was put under house arrest, and an ambush was set up in his apartment so that everyone who came to see him was arrested as well. [For a more detailed description of this incident, see Grigorii Aronson, *Martov i ego blizkie: sbornik* [Martov and Those Close to Him (New York: Rausen Brothers, 1959).] Official motives for this action remain unknown. At the same time all the employees of the editorial office of *Delo Naroda* were arrested as well. This newspaper of the Socialist Revolutionaries had been coming out in Moscow since the "legalization" of the SRs. [*Delo Naroda* published only ten issues in the second half of March.] Numerous other Socialists were arrested. Among them were those who used to be members of the Moscow city duma [in 1917]. They also arrested some Mensheviks and SRs who were members of the factory committees and were popular among the workers. They say that the total number of those arrested was about three thousand. But even if this figure is exaggerated, it is certain that the number of arrests was very high. This was the second time within a short period that arrests en masse had been made. The first time, Soviet authorities said that they were arresting "deserters." The same pretext was also used in regard to women; Mrs. Gorev and Miss Wolf, the secretary of the Central Committee, were arrested as well.

When I left Moscow there was no longer any Social Democratic press being published. For a short time, the newspaper *Vsegda Vpered* was coming out, but production was very difficult, above all due to the lack of paper because Glavbum (Central Directorate of Paper) allocated insufficient amounts to us. The hundred thousand copies we published could not satisfy demand even in Moscow. Publication was suspended at the beginning of March. After that we published the first and only issue of *Rabo-*

---

The author of this letter is not known. The text is translated from a copy of the letter in French that was published in *La Republique Russe,* no. 11 (13 August 1919), p. 3, a Social Democratic newspaper in Paris.

*chii Internatsional.* The chairman of the Cheka ordered the CC [Central Committee] and the printing shop to cease publication. (Number two was confiscated after it had been printed.) The first issue came out with the authorization of the "liberal" chairman of the Moscow soviet, Kamenev.

That our party has influence among the workers is incontestable. Our organizations enjoy great authority, particularly in Moscow, Tula, Sormovo, and above all among the railway workers. [Recent research on the subject confirms these observations. See Peter Scheibert, *Lenin an der Macht: Das Russische Volk in der Revolution, 1918–1922* [Lenin in Power: The Russian People in the Revolution, 1918–1922] (Weinheim: acta humaniora, 1984), p. 289.] Our party's activity has intensified since the conference in Bern, when we expected the arrival of the delegates of the International. [This conference, which was held in Bern from 3 to 10 February 1919, was the first conference of the Second International after the end of World War I. One of the conference's resolutions was to send a commission of inquiry into the conditions in Soviet Russia, a proposal made many months earlier by Pavel Axelrod. The SDs perceived the acceptance of this proposal as a major victory, especially because Lenin was planning to convene his own Communist International in March 1919. The Mensheviks believed that if an impartial international commission investigated the true workers' situation in the country of the "victorious proletariat," Lenin's propaganda would fall flat. Because of visa complications, the commission never arrived in Russia, and Lenin continued to portray Soviet Russia as a workers' paradise. See Konrad von Zwehl, ed., *Die Zweite Internationale 1918–1919,* p. 666.] One gets news from the outside world through *Izvestiia* only. To the extent that the chances of their [the delegates] arrival diminished, people's morale went down as well. . . .

Of course it is difficult to expect great activity from the masses in the conditions of exhaustion and total isolation to which we are subjected. Here are some examples. The food rations are very low. One has to resort to the services of bagmen and other speculators. The prices are astounding. At the time of my departure, the price of bread was 33 rubles. It used to be 40, but it fell when bagmen began to engage in travel and trade. Potatoes cost 13 rubles, butter 120 rubles, sugar 120, flour 40 rubles a pound, and soap of bad quality 70 rubles. The typhus epidemic has driven the prices up. Linens are seldom white and, if so, for a very short time.

The situation in Petrograd is much worse. Most apartments that had central heating are not heated anymore, and the pipes have burst. The temperature in some houses is about zero. The trams are not running. In addition to all this a typhus epidemic broke out. The authorities were not prepared and did not know where to house the sick. Some stayed in the corridors of hospitals, right on the floor. It was terrible to hear the doctors tell how they had to maneuver between rows of improvised "beds," stepping on vermin, which produced a dry, cracking noise. There was a very high mortality rate among the doctors (60 percent), whereas among the rest of the population it was about 6–7 percent.

We have become fatalists and now look at things in a philosophic way: We have maintained our capacity to live and work and "create," but for God's sake let us not "create socialism" in a country that is half dead! The metallurgical, textile, and rubber industries have stopped. There is a lack of fuel, and raw materials are exhausted. Whatever the people in the cities still have, they bring to the countryside and exchange for bread and potatoes.

As to the imaginary world of the Soviets, up there, they continue to anticipate world revolution and to elaborate nonstop on all kinds of "schemes" and "projects" devoid of meaning.

---

DOCUMENT TWENTY-SEVEN

---

## From Odessa to Tbilisi

[Summer 1919]

After the Bolsheviks entered Odessa I stayed there for one month. [The Bolsheviks entered Odessa on 5 April 1919 after the French expeditionary forces withdrew. The Bolsheviks remained in the city until 25 August, when the White Army of General Denikin captured the city. The author must be referring here to a period from 5 April to 5 May 1919.] Their entry into the city was not accompanied by any excesses. Until twenty-five Cheka agents arrived from Moscow, the Bolshevik leaders exhibited more mildness in their activity than last year, even though before their arrival a provisional local Cheka practiced executions without trials,

---

This clipping is from the newspaper collection. The article appeared in a Russian-language newspaper *Bor'ba* [Struggle] in Tbilisi, the capital of independent Georgia. Unfortunately no date was written on the clipping, only the number of the newspaper, no. 146. Yet it is clear from context that it was mid-summer 1919. The Georgian Social Democratic party was the ruling party in independent Georgia. Many Georgian Social Democrats continued to refer to themselves as Mensheviks, even though they had not been part of the Russian Social Democratic party since Georgia proclaimed its independence from Russia in the spring of 1918.

following the example of the volunteers [the volunteer White Army of General Denikin].

At first there were characters with a shady past among the Bolshevik leaders. Either a chairman or a commander of the Cheka was one M. N. Eniankov, a well-known black market currency dealer from Petrograd, who was removed from his post and arrested after two weeks in office. In the very first days after the seizure of power, the Bolsheviks abolished the courts, the jury, and the local city government. They closed all the banks, except the state bank. Justices of the peace, the circuit court, and the chamber, as well as all defense lawyers and prosecutors, had to hand over all business to the liquidation commission, under the Bolshevik commissar of justice.

The arrival of the Bolsheviks caused panic, and the ban they imposed on free trade of bread, as well as their requisitioning of the most essential goods, caused sharp increases in the prices of bread and all other foods. During the first two or three days, the public was very much afraid to leave their homes, but then little by little, they got used to the Bolsheviks. Nevertheless, there was a shortage of bread even for the Red Army. Residents [of Odessa] had either to get by without bread or be satisfied with a quarter of a pound of bread made of pea flour, available every three days. On the free market [black market] there was no bread at all, and if one was lucky enough to find it, one had to pay 40 rubles a pound. After three weeks, the authorities legalized free trade of bread, and immediately bread and flour reappeared in great quantities. When I was leaving Odessa, black bread cost 12 rubles and white bread 15 to 18 rubles a pound.

There is no fuel in Odessa at all. Firewood costs 50–55 rubles a *pud* [old weight measure in Russia]. The water supply system required 20,000 *puds* of firewood daily. To keep the system running, the Bolsheviks destroyed a wooden pier in the port. To destroy it was easy, but how long can they get by with that wood? The pier gave them 250,000–300,000 *puds* of firewood, which was enough for the water supply system to last for only about ten to fifteen days. All factories and plants are idle, and the Bolsheviks have to subsidize all workers. About fifty thousand workers are listed as unemployed.

To improve the financial situation, the Bolsheviks imposed an indemnity on the bourgeoisie [The defeated party in a war has to pay an indemnity. The Bolsheviks waged a war against the propertied classes, and their widely practiced policy was to impose an indemnity on the defeated class enemy—the bourgeoisie. In practical terms this was indistinguishable from arbitrary requisitions of food, clothing, houses, and the like.] in the amount of five hundred million rubles. They arrested those who refused to pay the indemnity. Among others, they arrested a well-known lawyer, A. I.

Brodsky. They also arrested several doctors. In violation of paragraph 16 of decree no. 115 issued by the Ukrainian Council of People's Commissars, which stipulated that foreign citizens were not subject to arrest for refusal to pay the indemnity, they arrested foreigners anyway. Even though a plenipotentiary for foreign affairs wrote requests to the commandant of the city urging him not to violate the law and release arrested foreigners immediately, the latter ignored those pleas completely. To one relative of a foreign national, the commandant said that he granted foreign nations just one privilege, namely, that they would not be executed for refusal to pay the indemnity, unlike the citizens of the Soviet Ukraine.

About eight hundred persons in Odessa declared themselves followers of Grigoriev [N. A. Grigoriev was the leader of the anti-Bolshevik peasant rebellion in June 1919 in the Ukraine. The background of this movement is described in the introduction.]. On the retreat from Odessa along the Fontanskaia road they staged a pogrom. Rumors estimate that two hundred people suffered. In Odessa itself, there was no pogrom of any kind. With the arrival of the Bolsheviks, there was no looting, but one could say that there are a lot of criminals in the Bolshevik detachments. The Ukrainian Bolsheviks are handling the national question coquettishly. Decree no. 115 recognized all newly created states of the former Russian empire as independent states, except for Belorussia and Lithuania, where Soviet power has been established. It follows from here that the Bolsheviks will recognize the independence of Georgia until Soviet power is established here as well. As soon as such [Soviet] power appears here, Lenin will immediately reach out his hand to take Georgia.

In mid-May [1919] the Bolsheviks organized a week of "the poor." In practical terms this meant that they went door-to-door collecting all kinds of goods by compulsion. To the owners, the Bolsheviks left three pieces of underwear per person and one piece of other kinds of clothing. This campaign collapsed, though, because the workers rose up against it and beat up members of the two commissions. Three hours later searches and requisitions were stopped. On the next day the Bolsheviks organized rallies to convince the workers that the decision of the city EC was correct. At the rallies they tried to convince the workers that requisitions would not harm them, but the workers did not succumb to Bolshevik persuasion.

The union of sailors in Odessa is clearly anti-Bolshevik. It consists of nine thousand members and has ninety representatives in the city soviet. The sailors elected only representatives without party affiliation to the soviet, contrary to the wishes of the Bolsheviks. Putting their own candidates on the ballot, the Bolsheviks declared that they would not admit sailors' representatives to the soviet if they were not on the Bolshevik list. There are no representatives of peasants in the soviet. Elections to the soviet went on under pressure of armed force and threats of execution. I can attest with confidence that the workers in Odessa are against Denikin, but they are not for the Bolsheviks either. The property of all persons who had left the city before the Bolsheviks' arrival has been declared property of the Soviet republic. Their apartments are being taken over by Soviet institutions and employees.

Executions have taken place quite often. During my time in Odessa about two hundred people were executed. The names of thirty-six of them were published in the local *Izvestiia*. Moreover, it was stated that they were executed for belonging to the Union of Russian People [the official name of the anti-Semitic organization better known as the Black Hundreds]. There were two women among those executed.

The Russian Social Democratic party has split into two wings. The majority kept the party's old political positions, and a minority consider themselves independent Social Democrats who recognize Soviet power. [The author must be referring here to the differences between the center-left Mensheviks, who accepted Martov's policy of supporting the Soviets in the civil war against the Whites, and the right Mensheviks, who opposed the Whites but did not want to support the Bolsheviks.] The Left SRs used to work together with the Bolsheviks and even held some positions of authority, but a few days before my departure the EC fired them all. The Bolsheviks had a suspicion that the Left SRs wanted to stage an uprising against Soviet power. The Bolsheviks also expelled the Social Democrats (Mensheviks) and the Right SRs from the soviet. The Social Democrats (Mensheviks) and the Right SRs were compelled to go underground. There also appeared a new party of Ukrainian Socialist Revolutionaries-Communists. [The author must be referring here to the Ukrainian Party of Left Socialist Revolutionaries, which was formed in March 1919, splitting away from the Left SRs. Like Martov's Mensheviks, they remained critical of Communist policies but refrained from armed struggle against Lenin's government.] Not a single non-Bolshevik newspaper comes out.

The uprising of Grigoriev caused great difficulties to the Bolsheviks. His detachments are anti-Semitic. They wanted to stage a pogrom in Odessa, but measures were taken to prevent it. Grigoriev himself went to Elisavetgrad, having taken with him several railcar loads of bolts of cloth, which he gave away to peasants for free. Grigoriev went to Elisavetgrad with the slogan: "Beat the Jews, Save Mother Russia!" Having taken the city, Grigoriev's troops staged a pogrom. It was said that there were several thousand victims.

M. D.

## DOCUMENT TWENTY-EIGHT

## Uprisings in Samara and Simbirsk Provinces

[March 1919]

We have just received Bolshevik newspapers from Samara and Sim-birsk clearly depicting several peasants' and Red Army soldiers' uprisings that have taken place in these provinces. The main theme that stands out in all the official reports and orders is the unbearable conditions prevailing in the provinces, which are virtually given away for plunder to all kinds of commissars who are conducting the "irresponsible policy" of requisitions, pillage, and looting. A number of spontaneous peasant uprisings rolled across these provinces. They were suppressed with horrifying brutality. The Bolsheviks are trying very hard to calm down popular discontent, and they are promising all kinds of improvements in local government. In this con-nection they issued a whole lot of orders and appeals, like this one:

*ORDER NO. 4*
*FROM THE MILITARY-REVOLUTIONARY COMMITTEE*
*OF THE SAMARA PROVINCE*

In some parts of Samara province the Kulaks-Kolchakovites have man-aged to make their way into positions of authority [in local government]. By their criminal behavior they undermined the trust of peasants in Soviet power and in this way they caused indignation against the Soviets in some places. It is announced that all persons who abuse their power will be immediately put on trial by the Military Revolutionary Tribunal. We will deal mercilessly with those scoundrels who undermine Soviet power.

The official paper of the Samara Bolsheviks, *Samarskii Kommunar,* published the following announcement of the Military Revolutionary Com-mittee about peasants' and soldiers' uprisings in the Syzran region:

---

The author of this report is most likely a Socialist Revolutionary. It was published in one of the last issues of *Delo Naroda* three days before the newspaper was closed forever. "Podrobnosti vosstanii v Samarskoi i Simbirskoi guberniiakh," *Delo Naroda,* no. 7 (27 March 1919) Hoover Institution Library.

Adventuristic uprisings are beginning to draw to an end. On the basis of the general data, it is possible to ascertain the fact of a well-prepared uprising aimed at disorganizing our rear and producing an impact on frontline operations. All uprisings start according to a certain pattern: At first an agitator [in Bolshevik perceptions, anyone who articulated political demands of the local populace. This agitator should not be confused with professional Bolshevik agitators and their trainloads of propaganda.] appears. He climbs the bell tower and begins to sound the alarm bell. Then he invites those gathered to rise against the requisitioning of cattle, grain, and against the extraordinary tax. Every uprising begins with the killing of the Executive Committee chairman, members of the soviet, and the Communists. Data are that in one of the villages, headquarters have been located that coordinate the actions of the insurgents. These people probably put forward the slogan Down with the Communists, and Long Live Soviet Power [It is difficult to identify party affiliation, if any, of insurgent peasants on the basis of a few slogans. Yet this was certainly the Left SRs' slogan. In its other variation, Long Live the Soviets, but Without the Communists, it was popular among the Kronstadt sailors in 1921.]—a slogan that is put forward in all uprisings. The priests are taking an active part in insurgencies. Also the entire Black Hundreds' scum have crawled out with their own slogans. [Although the authors do not cite the slogans of the alleged Black Hundreds, most likely they refer to anti-Communist and anti-Jewish slogans, perhaps monarchist, but most certainly not favoring Soviets of any kind. It is unlikely that the people, identified here as "Black Hundred scum," actually were members of the Black Hundreds, especially in that part of Russia. The Bolsheviks tended to identify indiscriminately many of their political opponents as Black Hundreds, including the Tula workers (see document 36). It was merely a convenient label, like "enemy of the people" would be later.] All these contradictory slogans muddle the consciousness of the peasant masses. Because of this confusion, a decomposition began in the insurgents' ranks. All the insurgents' organizations in some places united under the heading The Bloc of the Toiling Peasantry [Too little is known about these organizations to identify their political character. Yet this name was used in Tambov province by the SR peasant organization. Because that organization had always been strong on the Volga and because the insurrection occurred only six months after Samara had been the capital of the SR-led anti-Bolshevik government, it is likely that the SR influence among the peasants was strong.] or, in other places, The Peasant Section. The insurgents are led by an officer who calls and signs [apparently, the insurgent proclamation] himself as The Commander of the Peasant Section, Colonel Pavlov. The rebels practice terrible cruelties in regard to those whom they take as prisoners of war: they cut off their ears and noses, they chop off their hands and fingers. The losses of the detachments sent out against them are, nevertheless, not high in comparison with the destruction of the rebels. [In Russian, *poteri neveliki v sravnenii s unichtozheniem miatezhnikov*. This ambiguous formulation may mean that casualties were not high enough to achieve the goal of liquidating the rebels, or it may mean not high compared with the number of those destroyed among the rebels.] The Revolutionary Committee issued an order to shoot mercilessly those who resist. Concerning those already captured rebels in Syzran (about four hundred), the strictest possible investigation is being conducted. [This is an attempt to render illiterate Russian, *Nad . . . plennymi . . . rassledovaniia*, into English.]

As far as the internal causes that drove the peasants to insurgency are concerned, comrade Iu. Milonov, member of the Province Revolutionary Committee and member of the Presidium of the Council of Trade Unions, explained at the plenary session of the Samara Council of Trade Unions:

The speaker characterized the disorders in Stavropol [a *uezd* (similar to a county) in Samara province], now liquidated, as a kulak movement that relies [The present tense (in the original) is contradictory: if the disorders were liquidated, the movement could not have continued to rely on anything. Most likely, the movement was not liquidated.] on deserters from Red Army units and on part of the middle peasantry. The causes of the uprisings are that Soviet power violated kulak interests by introducing a revolutionary tax, a monopoly on grain trade, and, linked to that monopoly, requisitions of grain as well as carting and other obligations [*povinnost;* this term is reminiscent of the age of serfdom, for it meant that peasants were required to deliver goods, mostly grain, without compensation.]. The deserters joined the uprising (they were afraid of revolutionary justice for their treason) in a flight from the ranks of the heroically struggling Red Army. Middle peasants were driven to disorders by despair into which they were plunged by the provocative policies of the kulaks who had stuck to Soviet power [*primazavshiesia*] under the guise of its agents in [*volost*] and village soviets.

The insurgent kulaks explained their actions like this: "The Bolsheviks and the Communists are different. The Bolsheviks and the Communists struggle against each other. The Communists want to unite the peasants by force into agricultural communes; the Communists want to liquidate the church, and, finally, the Communists have replaced Soviet power by their own power." From here follows a logical conclusion: it is necessary to help the Bolsheviks struggle "against Communists and Jews," it is necessary to struggle for Soviet power against the dictatorship of the Communists.

In this survey, we have deliberately cited from exclusively Bolshevik and official statements. But even these show that the uprisings are not accidental and that they are not the work of the "White Guards and kulaks"—something that the Bolsheviks keep on repeating. In fact, peasant uprisings are rooted in much more serious causes. They clearly demonstrate that peasant life demands new forms and new conditions for its existence and development. In vain, the Bolshevik authorities are trying to convince everyone that the uprisings are White Guardist and kulak in character. Unsubstantiated allegations cannot convince anyone. It is clear to everyone that a long-term and complex process of rising discontent is going on in the countryside, discontent that will be impossible to put down either by appeals or by armed detachments.

---

DOCUMENT TWENTY-NINE

---

## A Letter from the Kiev Council of Trade Unions to the Workers of Western Europe

September 1919

Dear Comrades:

The enclosed materials will give you some information on the present situation of the trade union movement in one of the largest centers in the

---

This letter was written by a group of Social Democrats, leaders of the Council of Southern Trade Unions, in September 1919, immediately after the Bolsheviks had been driven out of Kiev by the volunteer army of General Denikin. The White Army held Kiev for only a short time and was not able to consolidate its position in the Ukraine. When Kiev was reconquered by the Communists, the Mensheviks were immediately charged with collaboration with the Whites. One of the key prosecution documents was this letter, which, from the prosecution's point of view, slandered Soviet reality and revealed sympathetic attitudes toward the Whites. The trial of the Kiev Mensheviks, which took place in Kiev 21–23 March 1920, was a failure for the Communists. Charges of collaboration were refuted by the leaders of the southern unions with statements and resolutions like the one on the Jewish pogroms (document 31). Nevertheless, four Mensheviks were sentenced to imprisonment in a concentration camp "for the duration of the civil war." S. Volin, *Mensheviki na Ukraine* (1917–1921) [The Mensheviks in the Ukraine (1917–1921)], Paper no. 11 (New York: Inter-University Project on the Menshevik Movement, 1962), p. 128.

south of Russia (the Ukraine) [The term *south of Russia* in regard to the Ukraine was offensive to the Ukrainians. That the Mensheviks used it, just as the Bolsheviks and the Whites did, is a clear indication that, despite ideological differences on other matters, these parties regarded the Ukraine as an integral part of Russia.] as well as on our current work. Because Russia is completely cut off from Europe now, materials on the workers' movement must be of certain value to you, even if they cover a short period and deal with local affairs. That is why we use this opportunity to inform you, at least partially, on behalf of our organization.

Several times during this year [1919] the civil war in the Ukraine has changed the political situation in which the trade union movement has had to develop. At present, the workers' movement has come out of a period of Soviet-Bolshevik power and entered a phase marked by a preponderance of reactionary forces. Bolshevik power was established in Kiev at the beginning of February this year, after the Bolsheviks had defeated the troops of the national democratic government of the Ukraine—the Directory. It lasted until September 1 [1919], when the uninterrupted offensive of the volunteer army, led by General Denikin from the south and from the east, rolled up to our city. The beginning of Bolshevik rule was doubtless marked by the growth of pro-Bolshevik attitudes among workers in the Ukraine and also in Kiev. This was a consequence of Hetman Skoropadsky's regime and of the German occupation, as well as the disintegration of the country. However, these attitudes began to disappear quickly. The rule of the "Communist" government was the same in the Ukraine as it was in other parts of Russia. It was the rule of an antidemocratic dictatorship of party cliques, bloodthirsty Cheka, relentless police arbitrariness, and the deadly terror. The Bolsheviks senselessly expanded the bureaucratic apparatus. Corruption was widespread among Soviet functionaries. The Communists suppressed independent workers' organizations. And, finally, they launched a utopian economic policy that worsened the financial and food supply crises and led to a break between the cities and the countryside. As a result, industry was dying out, the masses were pauperized, and peasant rebellions flared up with increasing frequency. These were the features of the period we have lived through. Pro-Bolshevik attitudes among the workers were disappearing very quickly under the impact of merciless terror and famine; the mood of total disillusionment and hopelessness was on the rise, combined with pent-up hatred of the Bolshevik regime, which had frustrated their hopes.

Outwardly it appeared as though the trade unions carried on with lively activity. Membership in trade unions was obligatory for the broad masses of workers. One had to be a member not only to obtain goods and services, but also in order to exercise legal rights as a person. [The authors mean that the right to vote, for example, was not a given for someone who was not a member of Soviet trade unions because a certain percentage of the seats in local soviets was allocated to trade unions.] The unions were subsidized by the state and artificially attached to the masses. No wonder they turned into bureaucratic agencies. They could not fulfill their true tasks. They gradually destroyed the very principle of union independence and self-rule and the principle of free elections in their own composition. Instead, they relied on appointments and orders. In the end, they lost touch with the workers and did not respond to their needs.

It is true, though, that during the past period of Soviet rule, the expansion of unions was sustained according to a plan. This was correct from the point of view of [Marxist] theory. Worker organizing and centralization of wage rates were maximized. Several local congresses and one general congress of unions took place. All local unions became branches of the All-Russian Union. All these results, however, were devoid of content because they were based on a distorted [from the Menshevik point of view because the unions were not independent of state authority] status of the unions. Only some unions succeeded in preserving their independence. Workers and members of Socialist parties could not achieve much in conditions of terror. Nevertheless, the nearer the end of Soviet rule, the more the few remaining independent unions relied on a growing sentiment of opposition among the workers. They were engaged in a protracted struggle to raise state wage rates. They were trying to alter a suicidal food supply policy and defend workers' rights against the terrorist regime.

At various workers' rallies, the pent-up resistance to adopting officially sponsored resolutions was increasingly obvious. One could hear criticism more and more often. On the other hand, the intensification of terror undermined the workers' strength. In August, Kiev was virtually surrounded by a tight ring of peasant insurgencies drawing ever closer to the city. The offensive of the volunteer army gained momentum against the background of peasant revolts and the distintegration of the Red Army in this period. Kiev was basically in a state of food supply siege. And on September 1, a new political period began.

On the very day of the Bolsheviks' departure, a new bureau of the Council of Trade Unions was elected that began its work in these new conditions. The workers entered the new period economically broken, weakened, and dispersed. There have not been such difficult internal conditions for the workers' movement for quite a long time. Because so many enterprises had been closed under the Bolsheviks, unemployment was very high and the workers' movement had a small social base. An unfavorable correlation of forces [between the entrepreneurs and the workers] in the economic struggle aggravated the situation. Now we face the basic task of recovering our strength. This task has to be fulfilled despite passive attitudes among the workers [in SD jargon, a lack of active class conscious spirit in the workers' struggle. In the context of September 1919, this meant that the workers were not inclined to oppose actively the White regime. It seems they displayed acquiescence and indifference at the very least, and evidence cited below shows that many of them supported right-wing groups.]. Disillusionment with the results of Bolshevik rule is so great that the protracted Civil War creates attitudes of weary humility. But the needs of a daily struggle for existence do stimulate the workers' activity and add to their energy. Our hopes are based on this reawakening.

The brutal experience under the Bolsheviks and the instructive experience of today's situation must necessarily lead collective thought in the right direction. Today's political situation has been predetermined by Bolshevik rule. The current rulers are reactionary. Bolshevik extremism and Bolshevik actions have generated a resurgence of widespread reactionary attitudes [in SD vocabulary this could mean intense hostility toward collectives, communes, and soviets of any kind; blaming the Jews for Russia's misfortunes; sympathetic attitudes to the Whites; or the staunch defense of private property] and prepared the ground for the supremacy of reactionary political aspirations. History has placed the banner of active struggle with the Bolshevik utopian regime for the unification of Russia in the hands of reactionary forces. Workers' social instincts have made them adopt a defensive position in the current situation. The declaration made public by the workers' delegation in the Commission for Labor Legislation [see document 30] characterizes the legal and political aspects of the workers' movement in the south of Russia. Here in Kiev, the situation is the same as elsewhere. The authorities do not allow the Council of Trade Unions to publish its own paper. They limit the number of permits for workers' meetings. They arrest union members. They are also trying to set up yellow unions in Kiev. [The authors refer here to an organization that sprang up in Kiev immediately on the entry of the Whites. Officially titled "An organizational Committee of Workers of Trade Unions in the city of Kiev," its leader, Kirsta Kiselev, an engineer, and his supporters tried to draw workers away from the Social Democrats. Their resolutions were marked by bombastic style, violent anti-Semitism, and hatred of the Communists and all Socialists. If a comparison could be drawn, it would be to the Black Hundreds in its anti-Semitism and even more to the German National Socialists in the 1920s.] They engage in political speculation full of impudent adventurism. They are trying to draw benefits from the workers' hatred of the Bolshevik regime and to use the workers' disillusionment and current gloomy disposition for ends that are far from those of the workers themselves.

In the long run, of course, the situation will lead the workers to gather around independent unions. Even now, this splinter yellow organization is very weak. It cannot defend workers' interests. It lives on paltry doles and produces only demagogical promises, copying Bolshevik methods. It corrupts the workers' milieu, resorts to any means to achieve its aims, enjoys obvious protection from the authorities, and is connected with right-wing circles. From our materials you will see with what energy we carry on the struggle against this pitiful organization, which undoubtedly enjoys the support of the overwhelming majority of workers in Kiev. [The previous passage makes it clear that the Social Democrats were very hostile to their rivals among the workers, which makes this admission all the more important.]

This unfavorable situation has been aggravated by the terrible events of the last few days. We are referring to a wave of Jewish pogroms. Extraordinary violence committed upon the peaceful Jewish population and uninterrupted pogroms in various parts of the city mark the latest period in the life of Kiev. These events have completely drowned normal life in the city. The population is living through unheard-of horrors. The activity of political organizations, including the unions, has died down, and the city still cannot overcome its state of torpidity. From the materials we enclose you will see what we have undertaken in this regard. You will also see what the role of the authorities has been.

This is the general situation. It is particularly morbid in this part of the Ukraine. It is still an area of shifting front lines, hence the utmost tension in nationality relations. The eastern and southeastern parts of the Ukraine have been under the authority of the volunteer army much longer than Kiev. The trade union movement there was much stronger than here in Kiev. In August, a conference of trade unions in the south of Russia took place in Kharkov. This conference elected its Council of Trade Unions. The council established contact with trade unions in the Crimea and North Caucasia. We have also established contact with this overall center of trade union movement. Unfortunately, we are virtually cut off from the entire southwestern Ukraine. The war going on with Petliura [a leader of Ukrainian national forces] and with the Bolsheviks has destroyed all means of communication.

The new authorities have abolished soviet legislation on labor and are currently working on new legislation. Civil law is being demolished. Many areas of the law are simply vacant. Everything is left to a "free play of forces." The struggle for workers' civil rights acquires great importance in this situation. Workers' attempts to take part in the deliberations of the Commission on Labor Legislation have ended in a fiasco. You must know that the entire right-wing press has launched a malicious campaign of slander against the workers' movement in order to distort our position and delude public opinion in Western Europe. They derive advantage from the fact that there is no independent workers' press.

During the past period we restored the unions' organizational apparatus as much as we could. However, the general situation and economic conditions hamper our work considerably. The Kiev Council of Trade Unions unites twenty-six unions with an overall membership of seventy thousand. The number of members paying dues is considerably lower. The council is trying to render help to the unemployed. It has set up a mutual aid fund. The strained financial situation of the council severely impedes its work. In the local councils a campaign is under way to create special funds for the unemployed, collecting donations and enlisting the help of city authorities. All over the south of Russia a struggle is going on to make entrepreneurs donate 2 percent of their wage rates to the fund of the unemployed. Due to the recasting of legal and social relations, the mutual insurance funds are in pitiful condition. Currently the council is establishing preliminary contacts with entrepreneurs on the question of collective agreements. The council has also tried to defend the latest minimum wage rate of twelve hundred rubles. In the Kharkov area there have been successful strikes for higher wage rates. We have also made sure that conciliatory boards be set up to resolve conflicts.

In this situation of continued Civil War—political changes, economic devastation, and the incurable passivity of the working class—our work has been aimed at recovering our strength, defending the elementary achievements of the workers, and consolidating their bargaining position in the new conditions. Gradually, disjointed efforts of organized workers are being unified and an intuitive policy becoming the chosen one. The process of Russia's political development has taken a complex and painful path. The struggle within the bourgeois camp determines the direction of that process. It is only through independent organizations and by defending its rights that the proletariat will be able to exert an impact on the course of events. We are deeply convinced that the organized forces of the proletariat will soon find the possibility of establishing true communication with the international workers' movement. Maybe this information will shed some light on part of Russia's reality.

In the difficult situation that surrounds us and defines our work, we send you, dear comrades, our warmest greetings.

# The White Threat
## *(1919)*

## Declaration of the Workers' Delegation to the Commission on Labor Legislation

August 1919

Only the regime of a democratic republic and only consistent implementation of the principles of general, equal, direct, and secret ballot for the working class and its organizations will make it possible for that class to achieve its final and immediate objectives. Only then will the conditions be created for a true defense of workers' interests and the interests of the majority of the population. Therefore, the workers' delegation considers absolutely hopeless any attempt to resolve complex problems of social legislation in any satisfactory way in conditions of uninterrupted civil war and in the absence of legislative institutions created by the free will of the population. [At this point the reading of the declaration was interrupted.]

The special conference under the commander in chief of the armed forces in the south of Russia is a consultative legislative institution under military authority and therefore cannot be recognized under any circumstances as authorized to express the interests of the people. In view of this, the workers' delegation eschews, in advance, any responsibility for the work in the Commission on Labor Legislation created under the special conference. Having received a mandate from workers' organizations in the south of Russia to defend working-class interests in this commission against encroachments on the part of the ruling classes and state authority, the workers' delegation states that the proletariat of Russia will not abandon under any circumstances its demand for freedom of associations, an eight-hour day, and all other achievements of the February Revolution. Considering labor legislation of the provisional government as a point of departure in its struggle, the working class will attempt to develop, add on to, and broaden this legislation in the future. At the same time, the workers' delegation considers that its utmost duty is to highlight the current political reality in which workers' organizations are forced to conduct their activity.

In the sphere of internal policy, the authorities are liquidating the

---

The text is incomplete. "Deklaratsiia rabochei delegatsii v Zakondatel'noi Kommissii pri Osobom Soveshchanii" (2 September 1919). It was published in Georgii Pokrovskii, *Denikinshchina, God politiki i ekonomiki na Kubani (1918–1919)* [Denikin's Rule: A Year of Politics and Economics in the Kuban (1918–1919)] (Berlin: Grzhebin, 1923).

democratic achievements of the revolutionary era. Democratic institutions of local self-government are being abolished and replaced by appointed boards. The new electoral law for the elections of local self-government is based on limiting working-people's rights. The election campaign and the elections themselves are beginning under conditions of a lack of civil rights and in the absence of political freedom. What we see is the rule of martial law and police terror.

Freedom of the press has been abolished, or, rather, only reactionary parties and right-wing press enjoy complete freedom. Most institutions of authority are controlled by former functionaries of the czarist regime and other elements inimical to democracy. The death penalty has become an everyday occurrence. Quite often executions are held without trial on the pretext of "an attempt to flee." Not infrequently, arrests and even executions have been conducted out of self-interest or revenge. There have been mass pogroms in a number of cities (Ekaterinoslav, Kremenchug, Elisavetgrad, and others) incited by baiting [minorities] and fueling national chauvinism.

In the sphere of politics, the authorities are liquidating workers' social welfare benefits. Freedom of association does not exist anymore. Threats of trying workers in military courts for strikes in effect puts the working class in a position of total dependence on the entrepreneurs. Arbitrary actions against workers' organizations continues, as does unlawful interference in their activities. Arrests and summary acts of violence are conducted against labor leaders under the pretext of struggle with bolshevism.

In Poltava, the presidium of the conference of trade unions was arrested for convening a discussion on whether to take part in the work of the Commission on Labor Legislation. After the union members were arrested, they were beaten up.

In Kremenchug, several trade union leaders were arrested despite the fact that the Society of Factory and Plant Owners as well as other organizations vouched for them.

In Ekaterinoslav, the chairman of the factory committee of the Bryansk plant was shot and killed for an "attempt to flee."

In Rostov-na-Donu, the authorities have refused a permit for the publication of a local council of trade unions.

Stating all these irrefutable facts (the number of such examples could have been multiplied), the workers' delegation declares that it would consider its participation in the work of the Labor Legislation Commission expedient only if the following conditions were fulfilled.

1. Complete freedom for the workers' delegation to communicate with trade union organizations and rank-and-file members by means of reports, bulletins, and the like.

2. Free activity for trade unions in all types of hired labor. Freedom for all workers' organizations, and freedom for workers' press.
3. Inviolability of the persons of the delegates and cessation of repressions against trade union members and workers.

WORKERS' DELEGATION

---

DOCUMENT THIRTY-ONE

---

## Resolution of the Central Council of Trade Unions in the South of Russia against Anti-Jewish Pogroms

A new wave of horrors, similar only to those in the Middle Ages, has rolled across the south of Russia, tormented as it has been by a two-year-long civil war. From various cities and shtetls in the former Jewish pale [a geographic area in the western provinces of Belorussia and the Ukraine where the Jews were required to reside under the old regime], news is coming in about pogroms, robberies, and savage violence committed on the defenseless Jewish population. The press is deprived of the right of presenting these facts to the public. Sinister rumors are spreading among the populace about more and more pogroms. Statistical data on pogroms are on the rise with the abundance of enough facts to stagger the mind. An absolutely unbearable atmosphere, poisoned by the evil of hatred of people, naked violence, and total impunity for the most horrible of crimes—murder of the innocent—has been created.

The images are resurrected from the times of the czarist autocracy, which, by inciting national hatred, tried to channel the discontent of the masses who lacked political consciousness into anti-Jewish pogroms. An unavoidable question arises. Is Russia again destined to go along the path that has already led it to a destructive civil war? We have heard from the authorities that the pogroms were unavoidable. We heard it first from the

---

"Rezoliutsiia protesta lugprofa protiv Evreiskikh pogromov," first published in B. Kolesnikov: *Professional'noe dvizhenie i kontrrevoliutsiia* [Trade Union Movement and Counterrevolution] (Kiev: Gosizdat Ukrainy, 1923) pp. 402–3. Hoover Institution Library.

governor of Ekaterinoslav and in recent days from the commander in chief, General Denikin. But these appeals are not entirely reassuring because the crimes remain unpunished and because the same individuals who defend pogroms in the press as a justified revenge of the population remain as heads of departments of social propaganda. The mood of total hopelessness for the cause of cultural regeneration in Russia embraces a broad stratum of the population where on one side the savage Cheka is shooting Russian intelligentsia in batches and on the other side "the army is committing violence against the Jews," as General Denikin put it.

In view of these facts, the Central Council of Trade Unions in the south of Russia, as a representative of the organized workers, considers it its duty to declare in the most categorical terms its resolute protest against those who have perpetrated as well as those who have inspired this new and shameful tragedy in the current Civil War. The organized proletariat is fully aware of those sociopolitical conditions that made the repetition of pogrom horrors possible. The proletariat is convinced that in a new and democratic Russia there will be no place for either an Inquisition like the Cheka or for savage pogrom bacchanalia. The process of creating such a new Russia still lies ahead.

To the present-day authorities who have assumed responsibility for the life and well-being of all citizens, regardless of nationality, the organized proletariat considers it necessary to point out that it is imperative to take the most decisive measures to stop the pogroms in all their forms and manifestations in the cities and on the railroads. It it imperative to open criminal proceedings against the culprits and instigators and to dismiss from all positions of authority those who in word or deed were involved in this shameful and criminal activity. The Council of Trade Unions resolves to recommend that all local councils put the question of pogroms on the agenda of all delegate meetings and general meetings of the local unions.

DOCUMENT THIRTY-TWO

## Report of the SD Delegation to the Central Committee

19 November 1919 (Tula)

Dear Comrades:

In accordance with the CC resolution of October 1, 1919, our delegation set out for Tula on October 11 and remained there until October 28. As far as the delegation's activity is concerned, it is necessary to draw the attention of Tula's working population to our mission, as well as the Tula authorities. After the arrests [which took place after a wave of strikes in Tula; see document 24] in the spring of this year, our party organization was not able to function legally. Even after most of the arrested Social Democrats were released, it was impossible to organize a single party gathering in Tula. Our party enjoys widespread support among the workers of the Tula plants. But in such conditions these sympathies could not be equated automatically with support for every aspect of our policy because our policy remained largely unknown. These were blanket [*blanco*] sympathies based on activities in the past. Whereas in party circles our policy toward Denikin did not arouse any ambiguity, among the workers and the Tula population at large, strange and even ridiculous sentiments prevailed.

The official Bolshevik press has been trying very hard in the course of the last several months to equate the Mensheviks with Denikin [to discredit the Mensheviks as counterrevolutionaries, as no better than Denikin]. As a result the workers sometimes said to us, "Well, if the Mensheviks are at one with Denikin, the Denikin is not that bad!" Bolshevik suppression of the press therefore has led to unexpected results. [Apparently, these workers reasoned that they did not know exactly what Denikin stood for, but did know what the Mensheviks stood for. If there was no difference between them and Denikin, thus "Denikin could not be that bad," a conclusion contrary to the one intended by the Bolsheviks.] In this situation, the main task of our delegation was to dissipate delusions and formulate the position of Social Democracy on the civil war with utmost clarity. During our stay in Tula, we gave speeches in the city soviet and at the trade union conference. We have organized one big rally in the city center and given one lecture in

---

Reports of the Menshevik delegation to Tula, Bryansk, and Tver were published in 1919 *Oborona revoliutsii i Sotsial Demokratiia*, a brochure put out by the Menshevik Central Committee. The edition was very small; this brochure is now a bibliographic rarity.

the house of music on the topic "Food Supply and Denikin." We have delivered four lectures to Red Army soldiers and taken part in four large rallies that went on simultaneously at the armaments and cartridge plants. We have also published three articles in a leaflet explaining the position of our party.

In all our public speeches we pursued two objectives. The first was to clarify our position on Denikin's offensive and to call on the workers to rebuff energetically the all-Russian reactionary forces. The second was to emphasize the oppositional character of our party in regard to Bolshevik authorities and to explain that our support of the Red Army does not in any way signify our capitulation to the Communists. Attentive and serious attitudes to our speeches, auditoriums filled to overflowing, and dozens of note cards with questions for our speakers showed that our work was not in vain. We managed to accomplish a great deal and succeeded in dissipating much confusion and misunderstanding. As far as the vigor and fighting spirit of the people is concerned, clearly, much could not be accomplished in just two weeks. One could not realistically expect that the working masses, exhausted by hunger and indignant over repressions against the opposition, would become inflamed and rush to battle instantaneously after one word from a Social Democrat. For this one needs much work over a long period of time and a different political atmosphere.

It is important to point out a few things about the current political situation in Tula. The Mensheviks' campaigning in support of the Red Army is such a "problem" for the local Bolsheviks that they simply cannot resolve it. To prohibit our work makes them objects of derision, but to allow us to work is also frightening. What if the Mensheviks become a powerful political force? Nothing would be left of the Bolsheviks' assured monopoly on power, and, even if the army won, one would have to part with many attributes of power. When we arrived in Tula, we asked the military authorities (the War Council), the only authority in the city, for a permit to campaign. The War Council vacillated for three days, and on the fourth day, after long consultations with Moscow, allowed us to work. As it turned out, this was not good enough, for the provincial EC [Executive Committee] decided to have its say. The provincial EC controls, among other things, all auditoriums suitable for meetings. Again, tedious negotiations dragged on for three days, and after an internal struggle, the provincial EC arrived at a wise decision: to grant permission to campaign to the delegation that has arrived from Moscow, but to refuse such a right to the local Tula Mensheviks. [This incident shows how much authority the local Bolsheviks enjoyed. Strictly speaking, this ruling was unlawful because the Central Executive Committee decree, which legalized the Social Democratic party in December 1918, was still in force. There was no legal basis for refusing to recognize the local organization of a legal opposition party. What mattered, though, was not the letter of the law but the distribution of political power. Local dictators jealously guarded their dictatorships from any encroachments, be it an opposition party or Moscow.] We were allowed to campaign under a rather clumsy and long title: The Tula Commission of the RSDWP to Implement the CC Resolution of October 1. The commission included two from Moscow and three from Tula. The commission was elected at a secret [because the local Social Democratic organization in Tula was still regarded as banned by the Bolshevik authorities] meeting of our Tula organization in the hotel where we were staying.

All our protests [aimed at making the banning of local Social Democrats unlawful] have achieved only a promise to consider the question of legalizing our Tula party organization in a week or two. During our entire stay in Tula, Bolshevik policy was characterized by ups and downs, undecidedness, and petty infringements on our work. Our status can be described as semilegal. They prohibited us from announcing on posters that the sponsor of our meeting was the Tula SD organization. We were prohibited from collecting monetary donations to support our commission. We could not even mobilize our party members in the Red Army because we could only gather our party members once. Most Tula Bolsheviks are incapable of understanding the idiocy and absurdity of this policy. They are nearly all solid bureaucrats who value their secure positions above all and cannot comprehend what this historic situation demands from them.

The Tula delegation of the CC has applied to the CEC demanding full legalization of our Tula party organization. The demand was sent on October 30, but to this date no answer has been received.

D. D.

---

## DOCUMENT THIRTY-THREE

---

### The Bryansk Region
#### (excerpt from the report of the local SD organization to the Central Committee)

[November 1919]

On November 10, a delegation of the CC headed by Pleskov and three members of the Moscow party committee set out for Bryansk. The delegation had been entrusted by the CC to rally local workers to repulse the counterrevolution [to convince local workers to support the Red Army against Denikin's offensive]. On arriving in Bryansk, our delegation convened a session of the local SD party committee. We proposed to discuss the CC resolution of October 1 and the measures to be undertaken to carry it out. After a lively debate, the local committee resolved to organize several meetings with the workers of the city. During the debate it became clear that, for the past several months, the Bryansk and the Bezhitsa party organizations could not engage in any open, broad-based political activity because of the repression prevalent throughout Soviet Russia. As a result, contact with the broad workers' masses has, to a considerable degree, been lost [a disguised reference to the arrests of workers and Social Democrats after the strikes in the spring of 1919].

In the course of our negotiations with the Communists, we managed the following: after some hesitation they announced that they would not put obstacles in the way when we organize rallies. They were also ready to tone down their speeches against the RSDWP and to make them more correct, if we in turn would not emphasize our disagreements with them. The first rally we organized at the arsenal (attended by 400 people) showed that the apathy among the broad workers' masses was much more pronounced than expected. The workers listened listlessly to our speeches and those of the Communists. One could see that the masses had lost faith, that they were exhausted by the conditions of the present economic and political ruin. Furthermore, the ruling party has not shown any sign that it will change its policy in the direction of democratization. This paralyzed all

---

Bryansk—an industrial city in Orel province at the southern edge of the central industrial region around Moscow—was the site of one of the oldest locomotive plants, with several thousand workers. Orel, the province capital, was taken by Denikin's forces on 14 October 1919. Thus Bryansk was very close to the front line when this report was written.

appeals for active struggle against Denikin's counterrevolution, which at that time operated only a few dozen *verst* [a measure of distance in prerevolutionary Russia] from Bryansk.

During our two-week-long stay in Bryansk and the neighboring area, our delegation managed to take part in seven workers' rallies: two large rallies in Bezhitsa (up to 500 participants at each rally), two in Bryansk (from 400 to 500 took part), one in Liudinov (about 1,500 were present), one at a sugar refinery near Bryansk, and one in Raditsa (about 300 present). Some of them were organized by our Bryansk and Bezhitsa comrades, and some were convened on the initiative of the Communists. In addition the delegation organized two party meetings in Bryansk and two in Bezhitsa.

Workers' attitudes, that is, how they received our speeches and those of the Communists, differed depending on local conditions. For example, in Liudinov (Maltsevsky region), where the Cheka repressions were strong and directed against individual workers, the masses were clearly hostile to the Communists, and no appeals to struggle with Denikin would soften their mood. In Bezhitsa, on the other hand, where repressions were not felt as sharply and where the Bolsheviks were quite correct in their speeches, the workers' mood was not as depressed as in other places. The same applies to the rally at the workshops of the Moscow-Kiev-Voronezh railroad line.

Summing up the results of the entire campaign, we must admit that they were very insignificant. It could hardly have been otherwise in an atmosphere where workers are intimidated by Bolshevik terror, by food supply crisis, by general economic ruin, and by the evacuation of enterprises. [The authors of this report mention the problem of the evacuation of enterprises only in passing. Some years ago I interviewed an old Menshevik, Lazar' Pistrak, one of the three delegates to Bryansk, who told me that the issue of evacuation was explosive. The Mensheviks defended the official Soviet position that if the enemy approached the area in question, industrial enterprises would have to be evacuated. This line of argument caused, according to Pistrak, a great deal of discontent among the workers, who wanted to keep their jobs and guard their enterprises no matter what: if the Bolsheviks had to go, let them go, but the plants were going to stay. This testimony suggests that a widely held view—that the workers opted for Bolshevik victory when confronted with White takeover—has to be revised. There seem to have been workers who displayed a lack of enthusiasm for the Bolshevik cause and, as the next paragraph in this report puts it, a "sympathetic attitude to Denikin."]

This atmosphere could not help but influence workers' attitudes in the most oppressive way. Nevertheless, as a result of our campaign, a sympathetic attitude to Denikin, or indifference to the fate of the revolution at best, which undoubtedly was prevalent among the broad working masses, now has cleared to a considerable extent. And this is a positive result.

---

## DOCUMENT THIRTY-FOUR

---

## In Tver

[October 1919]

The city of Tver is very similar to Tula and Bryansk: there are several large enterprises in Tver, and it is a large provincial proletarian center. The differences are that the textile industry predominates and that the workers in Tver have much stronger links to the countryside. Because of this, the cultural and political level [*niveau*] of workers and the degree of their organization are lower than in Tula or Bezhitsa.

Comrade Ermanskii [O. A. Ermanskii, a member of the Menshevik Central Committee, in 1921 tried to leave Soviet Russia, but was caught, repented, and became a loyal former Menshevik; he published a book: *O perezhitom.*] visited Tver. He was invited to give several lectures, and the party CC entrusted him to campaign in favor of voluntary mobilization in the Red Army to repulse the counterrevolution. From October 11 to 14, Comrade Ermanskii stayed in Tver and spoke at workers' rallies at the Baltic plant, supply workshops, the Morozov textile mill, the Berg factory, and the railroad workshops. Because of the lack of posters, only about two hundred to five hundred people attended each of them. The topic of his lectures was "What Is in Store for Workers Tomorrow?" The speaker criticized certain aspects of Bolshevik domestic policy and suggested that these could be corrected only through the efforts of the working class. Such corrections to policy were possible in Soviet Russia, but they would be unthinkable if Denikin were to triumph.

The speeches were successful as far as the effect on the audience was concerned. A lively debate followed, and the speaker received numerous notes from the floor. Workers asked him to come to Tver again and proposed to publish his speech in the local *Izvestiia*. However, one cannot speak in this context of a great impact on the workers' will or about raising the degree of their involvement. There is too much discontent among the workers over current policies. [The author is very cautious in his assessment of popular anti-Bolshevik attitudes. Compare his assessment with those of the Tver Bolsheviks themselves, one of whom said at the provincial party conference in the summer of 1919, "The peasants, almost entirely, almost all of them are armed against us, against the Bolsheviks." *Izvestiia Petrogradskogo Soveta,* no. 155 (12 July 1919, Petrograd).] There is much antisocial passivity in workers' attitudes. The predominant mood is "for bread," especially among factory women.

Local authorities were tolerant of Comrade Ermanskii at first. But then they discovered that the popularization of SD ideas was making them uncomfortable. This attitude was finally formulated in a statement: "The gain from these speeches is five kopecks, but the loss is a ruble." In practical consequences, this conslusion led to a ban on further campaigning. The Social Democratic organization in Tver tried to continue campaigning after Ermanskii's speech. It sent its own campaigners to smaller towns in the province. Comrade Leikardt even received a paper from the provincial EC that there would be no obstacles to his campaign. But when the Tver organization elected Comrades Ostrovsky and Rudakov to organize similar speeches in Tver, Ostrovsky was arrested on the eve of the first planned meeting. No reason was given, but he was subsequently released.

# War Communism and Popular Resistance
## *(1920)*

## Rafail Abramovich to Pavel Axelrod

30 May 1920

Dear Pavel Borisovich:

In addition to what Iu. O. [Martov] and F. I. [Dan] are writing, I would like to bring you up to date on what is going on in Moscow and tell you about the conditions of our lives. You know that during the past year we [the Social Democratic party] have been in a kind of semilegal situation. They have put up with us, yet have not allowed us full legalization [that is, the possibility of functioning as a legal Soviet party protected by law in accordance with the constitution] in terms of allowing us to publish a newspaper and so forth. When the Civil War appeared to be over [most probably, the end of 1919, when General Denikin's troops suffered an irreversible defeat. The author's wording suggests that another civil war, the war against the peasant rebels, was gaining momentum.] and the affair with the "militarization of labor" began to affect workers, our public activity intensified (speeches at congresses, congresses of Councils of Peoples' Economy, and so on). Moreover, our public pronouncements against government policy became perhaps sharper. This was the time [early 1920] that coincided with our party's electoral successes in numerous cities: Moscow, Kharkov, Tula, Smolensk, Bryansk, Samara, Vitebsk, Gomel, and others. Our party's influence increased noticeably, which, of course, alarmed the Bolsheviks, at which time [April 1920. For a discussion of the background to the Soviet-Polish war, see Norman Davies, "The Missing Revolutionary War," *Soviet Studies* 27, no. 2 (April 1975): 178–95.] the Polish offensive broke out. In accord with our entire policy, we took a "Defensist" position [During World War I, the "Defensists" were those Social Democrats who favored defending Russia from what they believed to be German imperialism. At that time, Abramovich was an Internationalist whose priority was not in national defense but in international workers' solidarity against the war. His use of the term *Defensist* in the context of the Soviet-Polish war emphasizes his loyalty to the Soviet state.] and presented it in a special declaration, which we are sending to you. At the same time, however, we found it necessary to emphasize our disagreements with the Bolsheviks

Nicolaevsky Collection, series 16, box 45, folder 5, papers of Pavel Axelrod. The text of the letter is translated from a copy in German. Another copy of this letter in Russian is in the Axelrod Archive, 1/1, at the Institute for Social History in Amsterdam.

over foreign policy. Iu. O. [Martov's] speech, even though loyal in general [Martov's speech on 5 May 1920 at a session of the Moscow soviet was loyal in the sense that it supported the Soviet government in its defensive posture vis-à-vis the Poles and created "bad feeling" because Martov criticized Bolshevik policies in the Ukraine. Because Kiev had just fallen to the Polish troops, the Soviet record in the Ukraine did not generate support for Soviet power. Martov demanded a "profound change of policy in regard to the Ukrainian peasant." See "Deklaratsiia RSDRP," Nicolaevsky Collection, series no.6, box 5, folder 25. For a discussion of Martov's policy during the Soviet-Polish war, see D. Dalin, "Politika Martova v Pol'sko-Sovetskoi voine," *Sotsialisticheskii Vestnik,* nos. 7–8 (7 April 1943): 76–77.] created a lot of bad feeling. At a time when the Bolsheviks were making advances to Russian society [that is, with non-Communist intelligentsia] and flirting with [General] Brusilov [A. A. Brusilov, a Russian general famous for his command of a successful offensive against Austrian forces in June 1916. The alleged Bolshevik cooperation with Brusilov and other czarist officers is much exaggerated here. In 1920, Brusilov's role was limited to being a military consultant.] and when Radek was publishing an article on the national character of the war [In the early stages of the war, when Polish troops took Kiev, the Communist government in Moscow attempted to exploit patriotic feelings and for a short time emphasized not the international proletarian solidarity, but the patriotic unity of all Russians.], Martov's speech did not have any damaging consequences for us. At that time in almost all southern and southwestern cities, our party organizations and those of the SD Bund mobilized their members for the needs of the front. (You know of course that the Bund has split.) [A Social Democratic political party of Jewish workers in Russia, the Ukraine, and Poland that throughout its history was closely associated with the Menshevik wing of Russian Social Democracy in 1920 split into Social Democrats, whose political position was hardly different from the Mensheviks and Communists. Those who supported the creation of the Communist Bund hoped that the Bund thus would be in a better position than the Social Democrats to safeguard what had always been its chief priority, representing Jewish workers. These hopes were soon shattered. Lenin's Communist party was not going to tolerate any separate autonomous organization. Soon the Communist Bund was absorbed into the Communist party. On the Bund history, see Arye Gelbard, *Der Judische Arbeiter-Bund Russlands im Revolutionsjahr 1917* [The Jewish Workers' Bund in the Revolutionary Year of 1917] (Vienna: Europa Verlag, 1982).] It seemed as though the *Burgfrieden* [social peace] had muffled the Bolshevik fear of our strengthening and suppressed the growing wrath against us.

But then the English delegation arrived. Our first speech in the Moscow soviet (minutes enclosed) was also quite loyal in our opinion. But, of course, during our meetings (there have been two so far) with the English, we could not hide from them the true state of affairs. To their detailed questions we gave detailed answers, trying to be objective. [The Menshevik Central Committee presented a detailed report to the British delegation entitled "Economic Conditions, 1920." The full text, which is in the Nicolaevsky Collection, series no.6, box 5, folder 40, contains much valuable information on the structure of the Soviet system in theory and practice, as well as exhaustive data on the Soviet economy. For lack of space, this data cannot be included in this collection.] The Bolsheviks knew about our meetings, which vexed them terribly. But what really exhausted their patience was a rally at the printers. This was a huge workers' gathering (four to five thousand), something that has not happened for a long time. At that rally the workers did not want to listen to the Bolsheviks. The printers Kamermakher and others spoke. F. I. [Dan] spoke, and then, all of a sudden, Chernov [Viktor Chernov, formerly the chairman of the Constituent Assembly and one of the key leaders of the party of Socialist Revolutionaries, in 1920 was hiding to avoid arrest. His public appearance and speech at the time when the Cheka was trying to capture him were sensational political events that infuriated the Bolsheviks. See Viktor Chernov, *Meine Schicksale in Sowjet Russland* [My Fate in Soviet Russia] (Berlin: Der Firn, 1921), pp. 35–45; V. Volin, *Deiatel'nost' Menshevikov v profsoiuzakh pri Sovetskoi vlasti* [The Mensheviks' Activity in the Trade Unions under Soviet Power], Paper no. 13 (New York: Inter-University Project on the History of the Menshevik Movement, 1962), p. 93.] gave a speech. He was hiding from arrest and disappeared after the meeting.

This was an impressive manifestation, and the Bolsheviks could not stand it any longer. At about that time, the food supply situation got considerably worse in Moscow, causing several spontaneous strikes at the plants. We always came out against the strikes because of their inexpediency and our "Defensist" considerations. The Bolsheviks needed a scapegoat and also got even with us for the English delegation. And here again, just as a year ago, they made up a legend (this is a ritual by now) that the Mensheviks were "informers of Lloyd George" (through the English delegation) and that the Mensheviks were hypocrites who were fighting against the Poles in words only, but in fact supported them and so on and so forth. (I'll try to send you the papers.) They even created a theory that there were three kinds of arsonists and that we, according to the commentary, belonged to the category of those who created a moral atmosphere for acts of sabotage. Then they produced a slogan, "Traitors, turncoats, and arsonists—out from the workers' ranks!"

On June 2, Wednesday, there will be a session of the Moscow soviet that will expel us from the soviet. After that there will most likely be arrests and, in a word, a new period of underground existence. I am writing to you about it calmly simply because I am used to it and above all because there is nothing one can do. The masses are embittered against the Bolsheviks, but they are intimidated, passive, and so on. We, for our part, would not want to provoke any actions of the masses in this period of great external danger. We do not have newspapers, press, and so forth. Our mouths are shut. Twice already we were in such a situation [illegible] probably [illegible] the third time.

The SRs [Socialist Revolutionaries] have been in prison for a long time. (Just the other day Gots [A. R. Gots, one of the leaders of the party of Socialist Revolutionaries; see document 1. Little is known about Gots's subsequent biography. It was reported by eyewitnesses that he was living in Alma Ata in exile in the 1930s. In 1937 he was arrested, tortured, and executed. See "Socialists in the Soviet Prisons," Nicelaevesky Collection, series no.7, box 9, folders 1–2.] was arrested.) We have accepted the battle, of course. On Wednesday we will try to go on the counteroffensive [at the session of the Moscow soviet]. Alas, the outcome is predetermined in advance. Their tactics are clear. When there is external danger, they respond not by a policy of internal peace, as Radek advocated in his writings, but by a relapse into terror against internal opponents. Psychologically and politically, this terror is directed against different-thinking Socialists, those natural leaders of any opposition within the revolutionary classes. Some Bolsheviks also have another, merchantlike consideration: "You help us now in order to present a bill later. Because we do not want to pay the bill, we do not want your help either." Besides all this, these people are not used to a single word of opposition or protest. They cannot bear hearing a single objection. They have become used to living and ruling autocratically, without a word of criticism.

I do not know what it will be like in the long run, but now and in the foreseeable future, I consider the existence of any "soviet" opposition *unthinkable.* The existing government demands unquestioning, silent, and *total submission,* or it consciously and deliberately pushes the oppositionists to go from peaceful opposition to revolutionary opposition to the current regime. As far as we are concerned, this provocation is not going to succeed, but among the masses and in the different groupings of SRs and anarchists, it seems such attitudes are on the rise. Whose interests this serves is, *qui perod est,* clear without further elaboration. [Abramovich means that the Cheka would be a beneficiary because it could claim that it performed the indispensable function of rooting out subversive elements.] (Today in the newspapers they are again maliciously baiting us and at the same time flirting with Brusilov and with Denikin's officers. That's the way politics is now.)

It seems to me that our party faces a very difficult and important question about measures to be taken in order to go through the coming crisis and to solve the knot of problems that have caused the current situation. It will probably not be possible to go abroad. Now they would not let us go under any circumstances. [In fact, after much deliberation at the highest level, Martov and Abramovich were granted visas to go to Germany. Martov departed in September 1920 for what he thought of as a temporary absence but which turned into permanent exile.] Too bad. We have written a letter to the English explaining the situation. [In this letter, the Menshevik Central Committee informed the British labor leaders that the printers who had hosted them had been arrested. See "Pis'mo k angliiskoi delegatsii," Nicolaevsky Collection, series no. 6, box 5, folder 37.]

> I shake your hand.
> Hearty greetings to comrades.
>
> Yours,
>
> ABRAMOVICH

---

DOCUMENT THIRTY-SIX

---

## To the Central Committee of the Russian Social Democratic Workers' Party

17 June 1920

From a member of the Tula Committee of
the RSDWP and member of the Tula soviet
of workers' and Red Army soldiers

*REPORT*

On the instructions of the bureau of the SD faction in the Tula soviet of workers', Red Army soldiers' deputies, and the Tula organization of the

---

"Dokladnaia Zapiska," Nicolaevsky Collection, series no. 6, box 5, folder 52.

RSDWP, to familiarize the Central Committee with the events in Tula in recent days, I hereby relate the circumstances pertaining to the latest strike at the Tula armaments and cartridge plants and to the unlawful arrest of Tula soviet members for participation in their party meeting on 9 June 1920. I am authorized to ask the Central Committee to undertake the required measures for the liberation of the members of the SD faction [in the soviet] who were arrested without any grounds or concrete charges and who have been kept in prison for over a week.

On the morning of June 6, the workers in the tool-making shop at the armaments plant refused to work and demanded that the shop committee hold a general meeting of the workshop. The causes for the workers' agitation were as follows: (1) the order of the plant administration that work was to continue as usual on Sunday, which coincided with an important religious holiday, (2) that the authorities carried out labor conscription registration of women without prior and timely explanation. Worker discontent was also caused by rumors of unknown origin that one of the units of the Red Army sent the Tula workers (who produce arms for the Red Army), as a present, flour and fat that was allegedly divided up only among the Communists. The workshop committee asked for instructions from the Central Plant Committee, which in turn consulted the plant management and decisively rejected the organization of a general meeting in the tool workshop. Arsent'ev, a member of the plant management board and a prominent Communist, came to the workshop and, shouting loudly, ordered the workers to start work immediately. Those who would not obey his orders had to leave the workshop within two minutes. The workers did not leave and from their workstations expressed their resentment against women being signed up for labor conscription. Taking the wives away from their families would menace their [workers'] livelihood. Food rations were too small to provide for the family, and it was impossible to receive a day off to go to the countryside for food. Thus the wives were the only ones who could go. If workers' wives were going to be conscripted to work and, as a result, be unable to go to the countryside to buy potatoes from time to time, then the workers' situation would become absolutely unbearable. There were also complaints that the food supply situation was extremely bad, that the Communists had privileges, that they seized and took away flour and fat donated to workers, and that, by making them work on Sundays and holidays, the workers could not use those free days to go to the countryside for provisions.

On Arsent'ev's order, a military unit was called into the workshop. The workers continued to demand that a general meeting of the workshop take place. They neither resumed work nor abandoned the workshop. Many Cheka agents appeared and together with zealous Communists yelled at the workers and made harsh threats. They were rude and provocative and intensified the general agitation. After Arsent'ev's repeated shouts and threats, most workers walked out of the workshop. They were immediately arrested. The news spread instantly to all other workshops of the armaments plant.

In most of them, incidents similar to the one at the tool workshop were going on. The plant became flooded with Cheka agents and armed soldiers. The next day, the territory of the armaments plant, the cartridge plant, and the railroad station was declared to be under martial law. At the plants, revolutionary committees (troikas) were formed with broad authority to impose penalties. Announcements were published, signed by the Province Executive Committee (Osinskii) and by the City Executive Committee (Kaminskii), which stated that "the strike" had been caused by the underground work of Polish spies and Black Hundreds and that these elements wanted to use the difficult position facing Soviet power—the food supply crisis and workers' discontent—to provoke a strike at the armaments and cartridge plants and in this way weaken the might of the Red Army. These elements, they stated, and the workers who did not resume work immediately, would be dealt with as deserters from the front, with all the strictness of martial law up to execution and confiscation of property. A military revolutionary tribunal chaired by Kaul', the chairman of the province Cheka, and a commission of inquiry with broad authority were going to be set up to struggle with the strike and the guilty parties. For the time being the workers' food ration, equal to that of the Red Army, would be suspended and so on.

It is important to note that during these events at the plant, the trade union representatives were absent and their places taken by agents of the Cheka and soldiers. The plant was turned into a besieged fortress. More than three thousand were arrested during the first two days. Many workers simply stayed at home. Even though they were threatened with penalties, they did not come to the plant. Those workers who did come to the plant did not resume work, saying that normal work was impossible because a great number of their comrades (particularly the qualified ones) had been arrested.

Arrests continued. After the question "who is not going to work?" every day, in every workshop and in every workshift, a considerable number of workers were arrested by the Cheka [*chrezvychainiki* in Russian, which can be translated as perpetrators of excessive repression] and escorted to the barracks by armed guards. *So, in the beginning, the workers merely demanded that a meeting in the tool workshop take place to discuss and explain questions concerning labor conscription of their wives. They had no intention of striking, but senseless repressions drew them away from their original intention and into a strike that turned out to be an impressive demonstration of solidarity among the workers, a demonstration of passive protest against the bullheadedness and brutality of the authorities.* The cartridge plant joined the armaments plant. The strike of comraderie solidarity was initiated there by women, who began to volunteer to be arrested. More and more groups of women, escorted by armed guards, were led off to prison singing revolutionary songs.

There is absolutely no doubt that the strike could have been averted and that the Red Army would not have been put in such a difficult situation [The authors must have believed that a disruption of production at the armaments plants would adversely affect the Red Army's supplies, especially because in June 1920 the Soviet-Polish war was at its most critical stage.] if a general meeting had been held at the tool workshop. The authorities could have explained to the workers in a humane way, not by shouts and threats, that there was a misunderstanding over the labor conscription of workers' wives, that the stoppage of weapons production was harmful to the Red Army, and that it was possible to seek satisfaction of workers' needs in an organized fashion, through the trade unions and the Soviet of Workers' Deputies. [The authors are contradicting themselves. How could the workers seek satisfaction through the soviet when the arrests were ordered by the chairman of the Soviet Executive Committee? How could they act through trade unions when there were no trade unionists to be seen during the strike and their places were taken by Cheka officials? What the Menshevik authors are suggesting here would have reversed the authorities' course of action.] There is also no doubt that, even after the general meeting at the tool workshop had been banned, if the authorities had not resorted to repressions, rude and provocative shouts, threats, and the calling in of armed force, and if they had promised that a plenum of the soviet or of the trade union would be convened where the workers' discontent could be vented, the strike could have been localized and quickly settled by peaceful means.

But the Tula authorities lost their heads. They set themselves on a course leading not to a quick settlement, but to the lengthening and broadening of the strike. The workers were now in almost a state of psychosis. They simply could not remain on the sidelines as indifferent spectators, and they could not resume work (which was impossible anyway because hundreds and thousands of workers were arrested in different workshops, particularly in the tool workshop, which is the production center of the armaments plant).

Throughout these days workers kept volunteering to be arrested [*samozaarestovyvanie*, a term coined to express the idea that the workers volunteered to be arrested out of solidarity with those who had already been arrested]. Workers' wives sent their husbands not to the plant, but to demonstrations comradely solidarity. When groups of those arrested were marched along the streets, dozens of workers, seeing their workshop comrades among them, pleaded with tears in their eyes that the guards arrest them as well. *This mass psychosis also embraced Communist workers. More than a few of them were among those arrested and those who volunteered to be arrested. They did not want to work under the prevailing conditions.* Many worker-Communists asked me what could be done to stop this absurd strike. When I mentioned the harm to revolution caused by plant stoppages and told them it was necessary to resume production of weapons for the Red Army immediately, they answered with irritation that the workers had no intention of striking, that Arsent'ev had caused the strike and then deepened it by repressions, that people like Arsent'ev disgrace communism, and that they [the Communists] should not talk to workers like gendarmes. There were several cases of workers quitting the Communist party on these grounds.

It is impossible to ascertain exactly how many strikers have been arrested because the authorities conceal this information. They must, however, be aware of the absurdity of the situation: they had more "instigators" and "activitists," that is conscious perpetrators, than those arrested for strikes in any industrialized country for an entire decade. *It will not be an exaggeration to say that the number of those arrested and those who volunteered to be arrested during the period of 6–10 June, reached ten to twelve thousand.*

The "liquidation" of the strike began on the fourth day. The Revolutionary Tribunal held sessions in inaccessible rooms at the Cheka, *in the absence of the accused.* [This information suggests that the practice of sentencing political offenders in their absence and without a defense was not an invention of Stalin.] It sentenced 28 workers to hard labor for the duration of wars threatening to Soviet power. The second session of the Revolutionary Tribunal was public, in the presence of the accused. *Defense attorneys were not admitted, though.* Only prosecution witnesses were interrogated. On the basis of such informers' reports (Communists who were squaring their accounts with workers objectionable to them), the Revolutionary Tribunal sentenced all four accused to exile from Tula province and imprisonment in a hard labor camp for one, five, three, and one years, respectively. The Revolutionary Tribunal in some respects outdid the Court of the Versailles [the court that tried the defenders of the Paris Commune] in 1871.

When the Revolutionary Tribunal began its work, a "liquidation" of the strike by "peaceful" and "cultured" means was under way as well. The arrested workers were cooped up in terrible, overcrowded barracks in unbelievable, unsanitary conditions and slept on dirt floors. Food packages from home were forbidden. They were given only half a pound of bread and a lukewarm bowl of watery soup for lunch and dinner. Then they [the authorities] started bringing large groups of workers to the Cheka inner yard; after upbraidings accompanied by rude abuse and threats, they suggested that the workers sign a declaration, composed in the style of a repentant Ivan the Terrible: "I, the undersigned, a stinking dog and the greatest criminal to appear before the Revolutionary Tribunal and the Red Army, repent my sins and promise . . ." and so on and so forth. [The accused being forced to write a humiliating confession for their sins is reminiscent of the 1930s. Yet this incident took place in 1920.] For two whole days, with only short breaks for rest, a Communist of last year's crop, one Keftel' (formerly a white-collar Black Hundreds–type student, now a prominent Communist functionary—a member of the Trade Union Board) tirelessly conducted this admonitory and agitational work. He was transported with joy from humiliating workers who were tied hand and foot. Silently and with gloomy indifference the workers listened to these cynical speeches, silently they signed the already completed declarations, silently they took their places in the columns and marched, under the Cheka guard, out into the street. There they were released, upon which they silently returned to their homes. Angry, with tightened jaws, the workers who had been labeled guilty but who were guiltless, began to resume work. About two hundred to three hundred workers remained under arrest, in addition to those sentenced and those in the Social Democratic faction of the soviet.

The Social Democrats were groundlessly arrested and unlawfully kept under guard, either as political prisoners or as hostages for sins and crimes of the ruling party. According to some workers, it was the top echelons of the ruling party who were the true organizers of the "strike committee." [At first reading this statement may seem incongruous. How could the Communists organize a "strike committee?" What is implied here is that the Communists did so in order to accuse the Social Democrats and other activists of setting up a counterrevolutionary center. On many occasions local Communists set up fake committees and centers to remove undesirable elements, which is why the Social Democrats wanted nothing to do with the "strike committee" and why they were critical of the strike. Had they openly supported the strike, they would have been immediately accused of a "White Guards' conspiracy." One indication of this is that the Social Democratic faction in the soviet was arrested even though it was critical of the strike.] Work at the armaments and cartridges plants has been profoundly disrupted. It will not be easy to get things going again, and it will not be soon. At least two to two-and-a-half weeks have been lost in weapon production for the Red Army.

In connection with the events that took place at the plants on Monday, June 7, a session of the SD faction of the soviet took place in the city EC building. The following decisions were unanimously adopted. (I render them from memory in a much condensed form.)

1. During the current difficult period for the Russian Revolution, a decisive period when domestic and foreign counterrevolution is making its last attempt to strangle the revolutionary achievements of the laboring classes of Russia, and when there is a situation of general economic dislocation and a critical food supply crisis, an economic strike of workers, particularly at the defense industry plants, is, by its very nature, undermining the defense of the revolution and weakening the Red Army's might. Therefore, the Social Democrats are definitely against such strikes. They regard as their main task forestalling work stoppages by appropriate measures and if, despite this, a strike breaks out, to contribute to its speedy termination.

2. The latest strike at the armaments and cartridge plants, just as the previous strike (which was successfully settled by peaceful means with the active participation of the SD faction in the soviet), was a result of the generally hard conditions of the working class, a terrible food supply crisis, the alienation of the working class from political and professional organizations, and a lack of information and understanding brought on by the tactlessness and unskilled behavior of the ruling party's functionaries.

3. If measures such as persuasion and explanation had been undertaken in a timely manner, as happened before, work could have been resumed very quickly. The hasty and indiscriminate application of severe repression without prior negotiations with the workers; the tactless behavior of the Communist cells, which provoked the discontent of broad circles of workers; the absence of trade union and soviet representatives from the plant during the events—all these drew the workers into a strike they did not want. Now, however, a strike movement is under way on the grounds of comradely solidarity and the sheer impossibility of resuming work in the given conditions.

4. All this has brought about the current truly tragic situation, when the workers, who have been turned into strikers despite their intentions, face the iron bayonets of soldiers and a wall of Cheka agents. The workers are alienated from the authorities, from the trade unions, and from the soviet. Such a situation threatens to prolong work stoppage of the war industry plants in Tula for a long time and thus put the Red Army in a rather difficult situation.

5. The SD's task is to contribute in every possible way to terminating the strike. This can only be achieved in the following way: The trade union and the soviet, which were inactive at the moment when they could have and should have forestalled the sad events at the plant, must now act as intermediaries between the authorities and the plant administration on the one hand and the workers on the other. They must secure the immediate release of the arrested workers. They must explain the given situation to the workers, give them the opportunity to resume work immediately, and allow them to make up for lost time by intensive work. Malicious counterrevolutionaries, Black Hundreds agents, and spies, who had consciously been trying to provoke the strike, must be tried in a public court. If charges against them are proven by concrete evidence, they should be severely punished.

6. All comrades working at the plants should explain the true situation to the workers and call on them to terminate the strike.

7. Comrade B. D. Nikolau, the SD representative at the city EC, is entrusted with raising the question of the strikes' termination on the basis of these decisions at the session of the city EC on 8 June.

On Tuesday, 8 June, at the city EC session, Comrade Nikolau had the opportunity to air the SD decisions. He made a number of proposals concerning the termination of the strike. All of them except the third (about releasing the arrested and punishing the guilty) have been unanimously accepted by the city EC. Then, however, the chairman of the city EC, Kaminskii, introduced an amendment sanctioning repressions that had been authorized by Osinskii and Kaminskii. Comrade Nikolau defended the following position: "We consider the method of strike termination by means of repressions to be fundamentally wrong, inexpedient, and incapable of fulfilling the task." On the other hand, in a given situation it would have been inappropriate for the city EC to publicly and officially criticize the province EC, thereby entering into a conflict with the latter. Therefore Nikolau proposed to delete this item, leave this question open, and devote all attention and energy to mediating between the two sides. "It is necessary to involve the trade unions. This is the proper way to assure the speedy termination of the strike." This proposal was rejected. Instead, Kaminskii's amendment was approved, which in fact nullified Comrade Nikolau's proposal (just accepted) on peacefully terminating the strike.

On the following day, the local newspaper *Kommunar* published Kaminskii's amendment as the decision of the city EC. It is important to note that Kaminskii did not dispute our assertions that the strike would not have broken out if the authorities had acted the way they had during the preceding strike. Then, by means of persuasion and an agreement with the workers, the conflict was resolved quickly and easily. We argued that no matter how one feels about the admissibility of applying repressions against workers, warning measures and signals should precede them. That has not been done. A tragic situation exists wherein the strike is going on and hundreds and thousands of workers are being arrested every day. The workers, who had no intention of striking, are now in prison, and the authorities who are calling workers back to work are, in fact, sending masses of them to prisons. We argued that it was necessary to remove the bayonets and prisons because this alienates the workers from authorities, making it impossible to clarify the misunderstandings and resume work. Kaminskii saw as the main justification of repressions that, as he put it, other methods and concessions might create the harmful illusion in workers' heads that all they have to do is strike in order to get the authorities to make concessions. *"It is necessary to put an end to this once and for all. It is necessary to make the workers obey blindly and obediently all demands of Soviet power."* These are his own words.

On the evening of 9 June, a meeting of the SD faction of the soviet took place in the building of the city EC with the prior knowledge and approval of the EC secretary. The meeting was called at the demand of some members of the SD faction who declared that it felt morally wrong for them to remain any longer as mere spectators of the events at the plants where such a tragic misunderstanding was being played out. They could no longer resist the growing wave of comradely solidarity. At the meeting, Comrade Nikolau made a report about the latest sessions of the city EC, a number of reports from local branches were heard, and the following resolution was accepted unanimously. (I render it from memory in brief outline.)

1. Strikes are harmful for the defense of the revolution at the current difficult moment for the Russian Revolution.
2. To successfully struggle with the advancing counterrevolution and to supply the Red Army with arms, it is necesssary to terminate the strike at the armaments and cartridge plants by all means as soon as possible. The only way to accomplish this is for the trade unions and the soviet to act as mediators between the authorities and the workers and thus resolve the misunderstanding that has created an abnormal and dangerous situation. The trade unions and the soviet must try to secure the immediate release of the arrested workers so they can return to work and make up for lost time.
3. To familiarize the Council of Trade Unions, the Union of Metalists, the city EC, and the province EC with these proposals and suggest that they begin settling the strike.
4. The SDs must not evade arrest if and when workers are arrested in the workshops. Neither should the SDs volunteer to be arrested.

5. Those SDs who happen to be among the arrested workers must explain the SD position on the strike to the workers, suggest that they apply to the Council of Trade Unions and the Union of Metalists, and ask them to take on themselves the mediation between the workers and the authorities because the workers did not and do not want to strike, but the authorities, bristling with iron bayonets, refused to talk with them.

At the meeting of the SD faction, it was pointed out, among other things, that very few workers remain in the workshops. Next to every one stands an armed soldier, and Cheka agents are poking about. To call on the workers to resume work not only does not make sense, but is practically impossible. Worker-Communists have also not resumed work. Kaminskii complained to one of our comrades that the behavior of the SDs was far more satisfactory than the behavior of worker-Communists, who would have to be dealt with strictly later.

About twenty minutes after the meeting of the SD faction of the Tula soviet ended, a large horde of Cheka agents, accompanied by an armed sentry, came to the premises to arrest the members of the SD faction. Many of them who had already gone home were arrested in their homes several hours later and taken to the province Cheka. Also arrested were comrades who were not present at the meeting. Altogether nineteen persons were arrested: B. D. Nikolau, S. V. Medvedev, V. N. Chernosvitov, N. G. Brigadirov, B. A. Berlin, Zalesskii, P. I. Kiselev, A. P. Pastukhov, N. Saizonov, M. Morozov, A. P. Ryshkov, Shevkov, Nikolaev, Gerasimov, A. G. Tret'iakov, and A. P. Larin. I do not remember the names of the others. G. I. Degtereev, a member of the SD organization who had been arrested in his workshop with the other workers, was transferred from the Skobelev barracks to join the other arrested SDs in the Cheka. Degtereev [before he was transferred] chaired a general meeting of those arrested in the Skobelev barracks. At that meeting, a decision was unanimously adopted to petition the Union of Metalists with a statement that the workers did not want to strike, that circumstances compelled them to stop work, and that the union should make efforts to release those arrested so that they could resume work.

Comrade Nikolau was interrogated first in a session that lasted one and a half hours. In written form he exhaustively described the decisions adopted at the last session of the SD faction and answered a number of questions on the SD attitude toward the strike and on the character of the SD proceedings. Stating aloud that the session could not be regarded as unlawful because the Social Democratic faction of the soviet was a legal organization, organized in strict accordance with all the necessary formalities, he declared that a sad misunderstanding had caused our arrest and that this misunderstanding should dissipate with his testimony. He said that it was no wonder one could lose one's head during these truly extraordinary events in Tula and that, in view of this, he abstained from protesting our arrest because in the house of someone hanged it is inappropriate to talk about the rope.

Kontel'tsev, a member of the Cheka board, told our comrades that the matter concerned an unlawful meeting and that the decision should be reached in two or three hours, as soon as the Cheka board assembled. After Nikolau, they interrogated Comrades Berlin, Brigadirov, and Medvedev. Brigadirov confirmed Nikolau's statement. They did not interrogate any other comrades and did not arrest any other Social Democrats. It was clear that the Cheka understood that there had been a misunderstanding and that they kept us under arrest "just in case." Thursday, Friday, and Saturday were very busy days for the province Cheka and for the Tula authorities, who worked without rest almost around the clock and therefore could not devote much attention to us. They promised to release the arrested Social Democrats and members of the soviets in a day or two. Other than Comrade Nikolau, however, who had to lead a large group of food supply workers on a business trip to Siberia, all those arrested were transferred [from the Cheka] to prison, where they are now. It seems that they are not going to release them.

Bringing the above to the notice of the Central Committee, I request on behalf of the Tula organization of the RSDWP to undertake the necessary measures for the immediate release of those arrested and to protect the Tula Social Democrats from the shameless arbitrariness of the Communists.

A member of the Tula Committee of the RSDWP
A member of the Tula Soviet of Workers' Deputies
/SIGNATURE/

3 August 1920, Moscow

According to the information at the disposal of the Central Committee, the arrested comrades are still in prison at the present time.

Secretary of the CC of the RSDWP

SKOMOROVSKY

---

## DOCUMENT THIRTY-SEVEN

---

## Iu. O. Martov to S. D. Shchupak

26 June 1920

Dear Samuil Davidovich:

I was so glad to receive your letter and so grateful for its thoroughness, for it gave us a vivid picture of what is going on in Paris. I have just written a seven-page letter to Pavel Borisovich [Axelrod] and, it seems, have completely written myself out. Be sure to read it (ask him to send it to you) to familiarize yourself with the latest events.

What else should I write about? The atmosphere here is, of course, stifling. Two years without the press *ont abruti la racë* [has made people stupid], in my opinion. People have become stupider, and the Bolsheviks, who do not have a yearning for the printed word, even more than others. I think that fifteen years of a regime like this is enough to make people grow hair and begin barking. It may be necessary to grow hair earlier, though, for the lack of cloth. You should not think, however, that material conditions have become much more difficult since your departure. Although prices now are high—a loaf of bread, 500 rubles; sugar, 5,000; butter, 2,000 a pound; one egg, 75 rubles; a cup of coffee, 250 rubles; a cab, not less than 3,000 rubles; a barber, 400 rubles; to fix shoes, from 1,000 to 5,000 rubles; firewood, 30,000 rubles for a *sagen'* [2,134 meters]—the conditions for our middle strata have not become much worse. We do not eat meat for months on end, and our main food staple is millet porridge. But we do manage to obtain food without greater difficulties than before because despite all the decrees, and all the "averaging" [The quotation marks suggest that Martov meant that the tendencies of the Food Supply Commissariat policy were not in the direction of averaging food rations for various categories of employees, but rather of accentuating these differences, as evidenced by the rest of the letter.] tendencies of the People's Commissariat of Food Supply, more and more people receive the food ration of workers and

---

S. D. Shchupak, a Russian Social Democrat and a close associate of Martov's, lived in Paris in 1920 and worked on the editorial board of *La Republique Russe*, a Social Democratic newspaper. In number 13, July 1920, Shchupak published this letter, without identifying Martov as the author. When Martov found out he was furious and sent Shchupak an indignant letter saying that his (Martov's) observations were not intended for publication and that it was unethical to reveal the personal lives of politicians for political purposes. The text here is translated from the original in Russian: Nicolaevsky Collection, series no. 21, box 60, folder 1.

employees. [During war communism, the Soviet government introduced a tiered class system of food rations for the population in the cities. It was called a class system because the working class and its vanguard, the Communist party, received the highest food rations. The bourgeoisie, officially the class of exploiters, received a small ration. By 1920, there were hardly any bourgeoisie left. Numerous employees in the ever growing Soviet bureaucracy, however, began receiving rations as Soviet employees.] Thanks to this ration (which is quite good in some departments), households like ours manage to make ends meet almost without recourse to the free market. I am now living with Ab. Nikif [A. N. Aleinikov, husband of Rita], Rita [short for Margarita, one of Martov's sisters], and Zhenia [short for Evgeniia, another of Martov's sisters], and all of us except Rita receive food rations. I get one from the Socialist Academy. All this, of course, is at the expense of a certain number of workers, employees, and those unemployed old-time bourgeoisie who literally starve.

The speculators, that is, people who became rich at the beginning of the revolution; physicians with established practices; and those who provide for themselves at the free market pay "mad" prices for living expenses—400,000 to 500,000 a month, or even more. The wages are miniscule; the highest wage rate is 4,800 rubles a month. Through "awards," "overtime," and so forth, however, they very often stretch it to 15,000 or 20,000. There are "*spetsy*" [specialists, or bourgeois specialists, engineers, managers, and other skilled workers who were politically unreliable from the Communists' point of view] particularly on the railroads and in war departments, who are openly paid 50,000, 100,000, and even 400,000 rubles a month!! On the other hand, there are doormen, watchmen, and typists who receive only 1,500 or 2,500 a month. The unevenness in real income has become enormous.

As far as the "Commissars' Estate" is concerned, its superior standard of living [in English, in the original] (due to preferential food deliveries) is almost out in the open or should I say less concealed than last year. People like Riazanov, Radek, and Rykov, who had earlier fought against "inequality," now display on their tables white bread, rice, butter, meat, and (at Radek's and Rykov's) a bottle of good wine or cognac. Karakhan [L. M. Karakhan, a Soviet diplomat], Kamenev, Bonch [Bruevich] [V. D. Bonch-Bruevich, a close aid of Lenin in the party apparatus], Demian Bednyi [a poet and a writer], Steklov [Iurii Steklov, an editor of *Izvestiia*], et al. obviously enjoy life. Only Angelica [Angelica Balabanoff in 1920 worked in the Secretariat of of Comintern; however, she detested Zinoviev, became disillusioned with communism, and left Russia in 1921], Bukharin, and Chicherin [G. V. Chicherin, People's Commissar of Foreign Affairs] among the stars of the first caliber are still noted for their "simplicity of disposition."

Sadoul's [Jaques Sadoul—a French officer, a Bolshevik sympathizer, and one of the key links of the Bolsheviks to the French Socialists—helped bring French Socialists into the Comintern.] brother (an official and a wine dealer) lives in the "Soviet Hotel" and, on Karakhan's instructions, was transferred into the category of "convalescent," which means that he no longer eats in the hotel's common canteen where they serve moldy soup, but has the right to order what he pleases. To the question of a neighbor, he answered, *"Je n'ai jamais subi une maladie"* [I have never been sick].) And so he has a dictionary (he speaks only French) every day to order "beef-steak with asparagus and onions" or "veal chops with green peas," and the superindendent delivers all this to him from *Okhotnyi riad* [market in Moscow], making about 100 percent profit for himself (everything is paid for by the Commissariat of Foreign Affairs). I saw this example for myself; it is probably one of many. Dinner parties where timber businessmen and the like meet circles of "highly placed officials" and where the bills are up to several hundred thousand rubles are considered normal. There are also sanatoriums (a few, for the privileged) where rice, butter, *balyk* [type of ham], sturgeon, and caviar are ordinary items of food.

The atmosphere, as I said, is stifling. It is so dull with no strong sensa-tions at all, except that now and then they begin all over again their monoto-nous baiting of the Mensheviks accompanied by threatening catcalls. But even these manifestations of hysteria are becoming trite, devoid of enthusi-asm, and failing to evoke responses even in the Bolshevik masses. A pro-found stagnation of thought pervades bolshevism. There are no intellectual thrusts or anxiety for the morrow of the revolution. A typical representa-tive of the regime and of the ruling party is Kamenev, well fed, with piggish eyes, often with the manners of a paternalistic lord mayor who takes care of the "population in the provinces entrusted to him." Sometimes he breaks into menacing tirades against internal and external enemies, but without much conviction. They say that after a five-minute conversation about overall perspectives, he begins to yawn.

Trotsky thrust forward an Arakcheev-like utopia of the militarization of labor and "labor armies" in January. But he cooled off when he saw what truly Russian nonsense came out of it. And he was glad when Pilsudsky gave him an opportunity to return to his usual occupations: posting sentries, conducting parades, and presenting banners and orders. Radek came back from German captivity refreshed, excited, and critical. In private conversa-tions he allowed that he was "appalled" by "corruption," "*kazenshchina*" [comes from the adjective *kazennyi*, meaning state controlled, sterile, life-less], and the intellectual death of bolshevism. He publicly criticized plans for the militarization [of labor] policy and defended independent actions of the proletariat. They whipped [figuratively speaking] him a couple of times, and he came to the conclusion that under the given regime one can exert "influence" only when one wriggles into the Central Committee. So he crawled on all fours and made it, although with great difficulty, having betrayed the opposition that formed before the last [Bolshevik] party congress. He remained on all fours and now has become a clear-cut spokesman of the official party line: one day he argues that revolution in Germany is very far off and that therefore it is necessary to include the independent [Social Democrats] in the Third International, and the next day he says they should be chucked out because everything is ripe [for the Communist revolution. In the summer of 1920, the Bolsheviks conducted difficult negotiations with the Independent Social Democratic party of Germany (USPD) about the terms of its entry into the Comintern. The decision to join led to the split of the USPD.]. One day he assures us that our [Soviet] goal is to repulse Poland's attack and force Polish landowners to sign a peace treaty to be able to resume "peaceful construction," and literally the next day he declares that "we will not sign a peace treaty with the Polish landlords. We will march through Poland and establish Soviet power there and then push into Germany and extend our hand to the Communist revolution that will break out there in the fall." [Another characterization of Radek is as follows: "His image in the party was that of an erratic, cynical talker rather than a serious politician. During his last years he became thoroughly corrupted." Robert Conquest, *The Great Terror* (New York, Macmillan, 1968), p. 9.]

Even Larin . . . stopped writing proposals and lapsed into silence. Rykov, Tomsky, and Shliapnikov tried to kick up a row by defending the trade unions' input into management against one-man rule and militarization. Rykov capitulated at the [Communist party] congress, Tomsky, after the congress, and Shliapnikov was sent to Europe to break up the trade union movement there. After this treason of the leaders, the rank-and-file opposition was squashed without any trouble. One should note that [Communist] opposition was truly broadly based for the first time. It included highly skilled workers and many local functionaries who rebelled against the deadly grasp of supercentralization. It also included some idealists, indignant over Cheka personnel and corruption. In the Ukraine, they extirpate the oppositionists with "red-hot irons," transfer them to other places, or deport them to the front or other far-off places. The same is also true in other areas.

Just a few days ago, in Tula, they exiled two hundred workers (Communists), to the front; these workers had persistently tried to oust their committee and the [city] Executive Committee. As acknowledged by the Communists even here [in Moscow], half of the EC [in Tula] consisted of criminal elements. That a concealed struggle is going on within bolshevism is, perhaps, the most important current event, although its consequences will not be seen soon. The dictatorship within the party and the cult of Lenin hinder the formation of opposition and nip civil courage in the bud. It is already clear, however, that if peace with the outside world is established, if the threat that everything could be lost disappears, and if the atmosphere becomes more relaxed, then not only workers are going to raise their heads, but the Communists will bicker among themselves. What makes this inevitable is that, by sucking in the dregs from all parties (Internationalists, SDs, SRs, right and left, the Bund, Anarchists, and even Kadets), the original consistency of bolshevism has been diluted and is becoming more so now that the party has been saturated by all kinds of adventurists.

As far as defections to the Communists are concerned, our party has really distinguished itself in recent times. In addition to Khinchuk [L. M. Khinchuk, an old Menshevik, in 1917 was chairman of the Moscow soviet and a member of the Central Committee. After defecting to the Bolsheviks, he worked in the foreign trade apparatus.], Iakhontov [a member of the Menshevik Central Committee from 1917 to 1920], and Dubrovinskaia, Chirkin [a leader of the Printers' Union], Bulkin [real name F. A. Semenov], and Ilia Vilenskii [a party member since 1898] also left [All these party members were important political figures in the Menshevik past.], as well as Maiskii, who was expelled from our party. [Ivan Maiskii, a member of the Menshevik Central Committee from December 1917 to July 1918, was expelled from the committee in August 1918 for his unauthorized participation in the Socialist Revolutionary government on the Volga as a minister of labor. After defecting to the Bolsheviks in 1920, Maiskii made a career of foreign service.] Generally speaking, those who were on the extreme right go over to the Bolsheviks most often. Certainly not all of them defect for selfish reasons or for career considerations; many who "turn left" sincerely want to dedicate themselves, without Hamletism, to working for the good of society, which is now monopolized by the state. With all the muddle, some positive things are still being done in that sphere. . . . [The deleted passage deals with the aforementioned party members' personal motivations for defecting to the Bolsheviks.]

. . . The party lives and works by fits and starts, grasping at favorable moments like trade union congresses or elections to the soviets for an opportunity to stick its nose up to the surface. There is no consistent and permanent work, cannot be, and probably won't be as long as there is no peace with the Entente [Allies]. Will it come? Aside from the Entente, a lot depends here on the Bolsheviks, who are increasingly (including "himself" [Lenin]) led by inertia. Today it carries them away to fight Poland until there is a Soviet revolution there; tomorrow it sends them to arouse the Muslim Orient against England. Do not forget that, in addition to commissars, commanders, Cheka functionaries, and superintendents of huge supply institutions, a great number of people have a permanent stake in the war. (Just as it was in France in 1794.) All the fanatics and doctrinaires of communism fear peace and especially trade with Europe because that would undermine all their foundations. [Martov's letter goes on for two more pages; however, because he discusses only friends and family members, we decided to delete them here.]

IU. TSEDERBAUM

---

## DOCUMENT THIRTY-EIGHT

---

## A Letter to Pavel Axelrod

6 July 1920

Almost all active members of our [party] organization went [probably in the spring of 1920] to the front against the Poles. Now [must be the summer of 1920] our party work has been renewed, and we hope it will be successful. The only problem is that the increase of our influence among the workers causes repressions on the part of the authorities. These repressions push the proletariat far to the right and engender a conviction that only physical struggle [probably, armed struggle] can be fruitful. The Bolsheviks stubbornly prod the masses down a path that we have been trying to avoid from the October days onward, a path of civil war within the democratic camp, within the working class itself. [This reference to the Bolsheviks being part of the democratic camp makes it clear that the author was a left-of-center Social Democrat.]

After the horrors of the Kolchak regime, the Bolsheviks have done so much harm [Bolshevik requisitions caused numerous peasant rebellions. For a detailed treatment of these rebellions, see Mikhail Heller and Aleksander Nekrich, *Utopia in Power: The History of the Soviet Union*

---

This handwritten letter in Russian, identified as "a letter to Axelrod," does not indicate an author. I am certain, however, that this is part of a letter from B. A. Skomorovsky, the secretary of the Menshevik Central Committee, to Axelrod. In his letter, Skomorovsky included passages from letters of local Mensheviks to the Central Committee. The letter begins with one of these passages. Nicolaevsky Collection, series no. 6, box 5, folder 32.

*from 1917 to the Present* (New York: Summit Books, 1986), p. 103.] in Siberia that even the Communists say that they will probably have to conquer Siberia again soon. The cycle repeats itself over and over again: at first an enthusiastic welcome [to the Red Army], then cooling off [to the Communists], then disillusionment, discontent, and, finally, hatred. As an illustration, I am sending you the Tula document [on the strike in Tula in June 1920; reproduced here as document 36]. Just today a comrade arrived from Ufa who told us (he will write it down, and I will send it to you) how in March the authorities pacified the peasants: they burned entire villages, etc.—the usual practice of punitive expeditions. According to him, several thousand were killed just among the peasants. It is superfluous to talk about the attitudes of the population, who, on top of it all, are expecting a bad harvest. (The winter field crops have perished. If the spring crops do not make it, a time will come that will make the past few years seem like a golden age.)

The party conference is scheduled to take place on August 20. Would you please send a letter (preferably in advance, so that we could send it to the provinces) explaining your views on those questions on the agenda? Your opinion about the Socialist inquiry [One of Axelrod's chief preoccupations in 1919 and 1920 was informing the Western public and Western Socialist parties about conditions in Russia, and he insisted that the Socialist International send an impartial commission of inquiry to Bolshevik Russia. Although an international commission never came, delegations of European Socialists began to arrive in Russia in 1920. On their contacts with Social Democrats, see document 35.] (published in *L.R.R.* [*La Republique Russe,* a Social Democratic newspaper in Paris] in a translation from the Tiflis *Bor'ba* [a Russian-language Social Democratic newspaper in the independent republic of Georgia]) has been sent out in full to local organizations. If the wall between you and the party falls [Axelrod had severe reservations about Martov's policy line. See "Tovarishch Akselrod o bol'shevizme i bor'be s nim," *Sotsialisticheskii Vestnik,* no. 6 (20 April 1921, Berlin).], you would want to take part, of course, in working out the party line. The August conference promises much in this regard. We are now connected with Irkutsk, Tashkent, Arkhangelsk, and Baku. Today we received the first letter from Kiev (we rely not on the postal service [The Mensheviks had indisputable evidence that the Cheka was reading their mail.], as in the "rotten West," but on opportunities when someone is traveling). We expect a large number of delegates to arrive unless a new wave of repressions against the workers and our party spoils everything. During the last three years, the Bolsheviks have worked out a certain pattern: when our influence on the proletariat increases, they respond, just like in Saltykov-Shchedrin, "I'll crush you."

In *Izvestiia* you will find a subservient declaration of Cachen and Frossard. [Marcel Cachen and Louis Oscar Frossard came to Moscow in June 1920 on behalf of the French Socialist party to negotiate with the Bolsheviks on the terms and conditions of their possible entry into the Comintern. See Albert S. Lindenmann, *The Red Years: European Socialism vs. Bolshevism: 1919–1921* (Berkeley: University of California Press, 1974), chaps. 5–6.] It is written as if they were deliberately trying to confirm your opinion about the French "swamp" [a group in the party that was opportunistic and indecisive; here, the French Socialist party]. Some time ago I wrote to you my impressions of Soviet newspapers. I now have the opportunity to read *Populaire* and *L'Humanite,* and I am almost ready to agree with you that between those two, "'tis not worth choosing." The enclosed clippings from *Pravda* will make it clear that your heroic work in exposing Communist lies has not been for nothing. The Bolsheviks know what a dangerous opponent you are. No wonder they don't like you much or, if I may translate from Latin, *oderunt dum metuant*—"they hate because they fear." Among their most dangerous enemies, they have always listed you before Iu. O. [Martov] and F. I. [Dan]. You know that we responded very angrily to their attacks (see the "Otstan'te" articles in *Vpered*). But now Russia is silent in all its languages, and we can communicate only by underground leaflets. But we have an overwhelming majority of [revolutionary] democrats and the working class. When [in 1919] hired scribblers wrote day after day, "Denikin with Axelrod and Martov," they not only failed to discredit the White general, but made him appear to be not so bad. In many *workers'* districts they were waiting for Denikin, whom they did not consider frightful, thanks to the Bolsheviks and their foul work.

In semilegal conditions, working undergound, we explained to workers that our alleged alliance with the Whites was a lie, and then they went eagerly against the Whites. The Bolsheviks have an incredible capacity to undermine themselves (this is not so bad after all) and the most revolutionary elements of the revolution. From the Communists themselves we have heard that they may have to conquer Siberia again. (Just imagine what they must have done there, if the peasants are beginning to forget the horrors of the Kolchak regime and forming partisan detachments against the Communists.) Well, they had to conquer the Ukraine four times, why not Siberia? At present, as soon as an unarmed Communist finds himself among peasants, they will show him [*takogo propishut*] that he will be lucky not to be killed. [The copy of the letter in the Nicolaevsky Collection ends with two more sentences that merely repeat events already mentioned. In a continuation of the letter, which is available in the Axelrod Archive at the International Institute for Social History in Amsterdam, Skomorovksy asks Axelrod to inform the British labor leaders that the Printers' Union (which they had been greeted by) had been disbanded. He also mentions that the Menshevik Central Committee had sent information on the conditions in Russia to Zurich with the Italian labor delegation. Finally, he discusses setting up a permanent apparatus of mail delivery outside the state-controlled postal service. Because of restrictions at the International Institute, only part of the letter can be published here.]

---

## DOCUMENT THIRTY-NINE

---

## Persecution of Socialists in Russia in 1920

The year began with wholesale arrests in Kiev where, when Denikin's army retreated, the Bolshevik authorities found our party to be very popular among local workers, thanks to our energetic struggle against Black Hundred Zubatovite demagogues like Kirsta Kiselev (a prominent Communist in the past) who tried to organize workers, not without success in the beginning, around the ideas of "Christianity" and "purely Russian" nationalism. When the Bolsheviks saw, at the Non-Party Workers' Conference and at numerous trade union conferences, that the Social Democrats in Kiev were the leaders of the proletarian masses and that they were in danger of losing the coming soviet elections, they staged a sensational trial of Kievan trade union leaders for alleged "cooperation with Denikin." This "cooperation" was manifested in their view by organizing legal trade unions that had business contacts with Denikin's authorities. The Social Democratic organization published a statement taking full responsibility for the actions of its members in the unions. Then the authorities broadened the charges of cooperation to include all members of the party committee. Several dozen people were arrested, and twenty were put on trial.

---

This report was compiled by the Menshevik Central Committee on the basis of reports from local organizations in 1920. Some local reports circulated in underground bulletins. Some parts of these reports were published in the first issue of *Sotsialisticheskii Vestnik*, which came out in Berlin in February 1921. To save space, abridged reports were chosen over more-lengthy original reports in the underground press. Nicolaevsky Collection, series no. 6, RSDWP Central Committee, box 6, folder 7.

Among them were members of the Central Bureau of Trade Unions, the city party committee, and the city council. During the trial, huge crowds of workers demonstrated in protest on the square in front of the court. The city commandant posted a special announcement with the threat that at the slightest attempt at "disorders," they would use firearms. After the stormy deliberations at the trial, four members of the Central Bureau, including Kuchin-Oranskii and Romanov, a printer, were sentenced to unspecified terms of hard labor in a concentration camp. Members of the [city party] committee S. Semkovskii, L. Skarzhinskii, M. Balabanov, I. Bisk, and others were permitted to engage in public activity. On leaving the court, they were greeted with an ovation by the workers in the square. The verdict was offensive even to the Communists, and the Ukrainian government took advantage of the war with Poland that had just begun to "amnesty" those convicted.

In the beginning of March, the printers of Samara went on strike to protest the arrest of the delegates they had elected to the All-Russian Trade Union Congress [of Printers]. [The report from Samara first appeared in *Billiuten' TsKa RSDRP* (30 July 1920), an underground publication.] The strike spread to all the factories in Samara. In addition to their demand that all those arrested be released, they demanded freedom of the press and an increase of food rations. The local party committee issued an appeal that warned against the strike but supported an improvement of the food supply and the political demands of strikers. Immediately, all known Social Democrats in the city and several hundred strikers were arrested. Many strikers were drafted into the Red Army and sent to the front. Some members of our party as well as nonparty workers and the SRs were put on trial by the Revolutionary Tribunal, which sentenced Egorov, a printer, to seven years of hard labor and others to lighter terms.

In Petrograd, in the beginning of May, without any foundation, they arrested Shevelev, the secretary of our party committee, as well as metal worker Shpakovskii and some other party members. They were charged with being implicated in the so-called case of a group of Plekhanov's followers who distributed a May Day proclamation calling on the workers not to work on May Day despite the soviet's decision. Shmelev was sentenced without trial to two years of hard labor, and Shpakovskii, to six months. Somewhat earlier, a metal worker, Zimnitskii, was sentenced in the same fashion to three months hard labor for his alleged leadership of the strike at the Putilov plant. After the elections to the Petrograd soviet, Comrade Kamenskii, a member of the soviet and the leader of the SD faction in the soviet, was arrested and is in prison to this day [February 1921].

Also in May, the [SD] Don region party committee was decimated by

arrests in Rostov-na-Donu. [This report first appeared in the Protest Declaration of the Menshevik Central Committee dated 14 June 1920.] Immediately after the elections to the local soviet, at its very first session, B. S.
Vasil'ev, the chairman of our party committee, was expelled from the soviet
for reading our declaration. All our party committee members, fifteen
people, as well as other prominent activists were arrested. Among them
were, in addition to B. S. Vasil'ev (he was the chairman of the Rostov-na-
Donu soviet in 1917–[early] 1918), A. S. Lockerman, a prominent trade
unionist; S. M. Gurvich, who was the chairman of the Rostov-na-Donu
soviet in 1905 and was sentenced twice to czarist jails; V. A. Pleskov, also a
former exile under the old regime; and A. P. Bibik, a proletarian poet who
was formerly the editor of a Samara paper, *Nash Golos,* during the war.
Besides these, they also arrested S. Petrenko, Nadezhda Petrenko, P. M.
Melsitov, G. O. Levin, G. L. Popov, I. A. Viliatser, G. K. Borisenko, G.
R. Zaichik, A. F. Samokhin, and V. G. Leibner. The ensuing indignation
among local workers forced the Revolutionary Committee to announce
that they would try those arrested in a public court for their "cooperation
with Denikin and Krasnov," that is, for their legal activity during the White
regime, just as in Kiev. However, there was no trial. Instead the Rostovites
were secretly transferred to Moscow and imprisoned in the Butyrki jail,
where they sat until December 1920 [The year was added later.], when an
administrative order was issued without any trial. A. S. Lockerman and B.
S. Vasil'ev were sentenced to five years in a concentration camp, and
Gurvich, Pleskov, Bibik, and Melsitov, and two others, to three years. The
others were released.

After Rostov, came Tula's turn. [Information on events in Tula is drawn
from the report of the Tula Mensheviks, document 36 in this volume.] The
provocative behavior of a factory commissar caused a spontaneous outburst
of worker protest at the armaments plant supported by all workers in the
city, including the Communists. At first the protest took the form of a strike,
but following the arrest of some strikers, workers and their wives compelled
the Bolsheviks to arrest them, thus expressing their solidarity with the prisoners. In this way, several thousand workers were arrested. The reprisals were
severe, including wholesale deportations to the front. At the peak of the
trouble, twelve strikers were put on trial by a field court martial and sentenced to hard labor for life. In response to the initiative of the Menshevik
faction in the soviet to settle the conflict peacefully, the entire faction was
arrested during the session of the soviet. Other than Comrade Nikolau, who
was soon released, all the others were kept in prison for a month, and then
some of them were exiled out of Tula province.

In Samara, in June, the entire party committee was arrested [This first appeared in *Billiuten' TsKa* (30 July 1920).], and most of the well-known party members were exiled from the province. In Moscow, soon after the visit of the British delegation and their meeting, organized by the Printers' Union, the union was decimated. The entire management board and a number of influential workers were arrested (Buksin, Romanov, Deviatkin, Tsypulin, Yakovlev, Voronin, Zubakov, Chistov, and others). Chistov was soon released. The printers demanded in vain that a public trial be held. After three months under arrest, they were sentenced by administrative order to terms ranging from six months to two years of hard labor.

In Ekaterinburg, our attempt to take part in the elections to the soviet resulted in the arrest of the entire local party committee together with D. Dalin, Central Committee member, and six workers of the Upper Isetsky plant. A month later those arrested were released by an order from Moscow, but the elections were "successful" for the Communists. Of those arrested during the summer, the following should be mentioned: Shierov, a worker from Tomsk, Doctor Shour from Irkutsk (they falsely charged them with having participated in a White Guards' uprising and threatened to execute them both); Zaitsev, a worker from Moscow, and L. N. Nemoklinskaia from Cheliabinsk. She was arrested because, at a trade union meeting, she spoke against mobilizing union members in the Red Army for the Polish front. She suggested that only volunteers should be enlisted. She was sentenced by administrative order to imprisonment in a concentration camp until the end of the war with Poland.

Groups of people were arrested in Baku, Novosibirsk, Ekaterinodar, Iuzovka, Tyumen, Simbirsk, Tver, Novozybkov, Kursk, and Sormovo. In Penza, before the elections to the soviet, Comrade Kuzovlev, the chairman of the factory committee, received an order to leave to Murmansk. When he protested, he was arrested and tried for "labor desertion." Finally, at the end of August, the Cheka delivered two staggering blows to the party: wholesale arrests during the southern Russian and all-Russian party conferences in Kharkov and Moscow. [These events were described in letter number 12 of the Central Committee to the local organizations dated 28 September 1920. A copy is in the Nicolaevsky Collection and in the Axelrod Archive in Amsterdam; it was reprinted in Boris Sapir, ed., *Fedor Il'ich Dan: Pis'ma, 1899–1946* (Theodore Dan: Letters, 1899–1946) (Amsterdam: International Institute for Social History, 1985), p. 575.] In Moscow, they arrested 56 people, including the following CC members: A. Ermanskii, A. Pleskov, A. Troianovskii, as well as S. Ezhov, Guterman, M. I. Nazar'ev, Zimnitskii (both from Petrograd), Z. Gurevich and A. Gurvich from Vitebsk, S. Toper from Odessa, V. N. Maliantovich with his wife, V. M. Abergauz from Baku, M. B. Smirnov from Rostov, N. Zhelezniakov from Kiev, and others. The apartments of R. A. Abramovich and Martov

were searched. Later all the arrested were released, but the party conferences were disrupted.

In Kharkov all the delegates, altogether 120 people, to the southern
Russian party conference were arrested, most of them in their homes.
Among those arrested were B. Ber, Belovskii, A. Sandomirskii, Rubtsov,
Shulpin, M. Shtern, Zakharovich, members of the Ukrainian SD party
committee; B. Ia. Malkin, a member of the Kharkov committee; Levin, a
member of the SD Bund Central Committee; Kuchin-Oranskii, L. Skarzhinskii, and Chizhevskii, delegates from Kiev; and many others. In connection with this conference, Astrov and Korobkov were arrested in
Odessa. At the end of the year a "verdict" was passed by administrative
order that Astrov, Korobkov, Grossman, Babin, Tkachenko, Kuchin-
Oranskii, and others, fifteen altogether, were "sentenced" for "belonging
to the right wing of the RSDWP" to confinement in a concentration camp
for the entire duration of the Civil War. B. Ber, L. Skarzhinskii, M. Shtern,
Rubtsov, Zakharovich, B. Malkin, Shulpin and others, seventeen altogether, were sentenced to deportation from Soviet Russia to Georgia. The
charge was that they "tolerated the right wing in the RSDWP." The verdict
was passed by the Central Directorate of the Ukrainian Cheka; the Presidium of the all-Russian CEC tried to suspend the implementation but failed.
Eleven other comrades were exiled to Georgia, eight from Poltava and
three from Kremenchug. Soviet authorities there disbanded the local Council of Trade Unions, which was composed of the Mensheviks. Several party
members were sentenced to hard labor for five years for "cooperation with
Denikin," and the RSDWP was prohibited from engaging "in activity
within the Kremenchug province."

During the fall, the most severe arrests took place in Samara, Vitebsk,
Rostov-na-Donu, and Mogilev. Seventeen party members were arrested in
Samara. Twenty people were arrested in Rostov-na-Donu. During the campaign of elections to the soviet in Vitebsk, many party members were
arrested, among them A. Karavkin, Seredinskii, and a well-known party
leader, formerly a Central Committee member [in 1917], B. S. Tseitlin
[Baturskii]. Because of the terrible conditions in the prison, Baturskii
caught typhus and died. Comrade Karavkin began coughing up blood. The
Cheka offered to release them if they would stop campaigning. Naturally,
they refused.

In Mogilev the entire SD committee and the Bund committee were
arrested on November 1 in connection with elections to the local soviet.
Those arrested were charged with sedition on the basis of passages from
their pre-election speeches. The Special Department of the Cheka sentenced sixteeen comrades to confinement in various concentration camps
with the following document:

We find the following guilty of malicious criticism of Soviet power and its activities. Because such pernicious criticism has devastating effects on and puts a halt to the work of Soviet organizations in the frontline area, the Special Department, guided by revolutionary consciousness and proletarian understanding of the law, has resolved to confine in concentration camps for hard labor: Leonid Zozimovich in Ekaterinburg, Iosif Nevzner and Sofia Pinus in Smolensk, Iakov Ioffe in Perm, Ivan Veksler and Evsei Ioffe in Kazan, Zalmar Krichever and Iakov Rozinov in Samara, Lazar Ratner in Vitebsk, David Dobkin and Efim Zekenkovich in Tambov. All of them for the term until the end of the Civil War.

Verdict No. 2821

14 November 1920

Special Department at the Revolutionary War Council of the 16th Army.

In Stavropol, Nina Tsintolovich, Ivanov, and Fomin were arrested and sentenced to be transferred to Moscow to be under Cheka supervision. In Nizhnii Novgorod, Ivanov and Gofman were arrested. In Bryansk, Samsonov, a worker, was arrested. In Smolensk, they searched the premises of party members, including that of F. Dan. In Kazan, G. Denike, printer S. M. Efimov, Ostrov, and Balakovskii were arrested. In Saratov, Popov, a worker, was arrested. Arrests were also made in Sormovo, Kaluga, and Pskov.

# The Unforeseen Dictatorship
## *(1920–1925)*

## Report of the Right Mensheviks

[Spring 1920]

Dear Comrades:

We are cut off from the rest of the world by the Allied blocade, by the Civil War fronts, and by the cordons of Soviet power. We are deprived of the right to speak out openly and freely within our country. Thanks to your arrival, we can familiarize our foreign comrades, for the first time since the November [1917] overturn, with the events unfolding in Russia. We want to draw your attention to our point of view, first, because *any* evaluation will make it easier to find your way through the labyrinth of complicated developments in the Russian Revolution and, second, because we are not an insignificant current in the RSDWP; entire party organizations in different cities of Russia and many prominent party leaders are in our ranks.

Lenin said at one point, "Without an economic foundation, communism is not worth a penny." It is exactly that, however—the economic foundation—that is missing in Soviet communism in Russia and that defines our attitude to the entire policy of the Soviet government. The Bolsheviks seized power by means of a military conspiracy, relying on the soldiers, who were tired of three long years of war. The soldiers, then, expected that the overturn would bring about immediate peace, and the Communist party, took upon itself the hopeless task of bringing about a Socialist order in a backward peasant country where the economic and social preconditions for it were missing.

This effort also relied on the sympathy of a broad strata of the urban working population, which justly perceived the destruction of the bourgeois order as liberation from oppression and exploitation; yet it misjudged both its own weakness and its own unpreparedness for the great goal of proletarian movement and the many obstacles placed on the path to socialism by the economic backwardness of the country and its exhaustion by the war. The large and mid-sized bourgeois circles were isolated from those

This typewritten document was single spaced on thin paper with no date or author indicated. Its contents make it clear, however, that it was written in the spring of 1920 and intended for one of the delegations of Western Socialists scheduled to visit Soviet Russia. The author or authors, who must have been Right Mensheviks who disagreed with Martov's view on Soviet Bolshevism, most likely intended to express a dissenting opinion from Russian Social Democrats. Nicolaevsky Collection, series no. 6, box 5, folder 29.

urban and agrarian petite bourgeoisie who were tempted by promises of peace, bread, and land. This helped the ruling party crush the resistance of industrialists and clear the way for the sweeping takeovers of production and distribution by the state. Once in charge of economic life in the country, Soviet authorities were powerless to restore the war-ravaged economy. Moreover, they not only failed to slow down disintegration processes in the economy already under way, but hastened them by groundless experiments and by demolishing even those measures of state regulation [of the economy] that went beyond the confines of the bourgeois order but were necessary for the painless reconstruction of economic activity (for example, rationing).

Before the revolution, establishing workers' control was the fighting slogan of the Communist party. After its [workers' control] failure was officially acknowledged, a total nationalization of large and middle industry was hurriedly carried out in 1918. But nationalization failed to get industry going. Nationalized enterprises were shutting down, one after another, for lack of raw materials and fuel. New branches of large-scale industry (textile and chemical) are on the verge of demise. Their ruins are covered with offshoots of small private enterprises of a *kustar* [cottage industry] or semi-*kustar* variety. Already, on the third day after the revolution, bank capital was confiscated and private commercial banks were merged into a state bank. Yet speculation and usury, indistinguishable from criminal activities, were nesting in the cracks of the nationalized credit system.

As a result of the nationalization of trade, the entire nation became engaged in private trade. The municipalization of urban real estate ended in the decay of municipal construction, which, combined with a general decay of urban public services, created conditions in the cities favorable for the spread of epidemics comparable in magnitude to the Middle Ages. In addition to all this, a catastrophic disintegration of transport has led to the replacement of rail with cart conveyances even for long distances (hundreds of *versts*). This disintegration is tearing apart the already bleeding economic organism of Russia, hampering the functioning of the state production and distribution apparatus, and depriving factories and plants of fuel and raw materials and workers and urban dwellers of bread and firewood.

The most shattering blows to Communist construction, however, are inflicted by the peasantry, which is deeply hostile to communism. The countryside willingly supported Soviet power as long as it encouraged seizure and division of landlords' estates (spring 1918). After October 1917, this was the only sound contribution of the Russian Revolution. But when the Soviets encroached peasant property by their decree on Socialist land tenure, when they demanded that the countryside actively participate in

Communist construction by way of creating agrarian communes, or, at the very least, by subsidizing Communist cities with provisions at unprofitable fixed prices, then the countryside not only recoiled from Soviet communism, but openly came out against it. By passive and armed resistance, the small rural land proprietor stubbornly defends the economic foundations of commodity production and immediately patches up the breaches in it inflicted by Soviet policy. Peasant uprisings encompass large territories despite ferocious suppressions—artillery, executions, and flogging. Like forest fires, they subside, hidden underground, and then burst out to the surface (for example, the recent uprisings in Tula, Simbirsk, and Ufa provinces). The Civil War is sucking the last drops out of the economic organism of the country. It is so protracted because the interior of the country rests on the clods of the anti-Communist peasantry. And if Kolchak and Denikin's officers and volunteers had not yearned to restore the old regime, thus making the peasantry apprehensive about the fate of lands now in its possession, the Red Army would not have been able to crush the Whites, just as it is unable to crush the peasant insurgency.

The countryside has virtually declared a food supply blockade on the cities, which, in its consequences, is even more menacing than the peasants' armed resistance. Neither the holy war for bread, the courting of the middle peasants, nor even the commodity exchange can break this blockade. Both the state grain trade monopoly and the fixed prices on agricultural products, as well as compulsory grain collection, run aground on the rock of peasants' private ownership instincts. Only by coercively grabbing the grain from peasants, reminiscent of the notorious poll tax collection by district police officers and land captains, is it possible to collect from one-third to one-half the grain allotment targets. But even complete fulfillment would have provided only a starvation ration for the population.

The food supply blockade of the cities by the countryside is exacerbated by the activities of Soviet requisition detachments and by the entire Soviet food supply policy, which puts additional obstacles in the way of the already clogged-up channels of commodity circulation between the cities and the countryside. As the transport conditions disintegrate, the food supply blockade of the cities by the countryside is bringing the food supply crisis to the point of famine in the cities. This in turn causes city dwellers and workers to flee from the cities. Therefore, deficiency in the means of production is compounded by the shortage of workers, particularly qualified ones, which exacerbates the difficulties in restoring industry and transport.

Planting communism on soil not yet plowed by capitalist development but already covered with the weeds of military-economic decay has brought two contradictory processes into being. The first is that the nationalization of the economy is accompanied more and more by the regeneration of purely capitalist relations, in most cases in a particularly predatory and cruel form of primary accumulation. Under the guise of *kustar* and craft cooperatives, new capitalist enterprises emerge. These enterprises (forestry, construction industry, food supply, etc.) enjoy disguised or even open support of state institutions, which resort to the services of private suppliers and contractors more and more willingly. With the blessing of the latest congress of the Communist party, the internal order in the state nationalized enterprises is being recast along capitalist lines, whereby the workers do not have any rights. At a time when nationalized state enterprises have one foot in the grave, young capitalist enterprises display surprising vitality and adaptability to the most unfavorable external conditions, despite permanent threats of repression.

The lifting of the [economic] blockade [of the Allies] will open the inflow of foreign capital into the pauperized country, which must rapidly accelerate the regeneration of private enterprise in Russia, in comparison with the dying state industry. The accumulation of private capital inside the country combined with the inflow of foreign capital (soon to be expected) will lead to the re-emergence of domestic profit seekers (who keep quiet now). All this predetermines the failure of Communist construction in Russia, in our opinion. [Signs of regeneration of private enterprise in Russia confirmed the Right Mensheviks in their social analysis. The Bolsheviks also saw these signs, but, unlike the Mensheviks, were afraid of them throughout the New Economic Policy period, as witness their expression *kto kogo?* (who will beat whom?), private enterprise or "Socialist" enterprise. Communists of all persuasions were determined to prevent the rise of private enterprise if it would pose a threat to the Communist monopoly on political power.] The Socialist revolution in the West will not avert this fate because the impact of advanced nations on backward ones can only ease the birth pangs of the new order but cannot create it without necessary preconditions inside the country. [This answers the thesis propounded by Trotsky, among others, that is, that a Socialist revolution in the West would aid backward Russia.]

The second socioeconomic process to be seen evermore clearly in Soviet Russia is the ever greater transfer of the economic center, which means sociopolitical center of gravity, from the cities to the countryside. Just as in czarist Russia before the 1905 revolution, the village was degenerating; according to Shingarev's [see document 3] catch expression, in Soviet Russia today the cities are degenerating and dying. The urban and industrial population not only is decreasing in quantity but also is weakening in quality every day. To chase after a piece of bread requires resorting to all kinds of tricks and ruse, takes energy and time away from productive labor, and, at the same time, demoralizes the masses, weakens the feeling of class solidarity, and paralyzes intellectual interests and aspirations. That is why cultural initiatives of Soviet power, even the well-conceived ones, droop and go to seed on the stony soil of material privation and spiritual apathy. Because of this general weakening of the rhythm of urban life, the cities' intellectual influence on the more backward countryside is also declining. The city has ceased to be the vanguard of the revolution and instead is compelled to follow the village.

Simultaneously with the degeneration of the cities, the countryside is sliding backward; this had started during the war and is accelerating now. After 1905, due to high prices on the world market and the growing internal market stimulated by industrial development, the peasant economy was ceasing to produce for personal consumption only. Rather, it was increasingly becoming a market- and a commodity exchange–oriented economy, turning from unprofitable into profitable. In the peasant economy, the appearance of crops for market went hand in hand with the intensification and improvement of technical equipment. Thanks to market relations, village links with the economic and societal life of the country were being born and strengthened. The rise of the peasant cooperatives united peasants under the slogan Land and Freedom [This old slogan of the Socialist Revolutionaries dates back to a populist organization of the same name.] and made them one of the main social forces of the revolution.

At present, however, the collapse of industry deprives the peasant economy of the most necessary means of production. The shrinking of the internal market and the inaccessibility of the external market, combined with low fixed prices that in value are close to zero, as well as the devaluation of money and the disappearance of commodities, made it impossible to exchange agrarian products for even such necessary items as salt and cloth. All this throws the countryside backward, to producing for personal consumption. It forces the peasants to abandon market crops and return to the grain-growing, three-field system and to primitive methods of land cultivation. This general decay of agrarian production is exacerbated by the devastations of the civil wars, by endless recruit mobilizations, and by requisitions of livestock and grain. The transfer of hundreds of thousands in worthless paper money and of the last remnants of urban luxury items [In 1920 the starving urban population often sold furniture, pianos, and other similar items to peasants, reflected in numerous accounts of the time.] to peasants' hands in exchange for bread cannot hide the coming pauperization of the countryside.

The general decay of agrarian production, caused by the peasants' return to production for personal consumption, tears the links of the village with the outside world, shuts the village in its own shell of local interests, and weakens its organized institutions. Peasant cooperatives, which helped unite the peasants, are withering, Bolshevik repressions notwithstanding, in the face of the return to production for personal consumption. Therefore, the increase in the economic and sociopolitical weight of the countryside in relation to the cities is taking place in exceptionally unfavorable conditions.

All this is compounded by the lowering of the already low level of peasants, political consciousness and the degree of their social organization. Hungry for land, the peasants confiscated nine-tenths of landlords' lands, and now they are ready to support any government that would agree to recognize and confirm these acquisitions. Ready to sacrifice "freedom" for "land," they will follow any adventurist. The dying city and the exhausted, defeated, and weakened proletariat will not be able to stop (thanks to the entire Bolshevik policy) the newest variety of Bonapartism [meaning the rule of a dictator relying on peasant masses. The Mensheviks' concern was that a czarist general would grant land to the peasants and use their anti-Bolshevik movement for his own ends. The White generals, however, did not recognize the legitimacy of peasant land seizures, which was one reason for the weakness of their social base.], wherein lies a grave danger for the fortunes of the revolution. This danger stems from Communist policies that are unacceptable to the peasantry. The inability to install Socialist order in a backward and ruined country defines the overall policy of the ruling party.

The way the Bolsheviks seized power (by means of military conspiracy) and the "shameful" peace treaty of Brest alienated a broad stratum of democrats in the cities and the leaders of peasant cooperatives. The elections to the Constituent Assembly did not give the majority to the Communists, who then disbanded it by force and declared war on democracy. The social basis that Soviet power originally relied on shrank as time went on. The army, which had supported the Bolsheviks for the sake of peace at any cost, dispersed and went home. The middle [income] peasants had been ready after the October Revolution to regard the Bolsheviks as a force that would realize their cherished dream of "Black Repartition" [The word *black* in this age-old expression stands for black earth and *repartition*, a custom among peasants in central Russia of redividing the land periodically according to the number of eaters, tillers, or households in the peasant commune. Black repartition, then, symbolized the peasants' one day redividing the landlords' lands.] of landlords' lands. Yet Bolshevik encroachments on peasants' lands (socialization), interference in peasants' internal affairs (creation of "committees of the poor") to artificially inflame class struggle, and the "crusade for bread" [an expression used by the Bolshevik media to describe the

Bolshevik policy, adopted in May 1918, of sending requisition detachments to the countryside to collect grain by force] to the countryside—all this alienated middle peasants more and more.

And finally, in the cities, semiproletarian and isolated strata of workers had actively supported the Communists as long as their key slogan was "Loot the Looted" [This political slogan was on the front pages of the Bolshevik press during the so-called Red Guards' attack on the bourgeoisie campaign, October 1917 to March 1918.] (this is a translation into Communist language of K. Marx's concept: expropriate the expropriators). But when the flow of accumulated earlier wealth dried up, when the workers' standard of living began to sink under economic ruin and blockade, when workers faced even more stern demands for the sake of economic reconstruction, then their former enthusiasm over the overthrow of capitalist order began to dissipate. This often resulted in open demonstrations against the authorities. In the end, Lenin's government had to rely on a handful of Communist fanatics surrounded by a thick layer of commissars and other bureaucrats (who had come out of the workers' milieu) and on those adventurists and hangers-on who had stuck to the party simply for their own benefit [*primazavshiesia*, literally those who stick to the party, was not a Menshevik formulation. In early 1919 *Pravda* was full of articles denouncing opportunists and adventurists who joined the Bolshevik party only to derive benefits and privileges.].

Lenin's government began to employ the obedient bayonets and rifles of the Red Army against even the slightest opposition. When some groups of the population were openly, although passively hostile, when others were indifferent, and when still others were unprepared [for what is unclear] it was only possible to rule by repression. That is why the overall policy of Soviet power emerges more and more as a struggle against any manifestations of democracy, a curbing of political rights, a liquidating of civil liberties, a suppressing of the activities of all those who are not regime supporters, a bureaucratizing of government, and finally a militarizing of the entire social order that combines bureaucratic rule with the absence of civil rights for the population. *What is being created now is a new form of barrack-like socialism—unforeseen by Marxism* [emphasis added]—which is reminiscent of the Jesuits' experiments in Paraguay in the seventeenth century.

The policy of lawlessness and repressions has its own logic. The Soviet constitution is conceitedly compared with "bourgeois democracy"; yet it formally deprives all those who are manifest enemies of communism of their political and civil rights. The limitation and deprivation of civil rights first affected the bourgeoisie, but in fact applied to all except adherents of the ruling party. At present there is no press in Russia, except Communist state press, and no freedom of speech and assembly for anyone other than Communists. All parties and organizations, even Socialist and worker ones, have been driven underground or destroyed, except those that trail the Communists and take on their oath of allegiance.

Even within their own party, the Communist ruling circles feel compelled to suppress any opposition and to deprive their local organizations of even a trace of independence. To secure unity of will and action in the Communist party, they exile party functionaries, send others to the front line, and arrest by administrative order even elected members of Soviet institutions. For example, after the Soviet government recognized the Ukraine's right to political self-determination, the Congress of the Ukrainian Communist party elected a central committee objectionable to Moscow rulers. This central committee was disbanded, and a new central committee was appointed by Moscow.

But even in backward Russia political life and social activity find their way around these obstacles. Now and then, however, this takes ugly forms of political adventurism. The absence of political rights, the existence of an underground, and repressions create a fertile soil for conspiracies and political terrorism. Any manifestation of political activity must be suppressed because it does not fit into the confines of the Soviet constitution—which demands unconditional subordination to the orders of Communist party leaders. That is why the Cheka in Soviet Russia has acquired the same kind of unlimited power as the Okhrana [secret police] had in czarist Russia. The Soviet republic is ruled by emergency laws. There is inviolability of neither person nor domicile. Not only antigovernment activities, but antigovernment views are considered criminal offenses.

Concentration camps are periodically filled up with political prisoners of all ages and backgrounds, just as the czarist hard-labor camps [*katorga*] were in the old days. Execution by shooting has replaced hanging. What thrives in such abnormal conditions is boundless arbitrary rule, bribery, and corruption. In the end, when people are deprived of civil rights and subjected to repressions, *a new privileged estate* [soslovie] *of Communists rises over the rest of the population.* This estate has an exclusive right to enjoy the benefits of life and, closed to the public eye, willingly uses its dominant position to make arrangements of all kinds, unbound by any legal constraints. The corrupting effect of privilege penetrates deeper and deeper into the milieu of committed Communists and eradicates the difference between them and opportunists.

Lack of firm democratic traditions, lack of organizational habits, and pursuit of daily bread play into the Bolsheviks' hands. Apathy and defeat reign even in the workers' organizations, which have become voiceless instruments of the authorities. Compulsory membership in state trade unions in actual fact means paying dues on payday. Urban and village cooperatives have been turned into an auxiliary distribution apparatus under the Food Supply Commissariat. One has to resort to threats of punishment and compulsory mobilization to induce even Communists to fulfill their obligations. In a word, social and political activities, not exactly thriving earlier, are now coming to a standstill.

At the same time, owing to a comparatively low level of culture and of political consciousness among the workers, relatively few of them have the necessary skills to bring about a Socialist transformation of society. At last years' party congress, Lenin complained that a thin layer of the advanced proletariat had to shoulder a task too heavy for it. The situation could not have improved since then because the revolutionary-minded workers, those most loyal to communism, were sent to the Civil War fronts. Because the true prerequisites for Socialist construction (i.e., independent activities of the conscious proletariat) were missing in Soviet Russia, an attempt was made to fill in that void with surrogates. This attempt was doomed to failure. Hence such simple practical issues as the transition from collegiality to one man in control and the replacement of unqualified proletarians or Communists by specialists not belonging to the Communist party, or even hostile to it, were torn by conflict. From dictatorship of the proletariat to the rise of a dictator is how one Soviet journalist summed up the development of nationalized industry.

The same process can be seen in other branches of the economy and government, especially if the new dictatorial tendencies do not encounter resistance from the industrial workers. If there is no resistance, these resurrected methods of management result in the growth of the bureaucratic executive apparatus, which at first overshadows and then replaces self-government and independent activities of the population. Perhaps the most convincing example of this bureaucratization of social and political life is the fate of the Central Executive Committee and the local soviets. The Central Executive Committee has been turned into a rubber stamp of the Council of People's Commissars. The local soviets serve as a cloak to cover for local rulers who were not elected but appointed from above. If we add to this that local authorities intrude in every detail of everyday life because they distrust the population, one can see how far bureaucratization has developed in Communist Soviet Russia. In Moscow, the number of employees in Soviet organizations is double the number of workers in nationalized enterprises. Therefore, what is taking place is not the withering away of the state, as Engels had foreseen in a Socialist society, but the swelling of the state apparatus, which pervades not only all spheres of societal life, but also the most intimate sides of personal life.

The consequence of this bureaucratization is that normal work has been replaced by red tape. This is the end result of thirty months of Communist rule. What makes the slow and clumsy bureaucratic apparatus of Soviet government different from ordinary bureaucracies is that it is more cumbersome, inexperienced, and uncultured. And this apparatus, objectively incapable and often unwilling to perform, is entrusted not only with the functions of state government but also with the management of the economy. [The next sentence is illegible.] Soviet industrial bureaucracy is powerless to inspire workers to work, which is why it has to rely on coercion. In most cases, *subbotniki* [Saturdays that Communists volunteered to work without compensation, usually on the "transport front"] are voluntary in name only, for, unable to raise labor productivity by improvements in technology, the industrial bureaucracy instead intensifies its exploitation of the workers by lengthening the workday, introducing a bonus system, and so on.

At every step, Soviet labor laws are violated and repealed. For example, collective labor agreements have been placed by the bureaucracy's unilateral decrees on labor conditions. Wages are increasingly falling behind the cost of living. The latest wage rates—adopted in September [1919], when the price of bread was 30 rubles a pound on the free market— are still in effect, even though bread prices have risen to 350 rubles a pound. No wonder that, in these conditions, workers and employees are trying to look for a better ratio between wages and the cost of living in the countryside. Indeed, a shepherd hired at current free market rates receives several times more than the most qualified metal worker, be it at state enterprises or at the quickly multiplying private shops. The flight of the best employees and the lack of qualified workers are increasing with every passing day.

Their idea was to tie workers and employees to an enterprise, so they issued a decree that prohibited workers and employees from quitting their jobs and prohibited enterprise directors from firing their employees. The crowning result of this new system of labor organization was the militarization of labor. Trotsky and his military advisers have developed, and the highest authorities have adopted, this plan whereby labor armies are modeled on regular army units and whereby labor desertion would be punishable in accordance with wartime laws. Therefore, not socialized labor (K. Marx) but *a serf-like labor by coercion* that had already revealed its inadequacies at the lowest stages of capitalist development—this is now the foundation of Communist construction.

In pursuit of the hopeless cause of Communist construction in Russia, the Communist party has traveled a long way, beginning with the liberation of labor from capitalist chains and ending by enslaving labor in the Soviet bureaucratic state apparatus. Bureaucratization and militarization, Cheka and repressions, absence of civil liberties and arbitrary rule—these are not merely cancerous formations on the body of the Soviet republic, as some may think; these are the inevitable consequences of attempting to implant predatatory and exploitative Soviet communism in the spheres of politics and economics.

---

DOCUMENT FORTY-ONE

---

## Insurrectionary Movement
## (a letter from Moscow)

[June 1921]

The peasants' insurrectionary movement against Soviet power continues to draw the unrelenting attention of the government. "The movement of Antonov" has not disappeared, but continues to exist on the eastern bank of the Volga in the provinces of Samara and the Urals. Numerous detachments operate in these regions, two of them led by former Communists.

In the region along the rail track to Astrakhan and Uralsk, the insurgency is led by a former chairman of the peasant section of the Novousiensk soviet, Comrade Safonov. When Safonov worked in the soviet, he distinguished himself by his honesty and by his struggle against the abuses of his colleagues, but now he leads the armed struggle against Soviet power. When I asked whether Safonov still considered himself a Communist, the person I was speaking to, who has gathered all the information in that area himself, did not know what to answer, but said that Safonov's detachment considered itself to be a part of Antonov's movement. A little to the north, another detachment is in action, under the command of a former Communist, a

---

This text is a translation from "Le Movement insurrectionel" in French, which appeared in the newspaper *Pour La Russie* 92 (18 August 1921, Paris), p. 2. Although the author of the letter is unknown, it is most likely that he was a Socialist Revolutionary. In his book *The Unknown Civil War in Soviet Russia: A Study of the Green Movement in the Tambov Region, 1920–1921* (Stanford: Hoover Institution Press, 1976), Oliver Radkey relies extensively on another publication of that letter, "Povstancheskoe dvizhenie (Pis'mo iz Moskvy)," *Volia Rossii*, no. 264 (27 July 1921), p. 2. Radkey concludes that the letter was written on 8 July 1921 and describes the events of May and June 1921.

former member if not the chairman of the local Cheka in Uralsk. Next to these detachments, which are led by former Communists, on the eastern bank of the Volga there are many other peasant detachments. These formed spontaneously because everything that has anything to do with "commune" ignites the profound hatred of the desperate peasant.

The situation is even more grave in northern Caucasia and throughout the Kuban area. Industry, which actually began to revive under the regional parliament [*rada*], is now reduced to nothing. Agriculture, which has been put to the test of "agricultural communes," is in total chaos. The agricultural communes proliferate, but are hated by the entire population, including the cossacks, as well as by those who are called "people from other cities" [*inogorodnie,* in cossack lands, those settlers who did not have the full rights of the cossacks, the original settlers in the eighteenth century. The inogorodnie craved equal rights with the cossacks, who jealously guarded the rights and privileges granted them by Catherine II. The inogorodnie's lack of rights was a source of friction. The Bolsheviks used this situation to attract many inogorodnie to their side against the cossacks.] Quite often, the communes are mercilessly ransacked and commune members subjected to atrocious lynchings. It was in this manner that all twelve members of the commune at the Briukhovetskaia large village [*stanitsa*] were slaughtered by a detachment of the Green Army. The number of Greens is growing, and so far they have successfully evaded the Reds. According to the official data, in the Kuban region alone there are thirty thousand Greens. (This number seems low and should not be trusted.) That the Bolsheviks still hold power in Kuban despite this atmosphere of wrath and hatred can only be explained by the fact that the population is disoriented and dejected and the Green Army, dispersed and poorly provisioned.

In the struggle between the Bolsheviks and the Greens, both sides resort to terror constantly, which has painful consequences for the peaceful population. The widespread practice of taking hostages is reminiscent of the most barbaric times of the Middle Ages. If the Greens attack the Communists in any *stanitsa,* the Communists start executing their hostages, as they did just recently. They often execute every tenth or twentieth inhabitant no matter how innocent or inoffensive. However, no matter how cruel and wild the measures against the Greens are, they cannot put an end to this movement. In Tambov province, where the movement of Russian Greens was born, the so-called liquidation of this peasant movement is going on at the present time. [June 1921. For a detailed discussion, see Radkey, *Unknown Civil War,* chaps. 10–11.] This movement is extremely dangerous to the Bolsheviks and has irreparably damaged the Bolshevik domination of central Russia. The special commission [The full name of this commission was the Plenipotentiary Commission of the All-Russian Central Executive Committee of Soviets for Fighting Banditry in Tambov Province." See Radkey, *Unknown Civil War,* p. 12.] formed by the All-Russian Executive Committee of Soviets arrived in Tambov to begin the suppression.

On 11 June this year [1921] this commission published an order [Radkey identified this as order no. 171 and cited the provisions reproduced here. Radkey, *Unknown Civil War,* p. 324.], which I have reproduced here (it was published in the Tambov *Izvestiia*). It is worth examining

> Since the first of June the struggle against banditism has re-established order in the countryside. Soviet power systematically re-establishes peaceful work of the peasants. Thanks to the energetic actions of our troops, Antonov's band has been defeated and dispersed and its members have fallen, one by one, into our hands.
>
> To tear out the roots of banditism and of the movement of Socialist Revolutionaries, the commission has decided to supplement the existing regulations with the following clauses:
>
> 1. All citizens who refuse to identify themselves are to be shot on the spot.
>
> 2. In the villages that hide weapons, the political commission of the district or of the region is to *take hostages* who are to be *executed* if the weapons are not surrendered.
>
> 3. In cases where hidden weapons are found, the order has been given *to shoot on the spot and without trial the oldest member of the family present.*
>
> 4. The family in whose house the bandit is hiding is to be arrested and *exiled from the province* and *the oldest in the family is to be shot on the spot without trial.*
>
> 5. The families that provide sanctuary to the family members of the bandits or that hide the property of the latter are to be considered as families of bandits and *the oldest working member of such a family is to be shot on the spot without trial.*
>
> 6. If the family of the bandit succeeds in fleeing, *its property is to be distributed to the peasants who remain loyal to Soviet power and the abandoned houses are to be burnt.*
>
> 7. This order is to be implemented sternly and mercilessly. It is to be read at the assemblies of village residents.
>
> Signed:
> ANTONOV-OVSEENKO, Chairman of the CEC Commission
> TUKHACHEVSKY, Commander in Chief of the Army
> LAVROV, Chairman of the Province Cheka

The inhuman character of this order shows only too well that what the government calls "bandits" *is in fact the true movement of the masses, profoundly popular* and intrinsically *connected to the peasants.* Following their actions in Tambov province and in the surrounding area of central Russia and the Ukraine, the [government] evidently banished from eighty thousand to one hundred thousand "bandit" families "to the distant regions of exile in order to be condemned to particularly hard labor." At the present time, they are forcing into exile, from Tambov province to Murman[sk], the Urals, and the Aral Sea, more than thirty thousand [Radkey compared this figure with all other available evidence and concluded that it is correct. *Unknown Civil War*, p. 350.] persons, so-called deserters, and fifty thousand women and children, "families of the bandits."

A MOSCOVITE

---

DOCUMENT FORTY-TWO

---

# An Appeal to the International Proletariat from a Prison in Tobolsk

[1925]

To: The RSDWP Delegation Abroad, the PSR Delegation Abroad, and
the Party of the Left SRs Delegation Abroad
To: The Editorial Board of *Zaria*
(For publication, to inform the international proletariat)

Dear Comrades:
You already know that the Solovetsky concentration camp for political prisoners, Socialists, and anarchists has been liquidated. The Bolshevik

---

This handwritten letter has no title or date. To disguise the handwriting, the characters were printed. The text is in Russian, but the identification attached at the top is in German: *Aufruf an das Internationale Proletariat unterzeichnet von 121 Sozialisten, die Sich in einem Gefaengnisse Sibiriens Befinden* (An Appeal to the International Proletariat signed by 121 Socialists Who Find Themselves in One of the Prisons in Siberia). Unfortunately, the copy in the archive does not have any signatures. From the contents we know that the time of writing is 1925. Nicolaevsky Collection, series no. 6, box 6, folder 4.

authorities have informed the whole world about it. It is not a coincidence that the liquidation of the Solovki camp was reported in the press on the same day when armed Cheka guards surrounded the buildings in the Solovki camp and announced to the political prisoners that they would be transferred to the Continent. Tomsky told the Franco-Belgian labor delegation, which visited Moscow recently, about the liquidation of the Solovki camp. In foreign Communist papers as well, they are probably singing praises of the humaneness of the Bolshevik authorities who have liquidated the Solovki. Some workers unfamiliar with Bolshevik hypocrisy might really believe that a turnabout in the Bolshevik repressions has come and that finally Socialists and anarchists in Russia could breathe freely. Our duty to the workers of the world compels us as comrades to tell you the truth, the whole unsightly truth about the liquidation of Solovki.

Yes, the Socialists and the anarchists have been transferred from Solovki, but on these desolate lands, near the polar circle, cut off from the rest of the world most of the year, there still remain many political prisoners—workers-strikers, participants in workers' movements, peasants exiled for taking part in peasant movements, individual Socialists and anarchists who for some reason were not granted the status of political prisoners by the GPU [Chief Political Directorate; replaced the Cheka], and a large group of counterrevolutionaries sentenced for religious beliefs and so on all of whom are subject to a general penal regime for common criminals in Solovki. They are dying from hunger and backbreaking work; they are systematically beaten up and even shot without trial by the administration, which is accountable to no one and which was recruited from criminal scum. For all those who remain in Solovki, their situation is extremely hard because now that the main group of Socialists and anarchists has been transferred, the Solovki administration will display no restraint whatsoever and be even more merciless than before.

Although the Socialists and anarchists have been transferred from Solovki, six corpses remain, those killed on 19 December 1923. Their remains are in a common grave in Savvatiev [formerly a monastery] dungeon [skit] next to the grave of Comrade Borts, who suffered an untimely death when she was not transferred to the continent for medical treatment. In the next Muksalamskii skit is the grave of a young comrade, Sandomir, who committed suicide; two more graves contain Aronovich, who also committed suicide, and Martsinkevich, who underwent the regime for common criminals. Ten corpses in two years—the awful result of Bolshevik terror—is the price for the liquidation of the Solovki camp. After the shooting of prisoners on 19 December, a wave of indignation among the workers of the whole world made it impossible to keep the Socialists and anarchists in the Solovki camp. Not the humaneness of Bolshevik authorities, not the repudiation of cruel repressions against the Socialists and anarchists, but the protest of the entire proletariat forced them to transfer political prisoners from Solovki. Even while making concessions, however, the Bolshevik authorities—the most hypocritical and vindictive in the world—tried to wreak their anger on the inmates of Solovki.

In the morning on 17 June [1924], armed detachments of Red Army soldiers and Cheka men unexpectedly surrounded Savvatiev *skit,* the largest in the Solovki camp. Infantry, cavalry, and even a machine gun were deployed against a prisoners' bloc in which everyone was sleeping at the time; all this caused bewilderment on the part of the inmates, who naturally expected some new act of arbitrariness. Finally they announced that some prisoners would be transferred to the continent, but not which ones. They gave the prisoners three hours to get ready and subjected them to rudeness, humiliations, and ceaseless threats. The same was reported from other buildings. The inmates from Muksalamskii *skit,* for example, were forced to run three *versts* to the harbor, after they had already walked seven *versts* and were pushed by horses from behind even though there were women and sick persons in the column. The chief of the directorate of Northern Camps himself—one Kostev—and the director of the Prison Department conducted this operation. It was only because of the exceptional presence of mind and endurance of healthy prisoners, who took on themselves the blows and protected the weak and sick ones, that this last provocation did not end in tragedy or the passage end in casualties.

The ship that delivered the prisoners to the continent was so crowded that it was hard to breathe. In a cramped hold, stuffed to the limit, with hatchways closed and scuttles shut, the exhausted people who had just gone through a long walk could not lie down, but had to stand up most of the way. Here also were mothers with babies.

On arriving on the continent, the prisoners were split into groups and placed in railway cars, regardless of family ties. In one case, threatening violence, they took a pregnant woman with an eighteen-month-old baby away from her husband; he had to go to a place thousands of *versts* away without being able to say good bye or knowing where he was going or where his wife was going. The train cars were filled beyond any conceivable norm; instead of forty-two passengers in a regular car they stuffed in eighty-seven. It was midsummer and oppressively hot. Some comrades fainted, others had heart attacks. In these unbearably cramped conditions, we traveled nine long days. During all this time, we were given inadequate food, and there was not even enough fresh water. Those who were seriously ill among us received the same ration and could not escape the common lot.

The circumstances surrounding our transfer from Solovki did not portend anything good in store, but even so it exceeded our worst expectations. All Solovki prisoners were divided into two groups. The larger group was sent to Verkhne-Uralsk prison, and we, about a hundred of us, were sent to Tobolsk. We in Tobolsk so far do not have any information on conditions in the Verkhne-Uralsk prison. But we can tell you what awaited us in Tobolsk. We were placed in the former convict jail in the city of Tobolsk, in faraway Siberia. Even in czarist times, they considered abolishing Siberian convict jails because they were so far away and because conditions there were so hard. The Bolshevik authorities could not think of anything better when liquidating the Solovki than the old czarist convict jails in Siberia. All those transferred from Solovki were sentenced to detention in a concentration camp, not in a prison. Even though conditions in the Solovki camp were very hard and barbed wire surrounded our prisoner blocs, nevertheless, inside the barbed wire territory we enjoyed relative freedom. We did not have internal supervision in the prisoner blocs, our cells were open, and we enjoyed the right of free communication with each other from roll call to roll call. Instead of this, in Tobolsk we found ourselves in a real jail with locked cells, with a foul-smelling toilet poisoning the air, with cells completely isolated from one another, and with a staff of guards transferred from Moscow's internal prisons especially for us, who immediately set up their regulations here. We have received new and much harder punishments, even though no one had committed any new "crimes," and no one reconsidered our sentences. We were placed in common cells, fourteen to seventeen people in each, which made it impossible to do any serious study. Some prisoners had spent many years in czarist and then in Bolshevik prisons. Our food rations were cut considerably compared with those in Solovki and distributed without the participation of the prisoners. The prison administration refused to recognize elected elders as spokesmen for the prisoners. There is no special food ration for the sick and no hospital either (a little corner for three or four beds, without any medical supplies, cannot be called a hospital). Those who are sick are compelled to live in common cells without hospital food and with hardly any medical care, even though some have a bad form of tuberculosis and some have neurotic disorders. The cells in the first floor of this two-story jail are damp and dark. The sick prisoners live there, and the healthy ones always have to face the danger of falling ill.

We are some three thousand *versts* from the center [of the country] and some three hundred *versts* from the railroad. We are almost completely isolated from our relatives, and very few of us can count on their chance visits. But even that is not enough. They limit our correspondence, limit the number of addresses we are allowed to write to, and permit us to write only to our closest family members. They limit the number of letters, both sent and received. Even the czarist prisons did not light on this measure—the newest invention of the GPU!

The staff of prison wardens and Red Army soldiers have been selected especially for us. They have been taught to hate us and can't wait to put that hatred into action. Despite the fact that we received permission from the administration to look out the windows, they constantly threaten that they will shoot those who stand at the windows. Just since we have been here, there have been two cases of shooting at the windows, which fortunately did not cause casualties. But casualties are probable and the repetition of the Solovki shooting on 19 December is inevitable in the current atmosphere in Tobolsk, as demonstrated by the latest incident of shooting at the windows.

After they shot at the windows, the prisoners began to knock on the doors, calling for the superiors from the prison administration. The guards responded by threatening to shoot from the yard and the corridor and stuck their revolvers through the small openings of the locked doors. Swearing obscenely, yelling "Menshevik scum," and "traitors of Christ," the wild, clearly drunken wardens rushed up and down the corridors from cell to cell threatening to shoot people and, aiming rifles and revolvers at us, shouted "Don't save bullets"—all this shows the kind of people we had in Tobolsk prison, sent to us by the GPU. That's the kind of "humaneness" the Bolsheviks displayed toward the former Solovki inmates who had been transferred to the Continent. Other inmates of Tobolsk prison have also experienced this "humaneness," including those brought from Cheliabinsk. At Cheliabinsk they had unlocked cells, free communication with one another, and individual cells for the most needy—all of which had been won by several hunger strikes. Now in Tobolsk they found themselves in common cells, without individual cells even for the sick or those who had fifteen years of czarist and Bolshevik prisons behind them. Now they still have to face five to ten long years of imprisonment.

A group of anarchists transferred from the Yaroslavl prison has also experienced Bolshevik humaneness (among them, a pregnant woman). Placed with common criminals, they had to go on a hunger strike to attain their transfer to the ward for political prisoners. Many Socialist and anarchist prisoners also had to go on a hunger strike because the GPU refused to grant them the status of political prisoners. The Messrs. Tomskys [trade union leaders and thus Bolshevik authorities] are talking about humaneness, and the German, Swedish, and other workers' delegations are listening to their speeches and, in response, praising Bolshevik freedom. But why was the Solovki camp in the two years of its existence not shown to any delegations? The English trade union delegation did ask to see Solovki, but were told that navigation was not possible at that time, even though this was not true. Now the newspapers write about the German delegation's visit to a prison in Sverdlovsk (Ekaterinburg) and about their meeting with political prisoners. We do not know what kind of political prisoners these delegates talked to in Sverdlovsk because there is no permanent prison for political prisoners there. But why, we ask, did they hurriedly whitewash the dirty cells of the Sverdlovsk jail? And why did they transfer Borisenko, Zharkovsky, and Enukashvili to the GPU on 4 August, the very eve of the delegations' arrival? Why, we ask, has no one from the delegates visited the Tobolsk prison or the Verkhne-Uralsk prison, where hundreds of political prisoners are imprisoned? Why wasn't a workers' delegation admitted there? Why didn't they open the prison cells for them so they could see with their own eyes how, after the Solovki, the Cheliabinsk, and the Siberian convict jails, we are enjoying Bolshevik freedom on the continent. We would have told them all about that freedom and why we wound up in Bolshevik prisons. And they would have found out that the overwhelming majority of us were sentenced not by verdict of an open court—let it be partial, let it be Bolshevik—but by the GPU, which, just like the medieval Inquisition, is passing sentences in its secret offices. They would have found out that out of 121 political prisoners in Tobolsk prison, only 21 persons have a court sentence and that out of the 200 Solovki prisoners who wound up in Verkhne-Uralsk, only 1 had a court sentence. All the others were imprisoned by GPU resolution, not for any concrete crimes, not for armed struggle against the Bolshevik power (as Communist newspapers are shamelessly saying in Russia and abroad), but simply for belonging (in some cases in the past) to this or that Socialist party; that is, for daring to think and feel differently.

Only one prisoner in the Tobolsk political prison was sentenced for participating in uprisings, in this case, the Tambov uprising. (He was sentenced to execution, but his sentence was commuted to ten years imprisonment.) The 115 comrades we questioned have, altogether, spent 360 years in Bolshevik prisons and sixteen years in exile—that averages out to three years and one month per person! And some of us have spent five or more years in prison out of the eight years of Bolshevik rule. Moreover, none of the 115 we questioned received his latest sentence during the Civil War. Twenty-nine were sentenced in 1922, 53 in 1923, and others in 1924 and 1925, that is, when references to civil war did not make any sense. Out of the 360 years we have spent in Bolshevik prisons, 60 were in preliminary confinement and only 16 counted toward the full term. More than 43 years of preliminary confinement were not counted (and that is in court trial cases only). There are comrades among us who had one, one-and-a-half, and even two-and-a-half years of preliminary confinement not counted toward the prison term.

Three hundred and sixty years in Bolshevik prisons after we have already gone through 220 years of imprisonment, hard labor camps, and exile under czarism! Out of 115 persons, 53 suffered from czarist repression; that averages four years per person. Some comrades, however, have ten years and more of prison behind them, among them, eleven who had been sentenced to penal servitude (one was sentenced to execution by the czarist court). They spent seventy years in penal servitude. They have gone through solitary confinement, flogging, and torture. Nine of them are workers and have been workers since the age of nine or ten. One of them spent ten years and four months in penal servitude in Shlisselburg, three years in prison, four hundred days in punishment cells, and three-and-a-half years in exile. He is a worker, a turner [metalworker] who has participated in the workers' revolutionary movement since 1898. Now he has got ten years' imprisonment from the Bolsheviks. These, the majority of whom are old party activists who joined the Socialist and revolutionary movement way before 1917, are the kinds of "counterrevolutionaries" that the Bolsheviks throw in prison. Out of 115 people, 112 are members of political parties, 66 entered before 1917, and 28 before 1905, for an average of 13 years of party membership per prisoner! This is not exceptional. Such a composition of the political prisoners' population is typical in prisons and places of exile in Bolshevik Russia. These people, exhausted by long years of repression, must again resume the hard and desperate struggle for their human dignity and for their very lives in Bolshevik prisons. Any historian of this struggle knows about the "heroic deeds" of Bolshevik authorities, such as the beating of three hundred Socialists and anarchists in the Butyrki jail in 1921, the brutal beatings in the Yaroslavl prison at the end of 1922, and the shootings in Solovki in 1923. Hunger strikes in Bolshevik prisons have become an everyday occurrence to attain the status of political prisoners, to obtain an individual cell, or to improve their hard conditions. The extent of hunger strikes is greater than ever before. Individuals as well as groups go on hunger strikes. In the fall of 1924, 150 prisoners went on a collective hunger strike that lasted fifteen days in Solovki. Here in Tobolsk, out of 115, 85 have gone on a hunger strike at one time or another, that is three-fourths of all the comrades. As time goes on, the hunger strikes become longer and longer, beating previous records. The latest hunger strikes in Cheliabinsk, Suzdal, and Moscow set a record of twenty-four days.

One comrade has gone through two hunger strikes—one, seventeen days, and the other, twenty-four days long. Another comrade (a woman and a member of the SR party) was beaten until she lost consciousness on the fourth day of her hunger strike in the GPU's internal prison [in GPU headquarters]. Not surprisingly, some prisoners have lost faith in the effectiveness of hunger strikes and are resorting to suicide. Foreign workers' delegations would have learned all this had they been allowed free access to political prisoners. And they would have learned one more thing about Bolshevik freedom—something that the majority of European workers most likely does not know—that a Socialist in Russia, once in the claws of the GPU, can never get out unless he repudiates his banner and repents on the pages of Bolshevik newspapers. Only by paying such a shameful price can he buy freedom and a piece of bread for his starving family. Otherwise, he must bear his cross endlessly from camp to prison, from prison to exile, and from exile again to prison. . . . He would not have to commit any new crimes against the authorities to be sent on that journey. All he has to do is be true to his political convictions. Many of us are sentenced to three, five, and ten years in prison or camp. But what is it that changes for us, when, upon completion of our prison term, we receive not freedom, but exile in the Siberian tundra, Turukhansk, Obdorsk, Mezen, or Pechora, at the polar circle? This is not an exaggeration. Out of the many hundreds of political prisoners who have gone through camps and prisons in Bolshevik Russia, only a few were freed [on completion of the term]. Here are the data on the Solovki camp: out of forty-seven persons who completed their term in 1922–1925, twenty-nine were sent into exile with the stipulation that their freedom of movement was limited. Nine persons were prohibited from settling in big cities, three persons could choose their place of residence but were to be under GPU surveillance, and six persons could return home, but were also to be under GPU surveillance. Among them were women with children, sick people, old people with czarist prisons behind them, and young men that had only recently joined the workers' movement. Torn away from relatives and friends, without means, without a job, deprived by the GPU of the possibility and, in certain cases, of the right to work, this is how our comrades live in exile. And as soon as they get settled, they are sent away again to even more godforsaken backwoods. They finish their term and get a new exile. In some cases they get a new prison term, again years behind bars, for some nonexistent crimes committed in uninhabited backwoods. And it goes on like this without end.

. . . Surprisingly, the louder the Bolshevik press shouts about the rule of law, the more inventive the GPU becomes. Only three or four years ago, they used to exile to Turkistan, to the Urals, to Vyatka, and to other places in European Russia. Then they began to exile to Narym, then all the way up to Pechora, and now they've remembered about Obdorsk, which was seldom used even in czarist times. Neither the infamous czarist courts nor the bourgeois courts in Europe and America, which cruelly persecute revolutionaries, have known anything like this. This is what makes the Bolshevik terrorist regime so horrible. And Socialists and workers throughout the world must know this. In "free" Bolshevik Russia—a country that has long since come out of the state of civil war and that is boasting about the strengthening of its power—*Socialists* are beyond the rule of law. In that country, there is not a single Socialist or anarchist whose name is known to the authorities and to the GPU, who is not languishing somewhere in a camp, a prison, or in exile. As long as this "free" regime exists, none of its captives will see freedom. These are the facts, and let those who sing praises to Russian freedom refute them. We have told you all these facts, comrades, so that you know how hypocritical and false are all the speeches about the liquidation or even about the softening of terror in Bolshevik Russia and so that you know that terror reigns here in Russia in all its pristine strength and in recent times has intensified. The Solovki camp was replaced with the Tobolsk prison. Let your old slogan, the slogan of all Socialists and workers of the whole world, sound from your ranks powerfully and ceaselessly as it used to: Down with Terror in Russia!

FACTION OF THE RSDWP  FACTION OF THE PSR
Faction of the Left SRs and a Group of SDs in
Tobolsk Prison

# Bibliography

All materials published in this book are from the Nicolaevsky Collection; I especially relied on the following collections: series no. 6: Records of the RSDRP (m); series no. 7: Records of the PSR, especially Victor Chernov, *Kommentarii k protokolam TsKa PSR,* Nicolaevsky Collection, series no. 7, box 10, folder 3; series no. 15: Papers of Iraklii Tsereteli; series no. 16: Papers of P. B. Axelrod; series no. 17: Papers of Iu. O. Martov; series no. 20: Mensheviks in Exile (Collected Correspondence, 1927–1935); series no. 53: Papers of O. Iu. Rozenfeld, editor of *La Republique Russe;* series no. 89: Materials of the Cheka; series no. 100: The Ukraine (Collection of Documents, 1918–1932); series no. 114: Russian Revolution and Civil War in Southern Russia; series no. 232: Papers of V. M. Chernov; and a collection of Russian newspapers.

Alinin, K. *Tche-ka. The Story of the Bolshevist Extraordinary Commission.* London: Russian Liberation Committee, 1920.

Aronson, Grigorii. *Martov i ego blizkie: sbornik* [Martov and Those Close to Him]. New York: 1959.

Ascher, Abraham, ed. *The Mensheviks in the Russian Revolution.* Ithaca, N.Y.: Cornell University Press, 1976.

Bauer, Otto. *Die Russische Revolution und das Europaeische Proletariat* [The Russian Revolution and the European Proletariat]. Vienna: 1917.

Bernstam, Mikhail, ed. *Nezavisimoe rabochee dvizhenie v 1918 godu: Dokumenty i materialy* [Independent Workers' Movement in 1918: Documents and Materials]. Paris: YMCA, 1981.

————. *Ural i prikam'e, noiabr' 1917–ianvar' 1919: Dokumenty i materialy* [The Urals and the Kama Region, November 1917–January 1919: Documents and Materials]. Paris: YMCA, 1982.

British Labour Delegation to Russia 1920. *Report.* London: Offices of the Trade Union Congress, 1920.

*The Case of Russian Labour Against Bolshevism.* New York: Russian Information Service, 1919.

Central Committee of the Left SRs. *Otkrytoe pis'mo TsKa Bolshevikov* [An Open Letter to the Central Committee of the Bolsheviks]. Moscow: PLSR, 1919.

Chernov, Victor [Tschernow]. *Meine Schicksalle in Sowjet Russland* [My Fate in Soviet Russia]. Berlin: Der Firn, 1921.

Chessin, Serge de. *L'Apocalypse russe: La Revolution bolchevique, 1918–1921* [The Russian Apocalypse: The Bolshevik Revolution, 1918–1921]. Paris: Plon-Nourrit, 1921.

*A Collection of Reports on Bolshevism in Russia: Abridged Edition of Parliamentary Paper, Russia No. 1.* London: His Majesty's Stationery Office, 1919.

Committee to Collect Information on Russia. *Report (Political and Economic).* London: His Majesty's Stationery Office, 1921.

Daniels, Robert V. *A Documentary History of Communism.* Hanover: Published for the University of Vermont by University Press of New England, 1984.

Drobizhev, V. Z., ed. *Rabochii klass Sovetskoi Rossii v pervyi god proletarskoi diktatury* [The Working Class of Soviet Russia during the First Year of the Proletarian Dictatorship]. Moscow: Moskovskii Gosudarstvennyi Universitet, 1975.

Eichwede, Wolfgang, ed. *Sozial und Wirtschaftsgeschichte der UdSSR von 1917 bis 1941 in Quellen und Documenten* [Social and Economic History of the USSR from 1917 to 1941 in Sources and Documents]. Bremen: n. p., forthcoming.

Ermanskii, O. A. *O Perezhitom* [About the Past]. Moscow: Gosizdat, 1927.

Garvi, Petr. A. *Zapiski Sotsial Demokrata (1906–1921)* [Notes of a Social Democrat (1906–1921)]. Newtonville, Mass.: Oriental Research Partners, 1982.

*In the Shadow of Death (A Document. Statement of Red Cross Sisters on the Bolshevist Prisons in Kiev).* London: Russian Liberation Committee, 1920.

Kautsky, Karl. *Demokratie oder Diktatur* [Democracy or Dictatorship]. Berlin: n. p., 1918.

Keep, John, ed. *The Debate on Soviet Power: Minutes of the All-Russian Central Executive Committee of Soviets, Second Convocation, October 1917–January 1918.* Oxford: Clarendon Press, 1979.

*Kreml' za reshetkoi (Vospominaniia levykh eserov)* [The Kremlin behind Bars (Reminiscences of the Left SRs)]. Berlin: Skify, 1922.

Lockerman, A. *Les Bolcheviks a l'ouvre* [The Bolsheviks at Work]. Paris: Riviere, 1920.

Lorenz, Richard, ed. *Die Russische Revolution 1917. Der Aufstand der Arbeiter, Bauern und Soldaten, eine Dokumentation* [The Russian Revolution of 1917. The Uprising of Workers, Peasants and Soldiers, A Documentation]. Munich: Nymphenburger, 1981.

Mohrenschildt, Dimitri Von. *The Russian Revolution of 1917: Contemporary Accounts.* New York: Oxford University Press, 1971.

Partiia Sotsialistov Revoliutsionerov. *Che-ka: Materialy po deiatel'nosti* [The Cheka: Materials about Its Activity]. Berlin: izdanie biuro partii SR, 1922.

*Perepiska sekretariata TsKa RKP(b) mestnymi organizatsiiami. Sbornik dokumentov i materialov (aprel–mai 1919)* [The Correspondence of the Secretariat of the RKP(b) CC with Local Organizations. A Collection of Documents and Materials (April–May 1919)]. Vol. 7. Moscow: Gospolitizdat, 1959.

*Protokoly TsKa RSDRP(b), avgust 1917–fevral 1918* [The Protocols of the RSDWP(b) CC, August 1917–February 1918]. Moscow: Gosizdat, 1958.

*Protokoly VTsIK chetvertogo sozyva* [The Protocols of the CEC of the Fourth Convocation]. Moscow: Gosizdat, 1920.

Sapir, Boris, ed. *Theodore Dan. Letters. 1899–1946.* Amsterdam: International Institute for Social History, 1985.

———. *From the Archives of L. O. Dan.* Amsterdam: Stichting Internationaal Instituut voor Sociale Geschiedenis, 1987.

Sokolov, Boris. *Bol'sheviki o Bol'shevikakh. Sovetskie dokumenty i materialy* [The Bolsheviks about the Bolsheviks. Soviet Documents and Materials]. Paris: Franko-slavianskoe izdanie, 1919.

Stalin, I. V. *Sochineniia.* Vol. 4. Moscow: Gosizdat, 1951.

Sukhanov, N. N. *Zapiski o revoliutsii* [Notes on Revolution]. 7 vols. Berlin: Z. I. Grzhebin, 1922.

*Texte der Meschewiki zur Russischen Revolution und zum Sowjetstaat aus den Jahren 1903–1937* [The Texts of the Mensheviks on the Russian Revolution and the Soviet State from the Years of 1903–1937]. Hamburg: Junius, 1981.

Trotsky, Lev, ed. *Stalinskaia shkola fal'sifikatsii* [The Stalinist School of Falsification]. Berlin: Granat, 1932.

Tucker, Robert C., ed. *The Lenin Anthology.* New York: W. W. Norton, 1975.

*Uprochenie Sovetskoi vlasti v Moskve i Moskovskoi gubernii* [The Consolidation of Soviet Power in Moscow and Moscow Province]. Moscow: institut istorii. Moskovskii rabochii, 1958.

*Vos'moi S'ezd RKP(b) Stenograficheskii otchet* [The Eighth Congress of the RKP(b). Minutes]. Moscow: Gosizdat, 1959.

Ritter, Gerhard A., ed. *Die Zweite Internationale 1918–1919. Protokolle, Memoranden, Berichte und Korrespondenzen* [The Second International 1918–1919. Memorandums, Reports and Correspondence]. Berlin: Verlag J. H. W. Dietz, 1980.

## Secondary Sources

Aronson, Grigorii. *Rossiia v epokhu revoliutsii.* New York: Walden, 1966.

Baron, S. H. *Plekhanov, the Father of Russian Marxism.* Stanford: Stanford University Press, 1963.

Benvenuti, Francesco. *The Bolsheviks and the Red Army, 1918–1922.* Cambridge, Eng.: Cambridge University Press, 1988.

Brovkin, Vladimir. *The Mensheviks after October: Socialist Opposition and the Rise of the Bolshevik Dictatorship.* Ithaca, N.Y.: Cornell University Press, 1987.

Conquest, Robert. *The Harvest of Sorrow: Soviet Collectivization and the Terror Famine.* New York: Oxford University Press, 1986.

Drachkovitch, Milorad, and Lazitch, Branko. *Lenin and the Comintern.* Vol. 1. Stanford: Hoover Institution Press, 1972.

Erickson, John. *The Soviet High Command, 1918–1941: A Military Political History.* Boulder, Colo.: Westview Press, 1984.

Felshtinsky, Yurii. *Bol'sheviki i Levye Esery: oktiabr' 1917–iiul' 1918. Na puti k odnopartiinoi diktature* [The Bolsheviks and the Left SRs: October 1917–July 1918. On the Way to a One-Party Dictatorship]. Paris: YMCA, 1985.

Ferro, Marc. *The Russian Revolution of February 1917.* Englewood Cliffs, N.J.: Prentice Hall, 1972.

Fic, Victor M. *The Bolsheviks and the Czechoslovak Legion.* New Delhi: Abhinav Publications, 1978.

Galili, Ziva. *The Menshevik Leaders in the Russian Revolution: Social Realities and Political Strategies.* Princeton, N.J.: Princeton University Press, 1989.

Gelbard, Arye. *Der Judische Arbeiter-Bund Russlands im Revolutionsjahr 1917* [The Jewish Workers' Bund in the Revolutionary Year of 1917]. Vienna: Europa Verlag, 1982.

Glavak, T. V., ed. *Ocherki istorii Kievskikh gorodskikh i oblastnykh partiinykh organizatsii* [Sketches on the History of the Kiev City and Province Party Organizations]. Kiev: Politizdat Ukrainy, 1981.

Gleason, Abbott; Kenez, Peter; and Stites, Richard, eds. *Bolshevik Culture.* Bloomington: Indiana University Press, 1985.

Gogolevksii, A. V. *Petrogradskii Sovet v gody grazhdanskoi voiny* [Petrograd Soviet in the Years of the Civil War]. Leningrad: Nauka, 1982.

Heller, Mikhail, and Nekrich, Aleksander. *Utopia in Power: The History of the Soviet Union from 1917 to the Present.* New York: Summit Books, 1986.

Hunczak, Taras, ed. *The Ukraine, 1917–1921: A Study in Revolution.* Cambridge, Mass.: Harvard University Press, 1977.

Iakovlev, L. I. *Internatsional'naia solidarnost' trudiashchikhsia zarubezhnykh stran s narodami Sovetskoi Rossii, 1917–1922* [International Solidarity of the Toilers in Foreign Countries with the Peoples of Soviet Russia, 1917–1922]. Moscow: Nauka, 1964.

*Istoriia grazhdanskoi voiny v SSSR* [History of the Civil War in the USSR]. Vol. 4. Moscow: Politizdat, 1959.

Jansen, Marc. *A Show Trial under Lenin: The Trial of the Socialist Revolutionaries. Moscow: 1922.* The Hague: Martinus Nijhoff Publishers, 1982.

Joost, Wilhelm, ed. *Botschafter bei den Roten Tsaren: Die Deutschen Missionschefs in Moskau, 1918 bis 1941, Nach Geheimakten und personlichen Aufzeichnungen* [Ambassadors to the Red Tsars: Chiefs of German Missions to Moscow, from 1918 to 1941, According to Secret Documents and Personal Papers]. Vienna: Fritz, 1967.

Kenez, Peter. *Civil War in South Russia, 1918: The First Year of the Volunteer Army.* Berkeley: University of California Press, 1971.

———. *Civil War in South Russia, 1919–1920.* Berkeley: University of California Press, 1977.

Klevanskii, A. Kh. *Chekhoslovatskie internatsionalisty i prodannyi korpus* [Czechoslovak Internationalists and a Betrayed Legion]. Moscow: Nauka, 1965.

Koenker, Diane. *Moscow Workers and the 1917 Revolution.* Princeton, N.J.: Princeton University Press, 1981.

Kolesnikov, B. *Professional'noe dvizhenie i kontrrevoliutsiia* [Trade Union Movement and Counterrevolution]. Kiev: Gosizdat Ukrainy, 1923.

*Kratkaia istoriia SSR* [Short History of the USSR]. 2 vols. Moscow: Nauka, 1983.

Leggett, George. *The Cheka: Lenin's Political Police.* New York: Oxford University Press, 1981.

Lewin, Moshe. *Lenin's Last Struggle.* New York: Monthly Review Press, 1978.

Liberman, Simon. *Building Lenin's Russia.* Chicago: n. p. 1945.

Lindemann, Albert S. *The Red Years: European Socialism vs. Bolshevism: 1919–1921.* Berkeley: University of California Press, 1974.

Malet, Michael. *Nestor Makhno in the Russian Civil War.* London: Macmillan, 1982.

Mandel, David. *The Petrograd Workers and the Soviet Seizure of Power.* New York: St. Martin's Press, 1983.

Mawdsley, Evan. *The Russian Civil War.* Boston: Allen & Unwin, 1987.

Melgunov, S. P. *Krasnyi terror v Rossii* [Red Terror in Russia]. New York: Brandy, 1979.

Pipes, Richard. *The Russian Revolution.* New York: Alfred A. Knopf, 1990.

Pokrovskii, Georgii. *Denikinshchina, God politiki i ekonomiki na Kubani (1918–1919)* [Denikin's Rule: A Year of Politics and Economics in the Kuban (1918–1919)]. Berlin: Grzhebin, 1923.

Rabinowitch, Alexander. *Prelude to Revolution: The Petrograd Bolsheviks and the July 1917 Uprising.* Bloomington: Indiana University Press, 1968.

Radkey, Oliver H. *The Election to the Constituent Assembly of 1917.* Cambridge, Mass.: Harvard University Press, 1950.

———. *The Sickle under the Hammer: The Russian Socialist Revolutionaries in the Early Months of Soviet Rule.* New York: Columbia University Press, 1963.

———. *The Unknown Civil War in Soviet Russia: A Study of the Green Movement in the Tambov Region, 1920–1921.* Stanford: Hoover Institution Press, 1976.

Razgon, A. I. *VTsIK Sovetov v pervye mesiatsy diktatury proletariata* [The CEC of Soviets in the First Months of the Dictatorship of the Proletariat]. Moscow: Nauka, 1971.

Remington, Thomas. *Building Socialism in Bolshevik Russia: Ideology and Industrial Organization (1917–1921).* Series in Russian and East European Studies No. 6. Pittsburgh, Penn.: University of Pittsburgh Press, 1984.

Roberts, C. E. Bechhofer. *In Denikin's Russia and the Caucasus, 1919–1920.* London: W. Collins Sons, 1921.

Roobol, W. H. *Tsereteli, a Democrat in the Russian Revolution: A Political Biography.* The Hague: Nijhoff, 1976.

Rosenberg, William. *Liberals in the Russian Revolution: The Constitutional Democratic Party, 1917–1921.* Princeton N.J.: Princeton University Press, 1974.

Scheibert, Peter. *Lenin an der Macht: Das Russische Volk in der Revolution, 1918–1922* [Lenin in Power: The Russian People in the Revolution, 1918–1922]. Weinheim: acta humaniora, 1984.

Smith, S. A. *Red Petrograd: Revolution in the Factories, 1917–1918.* Cambridge, Eng.: Cambridge University Press, 1983.

Starikov, Sergei, and Medvedev, Roy. *Philip Mironov and the Russian Civil War.* New York: Alfred A. Knopf, 1978.

Tucker, Robert, ed. *Stalinism.* New York: W. W. Norton, 1977.

Volin [Wolin], S. *Deiatel'nost Men'shevikov v profsoiuzakh pri Sovetskoi vlasti.* [The Mensheviks' Activity in the Trade Unions under Soviet Power]. New

York: Inter-University Project on the History of the Menshevik Movement, paper No. 13, 1962.

————. *Mensheviki na Ukraine (1917–1921)* [The Mensheviks in the Ukraine (1917–1921)]. New York: Inter-University Project on the History of the Menshevik Movement, paper No. 11, 1962.

# Index

Abergauz, V. M., 220
Abramovich, Rafail, 27, 51, 122, 124, 127–28, 134, 139, 140, 142, 194–98, 220–21
Adler, Friedrich, 129–30, 139–40
Aleinikov, A. N., 210
Alekinskii, A., 141
Aleksandrovskii workshops, 161
Allies, 53, 102–3, 125–26, 135, 136, 146–48, 213–14, 227
All-Russian Union, 176
American Red Cross, 16–17
Amnesty, 89, 139, 140–42, 218
Anarchists, 197, 213, 237–45
Anti-Semitism, 18, 22, 26, 72, 170, 177, 184–85. *See also* Black Hundreds
April thesis (Mensheviks), 28–29
Arkhangel'sk, 98, 114, 121, 126, 215
Armament/cartridge plants, 157–58, 198–208, 219. *See also name of specific city, province, or plant*
Armanskii, A., 220
Armavir, 114
Army/Red Army: as the basis of Bolshevik power, 13, 60, 106, 109, 136, 162, 224, 229, 230; and the Bolshevik seizure of power, 39, 42–43, 44, 45, 46, 48, 51, 53, 56; Bolsheviks supported by the, 3, 4, 38, 44, 67; Bolsheviks undermine the, 162; and the bourgeoisie, 230; breakdown of the, 41; and the cadets, 45; in cities, 67; and Civil War, 48; composition of the, 109; and the Constituent Assembly dissolution, 61; and the cossacks, 24; in the countryside, 67, 101–2; criminals in the, 169; desertions from the, 17–19, 33n34, 33–34n45, 159, 173; disintegration/dispersal of the, 162, 176, 229; factionalism within the, 136; food supply for the, 168; and insurgents, 17; intelligentsia in

the, 42; and the Internationalists, 2, 11, 101; and the Mensheviks, 100, 152, 161, 162, 187, 188, 206; and the peace, 42, 44, 224; and the peasants, 18, 42; peasants drafted into the, 7, 17, 140; and the press, 111, 112; and prisoners, 239, 241; as a privileged group, 101–2; and the Socialist Revolutionaries, 60; in a society at war, 129; and the soviet elections, 5, 101–2; terrorism by the, 56, 59, 67, 71; as a threat to the Bolsheviks, 101; and the unions, 48; uprisings/mutinies by the, xvi–xvii, 9, 33n34, 39, 101, 161; volunteers for the, 191; and the workers, 15–16, 25, 60; workers drafted into the, 7, 11, 25, 26, 218, 220, 232. *See also* Officers; *name of specific city or province*
Arrests: voluntary, 201–2, 206, 219. *See also name of specific person, city, province, political party, or class*
Astrakhan, 114, 161
Austria, 53, 129–30
Avksent'ev, N. D., 41, 46
Axelrod, Pavel, xix, 3, 51, 166, 215, 216
Axelrod, Pavel—letters to: from Abramovich, 27, 194–98; from Dan, 4, 59–63; from Martov, 3–4, 38–54, 55–58; from unknown, 214–17

Bagmen, 73, 166
Baku, 215, 220
Bakunin, Mikhail, 112
Balabanoff, Angelica, 210
Balabanov, M., 218
Banks, 138, 168, 225. *See also* Nationalization
Bashkiria, 56
Baturskii, B. S. (aka B. S. Tseitlin), 48, 221
Bauer, Otto, 130

*About the editor/translator:*

VLADIMIR N. BROVKIN is an associate professor of history at Harvard University. He emigrated to the United States from the Soviet Union in 1975 and received his M.A. from Georgetown University and his Ph.D. from Princeton University. His most recent publications include *The Mensheviks after October: Socialist Opposition and the Rise of the Bolshevik Dictatorship* (1987). He has published numerous articles on Soviet history in such journals as *Slavic Review, Russian Review, Russian History, Soviet Studies, Harvard Ukrainian Studies, Jahrbuecher fuer Geschichte Osteuropas, Problems of Communism, Global Affairs,* and *Cornell International Law Journal.*